Venetian Academy of Indian Studies Series
No. 3

General Editor
Gian Giuseppe Filippi

Venetian Academy of Indian Studies (VAIS)

As a prestigious instrument of the Department of East Asian Studies, University "Ca' Foscari" of Venice, Italy, the Venetian Academy of Indian Studies has, since its inception, been involved with organisation of symposia, missions in field, publications, and cultural programmes that have some kind of relevance to Indological studies.

Foremost among its other academic/research concerns, however, is the VAIS' aim to promote scientific interaction and mutual understanding between Indian and European scholars, institutions, media and enterprises.

Kāmpilyamahātmya

Venetian Academy of Indian Studies Series, no. 3

Kāmpilyamahātmya

of

Durgadatta Sharma

Translated into English by
Corrado Puchetti

Venetian Academy of Indian Studies
Venice, Italy

D.K. Printworld (P) Ltd.
New Delhi, India

Cataloging in Publication Data — DK

Sharma, Durgadatta.

Kāmpilyamahātmya of Durgadatta Sharma.
(Venetian academy of Indian studies series; no. 3).
Includes bibliographical references (p.)

1. Kāmpilya (Extinct city) — Antiquities. 2. Mahābhārata — Geography. I. Puchetti, Corrado, 1963– II. Title. III. Series: Venetian academy of Indian studies series; no. 3.

ISBN - 81-246-0219-0
First published in India in 2003

Published with the cooperation of 'Italian Ministry of Foreign Affairs' and 'Italian Embassy, New Delhi'.

Published by:
Venetian Academy of Indian Studies
Department of East Asian Studies
"Ca' Foscari" Venice University
Ca' Soranzo, San Polo 2169
30125 Venice (Italy)

and

D. K. Printworld (P) Ltd.
Regd. office : *'Sri Kunj'*, F-52, Bali Nagar
New Delhi - 110 015
Phones : (011) 545-3975; 546-6019
Fax : (011) 546-5926
E-mail: dkprintworld@vsnl.net

Printed by: D.K. Printworld (P) Ltd., New Delhi

Foreword

KĀMPILYA has been one of the few towns of the Ganges Valley well known from the primordial times of the Vedic hymns.[1] The name Kāmpilya appears twice in the Veda as 'Kāmpilya Vāsinī', and is referred to in the accounts of the solemn horse sacrifice performed by its king Kraivya.[2] The town is also mentioned frequently in the oldest Sanskrit literature. The *Rāmāyaṇa* records that its founder was the Thaumaturge King Brahmadatta; at that period Kāmpilya seemed as fine as Amarāvatī, the heavenly capital of Indra's realm. The *Brāhmaṇa*s praise the wisdom, the perfect rituals, the education of the Pañcāla priests and mention the nobleness and generosity of its princes.[3] The *ṛṣi* Śvetaketu and King Pravāhana Jaivali,[4] Uddālaka,[5] Yājñavalkya,[6] who is among the most celebrated seers of the Upaniṣads, were born in South Pañcāla. The town was under the protection of the *yakṣa* Kapila,[7] later identified with the homonymous seer.

The *Mahābhārata* is the principal source of information on the town. The great Indian epic describes the political agreement

1. *VS*, 7.4.19.
2 *ŚB*, 13.5.4.7.
3. *ŚB*, 5.5.2.3-5.
4. *BAU*, 6.1.1; *ChU*, 5.3.1.
5. *ŚB*, 11.4.1.1-2.
6. *BAU*, 6.3.15; 3.7.31; *ŚB*, 11.4.1.1.
7. Ram Nath Misra, *Yaksha Cult and Iconography*, New Delhi, 1981, p. 169.

between Droṇa and Drupada and records the division of the Pañcāla Kingdom into two different states: Northern Pañcāla, with capital Ahicchatrā, and Southern Pañcāla, with Kāmpilya as capital.[8] Later, King Drupada organised in the neighbourhood of Kāmpilya the great *svayaṁvara*, the tournament of heroes, from among whom his daughter, Draupadī, was to choose a husband. It is well known that Draupadī then became the sole wife of the five Pāṇḍavas.[9] Kāmpilya participated in the *Mahābhārata* war allied to the five Pāṇḍavas and consistently maintained great political and religious prestige. Later, during the same war, Dhṛṣṭadyumna, the king of South Pañcāla, distinguished for his boldness, killed Droṇa, the murderer of his father Drupada.[10] It seems that he died without heirs and, after the war, Pañcāla became once more a united and prosperous kingdom under a Kuru dynasty, as is mentioned in the Purāṇas.[11] In Pañcāla, during the following period, the development of Jainism and Buddhism began. Mahāvīra as a pilgrim visited Kāmpilya where the thirteenth *tīrthaṅkara* Vimalanātha was born, entered *nirvāṇa* and reached final *samādhi*. Subsequently the town became an important Jaina centre. King Sañjaya renounced the throne and became a Jaina monk.[12] In the Buddhist *Jātaka*s, Kāmpilya is mentioned as a rich and peaceful town under the rule of another king called Brahmadatta.[13] The town, located on the bank of river Ganges, was a centre of pilgrimage

---

8. *Mbh*, 1.166; 1.138.73-74.
9. *Mbh*, 3.233.
10. *Mbh*, 5.192.15.
11. *VāyuP.*, 99.170-171; *ViṣṇuP.*, 4.19.11-13; *BhāgavataP.*, 9.21; *MatsyaP.*, 49.47.
12. *Mahāmagga J.*, 6.329. J.C. Jain, *Life in Ancient India as Depicted in the Jain Canon*, Bombay, 1947, p. 293.
13. *Jñātadharmakathā*, 74-78. K.D. Bajpei, *'Kāmpilyanareśa Brahmadatta aur unkā sāsankāla svarṇyug', Kāmpial Kalpa,* Varanasi, 1978.

and here the eighteen arts were highly developed. Pañcāla maintained its independence and fame over a long period of time up to the invasion of the new rulers of Magadha, the illegitimate dynasty of the Nandas, *c.* 350 BC. Under the domain of the Nandas and the following Maurya dynasty, Kāmpilya lapsed into two centuries of obscurity.[14] With the Brāhmaṇical restoration of the Śuṅgas, Kāmpilya and the whole Pañcāla Kingdom recovered importance and glory and enjoyed partial autonomy. It has been possible to identify the names of twenty four kings by means of numismatic studies.[15] This fact supports the view that the kings of Kāmpilya retained some degree of autonomy under the Kuṣāṇa Empire also.[16] In the middle of the fourth century AD Pañcāla completely lost its independence after the conquest by Samudragupta of the Imperial Gupta dynasty, though Kāmpilya was still eminent as a centre of commerce and pilgrimage. Also, under the new domain of Kanauj its strategic importance ensured its continuing renown which is confirmed by the accounts of Chinese Buddhist travellers.[17] The Pratihāra conquerors also favoured this area of the Ganges valley and the great King Bhoja ordered the construction of a high temple, located near Kāmpilya, in honour of Viṣṇu. The invasions of Mahmud of Ghazni, and later, of Muhammad Ghaurī represented a severe blow to the prosperity of Kāmpilya. This is evidenced by many broken sculptures found in the fields around the present village of Kampil, District of Farrukhabad (U.P.). Many ornate palaces of the Mogul era nevertheless prove the slow decadence of the old capital under Islamic power. During the British Raj it

14. H.C. Raychaudhuri, *Political History of Ancient India,* Calcutta, 1953, pp. 233-34.
15. K.D. Bajpai, *Indian Numismatic Studies*, New Delhi, 1974, p.9.
16. Vidula Jayaswal, *Kushana Clay Art of Ganga Plains*, Delhi, 1991, pp. 10-11.
17. R.S. Tripathi, *History of Kanauj up to the Moslem Conquest*, Delhi, 1964, pp. 32-55.

was thought that the village of Kampil could be the unrecognisable site of the glorious Kāmpilya town. Many broken sculptures found by the peasants in the fields, the presence of tall mounds, together with a great quantity of bricks, suggested to Cunningham the identification of Kampil with Kāmpilya.[18] This belief has now been supported by contemporary Indian archaeologists. Eighty years after his survey, the first scientific research of the site was initiated. In 1954 Prof. B.B. Lal noted the presence of the Northern Black Polished Ware (NBPW) in Kampil area. This is typical of the middle Indian Iron Age *c.* 600-500 BC.[19] The first official survey in Kampil was undertaken by a team from Deccan College under the direction of Prof. V.N. Misra.[20] The team recognised the great mound located in the north-western part of the village where a large quantity of Painted Grey Ware (PGW) along with fragments of NBPW was found. PGW is an older kind of ware and may be dated as early as the Iron Age though the presence of the NBPW in the same archaeological stratum has reduced the possibility of an earlier date of the site. Another survey was undertaken in 1976 by Prof. K.K. Sinha of Banaras Hindu University. During the BHU mission, six trenches were excavated and in all of them the virgin strata was reached. The results confirmed the dating of the contemporary NBPW and PGW.[21] In recent times, the Pañchal Research Institute at Kanpur has organised many surface surveys on the field. During one of these, Prof. K.D. Bajpai discovered the important inscription praising the great Viṣṇu temple of Bhoja, now at Fatehgarh Museum.[22] All the important specimens

18. A. Cunningham, *Archaeological Survey of India Reports*, vol. XI, 1871-87.

19. B.B. Lal, *Ancient India*, n. 10-11, p. 140.

20. V.N. Misra, *Indian Archaeology — A Review*, 1965-66, p. 48.

21. T.N. Roy, *IA*, 1979, pp. 51-52.

22. K.D. Bajpai, 'Pratīhār śāsak mihir Bhoj kā nayā śilālekh', *Yugon Yugon se Pañcāla*, Pañcala Śodha Sansthāna, Kanpur.

recovered, mainly post-Gupta sculptures as well as a few Kuṣāṇa's terracottas, were placed in a small museum annexed to the main Jaina temple, with the exception of a beautiful dancing Gaṇeśa in buff sandstone which at present is kept in the State Museum of Lucknow. Subsequent to the above-mentioned surveys no methodical excavation has taken place. Clearly, the reason is that the deepest human settlement stratum pre-dating the virgin ground at Kampil is too recent and thus cannot be the site of the ancient Kāmpilya of the epic tales. If the remains of human settlement in the Kampil mound was the splendid capital of Drupada, the deepest remains should have dated at least to 1200-1000 BC. The deception is quite understandable.

In March 1993 I was invited by the President of the Panchal Research Institute, Shree Hazari Mull Banthia, to make a surface inspection of Kampil village. The vast mound in the north-west corner of the village, the widespread quantity of terracotta fragments, the evidence of several medieval remains, the active local folk traditions and the Kampil epic toponymy all convinced me of the importance of the site. Moreover, information given by Mr. Banthia relating to some terracotta tablets and heads of the Kuṣāṇa epoch stimulated me to reopen the research. On my return to Venice a student of mine, already qualified with a degree in Geology, sought my advice on a topic for a thesis on the History of Art of India. Considering her formation, I entrusted Ms. A. Dallaporta with a research project on Kampil with the underlying objective of identifying the original capital of the *Mahābhārata* poem. No new research in the 1990s could ignore the vast resources offered by the new technologies which were non-existent at the time of the previous surveys. I contacted the eminent hydrogeologist of the National Centre of Research of Padua (Italy), Dr. Bruno Marcolongo, and invited him to collaborate in the research. He took charge of remote sensing and the related information technology aspects of the project.

His contribution has been of great importance in the discovery of another field of ruins nearby Kampil. Dr. Dallaporta visited Kampil in 1994 and during her surface survey reached the same conclusions as those of the previous above-mentioned studies. Kampil was certainly a historically notable town, but was not as old as the capital of the *Mahābhārata* war.[23] In 1995 the team composed of students and researchers from my Department of Indological Studies and of V.A.I.S. checked the findings by a satellite image under the guidance of Dr. Marcolongo. Our final opinion was that the original location of Kāmpilya does not exactly overlap that of present Kampil.

In February 1996 the same team under the guidance of Dr. Marcolongo and myself visited the area of Kampil. On the second day of surface survey we discovered, five km away from Kampil, a vast area surrounding a mound, covered by an astonishing quantity of terracotta debris. A preliminary evaluation suggested that they dated from 600 to 100 BC. This made us think that the human settlement was contemporary to the mound of Kampil. Maybe the great flood which ravaged Hastināpura in the sixth century BC induced the inhabitants to leave some old settlement and to found the big fortified city called Drupad Qilā by the inhabitants of the neighbouring villages.

In February 1997, the same team came back to the field of the discovery (Lat. 27°36'13"; Long. 79°12'30") for another surface survey and measurement. The results of the investigations were very interesting. The Drupad Qilā has a rectangular shape surrounded by walls, whose sides measure 780 × 660 m. The Drupad Qilā is accurately oriented with the compass, and its longest sides are positioned in EW direction. The walls, five-to-

---

23. Annamaria Dallaporta, *Kāmpilya, capitale del Sud Pañcāla*, unpublished Doctorate Dissertation, University of Venice, 1995.

six m high and four-to-five m thick in the emergent parts, have the structure with green bricks and baked bricks lining on the top. Inside the walls the surface is fully covered with terracotta fragments, evidently scattered by the floods of the Ganges. There are several mounds probably hiding collapsed buildings. The NE corner of the citadel, where now there is the human settlement of Dhonpura, is lost probably because of a violent flood. The Ganges now flows five kilometres NE from the Drupad Qilā, but many century ago its river-bed ran along the northern walls. Out of the city walls there are other several mounds covered by broken bits, mostly in the direction of the present villages of Nārāyaṇpur and Pahārpur. Between the villages the layout of another fort, called by the villagers Gaṛhī Qilā, is visible. Two other mounds stand under the villages of Jhinjauṭa and Mānikpur. The complex of Drupad Qilā is remarkable, covering approximately 1,000,000 sq m.

Some bricks of the Kuṣāṇa period, the epigraphy of King Bhoja and several broken but graceful sculptures in *kankar* or sandstone of the Gurjara-Pratihāra epoch, collected and kept under the sacred trees of the surrounding villages, indicate and testify to the continuation of important settlements in the area up to the beginning of the Middle Ages.

On 7 January, 1998, on the occasion of the official visit of the Italian Prime Minister to India, the Kāmpilya Project was presented at Rashtrapati Bhavan to numerous Indian and Italian ministers and authorities.

The other missions in 1997, 1998 and the excavations in winter 2000 were co-organised by my Department, V.A.I.S., C.N.R./IRPI, the Indian Archaeological Society and the Panchal Research Institute, under the patronage of the Archaeological Survey of India and the Italian Embassy in India. The scientific collaboration with the Department of Ancient Indian Culture and Archaeology of B.H.U. offered to Corrado Puchetti — one of my best students — the opportunity for a field research under the guidance of the eminent scientist Prof. Purushottam Singh. The research concluded with a dissertation (Ph.D.) by Dr. Puchetti which was discussed at the B.H.U. of Varanasi. During one of these missions, Dr. Puchetti found a copy of the *Kāmpilyamahātmya* which will become a landmark for future philological investigation of the archaeological site of Kāmpilya. The archaeological efforts of this young scholar have been achieved with the publication of this English translation of the *Kāmpilyamahātmya* under the auspices of D.K. Printworld, the same publishing house which brought out the first book on the discovery of Drupad Qilā in 1997.

At present, Dr. Puchetti is a member of the Kāmpilya Project team under the patronage of the Italian Ministry of Foreign Affairs.

Gian Giuseppe Filippi

Preface

BEING in the presence of Indian teachers for several years has given me a glimpse into the greatness of Sanātana Dharma, to which the Indian traditional society corresponds in all its facets; among these, to the *Sanātanadharma* (the perennial *dharma*[1], whose closest form is the *Hindu Vedicdharma*) a spiritual geography is also referred like a web spun throughout the whole *akhaṇḍa Bhārata*[2], as it is described by the *Purāṇa*.

In India there are many *tīrtha*[3] (ford) and *pīṭha* (the 'seat' of a deity), special pilgrimage sites maintaining the witness of saints and divine events which have entered into the course of time as metahistorical influences. The learned scholar should never forget that the source of all this manifestation is beyond time and space; thus, in a country such India, where a natural attitude towards metaphysics is continuously nourished by uninterrupted tradition, it is normal that historical facts can break with the ordinary material co-ordinates conceived by modern historians. Regarding this it is to notice the doctrine of the *avatāra*, divine manifestations, and the peculiarity of India to be the guest-land of such extraordinary personalities.[4]

---

1. From the root *dhṛ*, to be or exist; to continue; to mantain. It is shortly translated as the 'Universal Law'.
2. The 'complete' India, covering an area going from Beluchistan (present Pakistan) in the west to Burma in the east.
3. From the root *tṛ*.
4. Regarding this topic see: Karpattriji, 'Bharata hī meṁ avatāra kyoṅ?' from the collection *Bhakti-sudhā*.

Since immeasurable time, in force of their capacity to remind the Centre, these sites have attracted multitudes of pilgrims. Monks and sages have often chosen to live at such *tīrtha*, which, far from being just simple fords, are like bridges to cross the perilous rivers of worldly existence. The importance of *tīrtha*s is attested by both Vedic and Purāṇic literature, where the mere recitation of their names bestows spiritual merits to the devotees.

A necessary element for the vitality of the *tīrtha*s is their vicinity to a holy river or a pond, so that, keeping the same name or with some slight phonetic variations, these sites have changed place following the shifting of the river courses.

*Tīrtha*s denote different qualities according to the presiding deity and the grace conferred. Some of them grant to man immortality, while others success; others are more suitable to initiation or for the rites of post-mortem. This is the case of a *tīrtha* such as Kāmpilya, the capital of King Drupada and the origin place of Draupadī, of *Mahābhārata* memory, nowadays situated in the Gaṅgā-Yamunā doāb near the village of Kāmpil (district of Farrukhabad, U.P.). In the times when Kāmpilya was closely facing the right bank of the most sacred river of India, the ancient capital of southern Pāñcāla for some periods had the control all over the Pāñcāla realm, of both northern and southern parts, the river Ganges being the border between the two. In consequence of the shifting of the Ganges this place was deserted, leaving behind traces of the vestiges of an ancient urban settlement.

Kāmpilya has been the subject of my study[5], and the researches on the field have led me there to collect pieces of information. Besides the geo-archaeological data, I have also looked for the references on Kāmpil from the local tradition. In

5. *History and Archaeology of the Kāmpilya Region*, Banaras Hindu University, 2002.

one of these surveys at Kāmpil I was told by some learned residents about the existence of the *Kāmpilyamahātmya* text, a collection from *Mahābhārata* and some *Purāṇas*[6] on the qualities and important happenings that took place in the region of Kāmpilya. Reading and translating this *Purāṇa* I got the direct evidence to reappraise the concept, alas well diffused in Western academies, that the *smṛti* literature is just an old collection written in ancient times: a peculiar aspect of Indian culture is to re-write the traditional texts, either for adapting them to modern literary demands, by instance as for the *Rāmāyaṇa* written in Sanskrit by Vālmiki and after many centuries in Avadhī by Tulsidāsa, or to stress the peculiarity of a character or of a place in the form of a special eulogy dedicated to a circumscribed theme. In this way, through fresh forms tradition is maintained and new vitality is instilled in the readers.

Few but important personalities I would like to remember here.

First of all Prof. G.G. Filippi of the Ca' Foscari University of Venice and founder of the Venetian Academy of Indian Studies (VAIS), who has been the promoter of the last researches[7] on Kāmpilya giving them an international echo, and who has invited me to undertake my Ph.D. study at the Benaras Hindu University, under the supervision of the eminent archaeologist Prof. P. Singh, Head of Department of Ancient Indian Culture and Archaeology at the faculty of Arts, who has patiently supervised the planning, the development and the completion of my research, and to whom I express my lifelong gratitude.

---

6. *ajo nityaḥśāśvato 'yaṁ purāṇaḥ*. Bg. 2, 20. '*Purāṇa*' is indeed related to what fully pervades the three times, past, present and future.

7. Previous archaeological suveys at Kāmpil were done by A. Cunningham, 1878; B.B. Lal, 1954-55; V.N. Miśra, 1961; K.K. Sinha, 1976; G.C. Singh, 1979, and M. Gupta, 1992.

My reverent thoughts go to Sri Hazari Mull Banthia, President of the Pancala Research Institute, who has made possible the co-operation with the Italian team on dealing with the subject of Kāmpilya and Pāñcāla. A special thanks to his nephew Pukharaj, manager of the Śvetāmbara Jaina Mandir in Kāmpil, who personally gave me the book of the text of the *Kāmpilyamahātmya*.

Finally, I wish to profess my gratefulness to all those friends and colleagues who have helped and stimulated the finishing of the present work.

Corrado Puchetti

Contents

Introduction

THE town of Kāmpilya is among the most eminent capitals mentioned in the *Mahābhārata* but, at present, it is the only one that has not been identified with certainty.

The word *mahātmya,* besides its meanings of magnanimity, highmindedness, exalted state or position, and majesty, indicates the peculiar efficacy or virtue of any divinity or sacred shrine or a literary work giving an account of the merits of a holy place or object. Often a *mahātmya* is a collection made by references on the same theme from different Purāṇas, but it can also be part of a Paurāṇic text as in the case of the *Devī Mahātmya* which is a part of the *Mārkaṇḍeya Purāṇa*. The *Kāmpilyamahātmya* focusses its attention on the region of Kāmpilya, where the old capital of South Pañcāla was, a place which is strictly tied not only with the name of King Drupada and his celebrated daughter Draupadī, the five Pāṇḍavas and other characters of the *Mahābhārata*, but also has been the scene of some episodes of the *Rāmāyaṇa* and other Purāṇas.

A *Purāṇa* is characterised by *pañca lakṣaṇa* (five attributes): *sarga* (origin of the universe), *pratisarga* (continuous development from the primordial matter, its manifestation and dissolution), *vaṁśa* (description of the dynasties), *manvantara* (cosmic cycles, the reigns of the Manus) and *vaṁśānucarita* (history of a dynasty, genealogical list).

These five requiremets are described in the text of the *Kāmpilyamahātmya*. The origin of the universe, the development from the primordial matter are dealt with in the first chapter. The description of the dynasties comes out in the thirty-fifth chapter. The *vaṁśānucarita*, the history of the dynasty of King Brahmadatta, is explained in the forty-sixth chapter. The argument of the *manvantara* is not directly dealt with as in the main Purāṇas but we can argue about the cyclicity of the *yuga*s by the presence of some king's names such as Brahmadatta (Solar dynasty), Draupada and Ajamīḍha (Lunar dynasty). The cyclicity is also inferred from the fact that in some cases there is a description of the characters' different existences, who improve from birth to birth by virtue of asceticism and the grace of being at the *tīrtha* of Kāmpilya.

The conception of a meta-historical intervention into Indian history must be kept in the foreground. The possibility of the worldly presence of *avatāra*s in India should not be considered non-scientific just on the basis of a mere materialistic research.

The mentality from which the so-called historical perspective sprang excludes the bigger and greater 'integral' perspective illuminated by the Vedic and Purāṇic traditions. From incommensurable time this tradition has enlightened the everyday routine and the 'normal' path of the Hindus' lives, denoting a vitality which cannot nowadays be met with in any other place of the world. On the contrary this common patrimony, inherited through an interrupted chain of *guru-celā*, teacher and disciple, deserves a careful reading by the Western scientists.

The concept of the immanent and trascendent centre, which is the baseless base of the whole manifestation, is expounded from the very first lines of this *mahātmya*, and repeated all along the work. Fundamental principles of the *sāṅkhya darśana*, and the etymon of the name Kāmpilya are also explained in a mythological context in the first few chapters. The whole *mahātmya* lays stress on the significance of the origin of the Kāmpilya region, on the many pregnant events that happened there, and last but not least its effective importance for the rites of *śrāddha* to be performed in honour of the ancestors. The drawer tale is introduced by Vyāsa who relates the meeting between Śaunaka and other *muni*s with Sūta, but the main interlocutors are Vaiśampāyana and King Janamejaya. The cumulative effect of the opera instils the idea of the greatness of the Kāmpilya region into the reader's mind: lights of a glorious past, still transmitted to the new generations, even through the many shadows projected by the influences coming from the near and far West.

Corrado Puchetti

Bhūmikā

Introduction from the original manuscript

The author Durgadatta Sharma was invited by Goswami Bhairavagiri to compile this *Kāmpilyamahātmyam* after Śukratoṣanidhijī and Miśra Dūrgarnāthjī, two excellent poets, had already written a first *Kāmpilyamahātmyam* on the basis of the *Purāṇa*s. Unfortunately these two were not able to complete their work which was completely destroyed after their death. The author's uncle Rāmadattajī supplied the books on the subject. Among them there were also two books which were written by the grandfather and the father of the author regarding the tales of Rāmeśvarnāth, Kāleśvarnāth, the Draupadīkuṇḍa. With the help of the previous works and with Paurāṇic quotations, the writer was able to arrange an extensive compilation: it consists of 1363 *śloka*, stanzas, divided in 51 *adhyāya*, chapters.

Some people confuse the land of Pañcāla with Punjab (Pir Pantsal) but two pieces of evidence can be quoted to show this is not correct: (1) the presence of the Gaṅgā and the quotation of other sites in Pañcāla (*Mbh.*, Ādi-Parvan); (2) when King Yudhiṣṭhira after the rite of *rājasūya* in Indraprastha (Delhi) sent his four brothers on the four directions to proclaim his universal conquest, among them Bhīma was sent eastward and Nakula westward. After coming back, the former reported that among the conquered lands there was also Pañcāla, whereas Nakula referred to Pañcanada (Punjab). (*Mbh.*, Sabhā-Parvan, 29.32)

The land of Kāmpilya is important as *yogasiddhi bhūmi*: as a matter of fact, many *yogīrāja*s lived there, like kings Aṇuha,

Brahmadatta, Kṛta; it was the birthplace of many valiant heroes: Dhṛṣṭadyumna, Bhīṣma the most famous warrior of the Bhārata war, who fought against Droṇācārya, his *guru* (*Mbh.*, Droṇa-Parvan). Not only is the region of Kāmpilya the birthplace of great *vīras*, heroes, but also the *brāhmaṇas* of this area were well renowned for their eloquence. The *purohita* of the king of Kāmpilya was sent by the Pāṇḍavas to the Kauravas to perform the rite of *sandhi*. On that occasion all the assembly were struck dumb when they heard the very clear pronunciation of the *purohita*. Only Bhīṣma somehow could answer: 'O *vipravar* you are uttering very rigorous words'. '*Atitīkṣṇacate vākyaṁ brahmaṇyāditi manyate*'.

Kāmpilya is also an important Jaina site because it is the place where the thirteenth *tīrthaṅkara* Vimalanātha appeared. Some references about him, drawn out from the *Vimala Purāṇa*, have been written in this book. He belonged to the Solar dynasty, being a member of the family of King Ikṣvāku. His father was Kṛtavarmā and his mother's name was Śyāmādevī. In Kāmpilya his four *kalyāṇa* (name of the eleventh of the fourteen Pūrvas or most ancient writings of the Jainas; here it is correspondent to *saṁskāra*, consecration, a sacred ceremony which purifies from the taint of sin contracted in the womb and leading to regeneration) happened: *garbha-kalyāṇa*, on *kṛṣṇa daśamī*, the tenth lunar day of the waning moon, of the month of *jyeṣṭha*; *janmakalyāṇa*, on *māgha-sudī-cathurtī* (the fourth day of the waxing moon); *dīkṣā-kalyāṇa* on the *śukla pakṣa* of *māgha* (the waxing lunar fortnight of the month of *māgha*); and *kevalajñāna-kalyāṇa* on the *kṛṣṇa ṣaṣṭamī* of *māgha* (the sixth day of the dark-half fortnight of the lunar month of *māgha*).

Śvetāmbara, the whitedressed, includes all the householders, *gṛhastha dharma*. They keep a *mūrti* of Vimalanāthajī, well adorned with embellishments and dressed with rich garments. Sandalpaste and other offerings are also made. In the *mandir* there are the statues of Bhairava and Cakreśvarī Devī and the *pujārī* is a *brāhmaṇa*. In Kāmpil there is a temple of this *sampradāya* that was completed in 1902 of the Vikramāditya calendar (AD 1960) by the Jauharī Jaina of Lakhnau. The Śrīgaṇeśa, the rite of installation, was performed by Hindu *paṇḍitas*. In this *mandir* no special *melā*, fair, is held.

Digambarī worship Vimalanātha in his *paramhaṁsa* form. The *mūrti* is naked (*digambara*, lit. 'dressed with the space directions') and no direct offerings of sandalwood paste, rice, etc., are made, but the oblations are to be made only on a large flat metal plate kept in front of the statue. In this temple there is only the image of Vimalanātha and the *pujārī* is a Jaina. In this quite old temple two fairs, *melās*, are held every year. A little one occurs in the dark lunar-fortnight of the month of *kvāra* (around October). A more important fair takes place in the last day of the dark fortnight of the lunar month of *caitra*. During this *melā* several chariot-processions, *ratha-yātrā*, come from the area: Mainpurī, Eṭā, Kurāvalī, Kannauj, Farrukhābād, Kāyamgañj and other towns around Kāmpil. On the first day the *ratha* of Mainpurī drives out with great pomp. In front of the chariot a pavement is laid, on which the devotees sing the glories of their *iṣṭa-devatā*, their favourite god, and dance. This fair lasts for five or six days. It is also an occasion for Jainas to arrange their daughters' meeting with their prospective bridegrooms. In the temple of the Digambara a *dharmaśālā* was built, from which four long-lasting wells issued.

In the *Vimala Purāṇa* there is a description of the area of the settlement of Kāmpilya, 12 *yojana* long and 9 *yojana* wide, but it seems exaggerated.

It is also important to mention two main reasons that link the Kāmpilya region with the Sūryavaṁśī kings of Ayodhyā: (1) the installation in Kampil of a *Śivaliṅgam* named Rāmeśvarnātha by the hand of Śatrughna, brother of Śrī Rāmacandra; (2) Hiraṇyanābha, of the Ikṣvāku progeny, was the seventeenth ruler of Ayodhyā after Śrī Rāmacandra. He was a great preceptor of Yogic science and had a relation of *guru-śiṣya* with the King of Kāmpilya, Kṛta. In the *Harivaṁśa* after King Rāmacandra the name of Hiraṇyanābha does not appear in the traditional dynasty, but it occurs in *Bhāgavata*, in *Śiva-Purāṇa* (*Umā-saṁhitā* 39,

25) and also in the *sarga* 28 of the *Raghuvaṁśa* of the *mahākavi* Kālidāsa.

In February AD 1935, during his annual inspection in the town of Kāmpil, Mr. Wallace, hearing about the compilation of the *Kāmpilyamahātmyam*, asked the author up to which period the description of the greatness of Kāmpilya was. He was answered that it reached the *Mahābhārata* times. In fact, after those times there are not many references to Kāmpilya. But following Mr. Wallace's advice further research showed that around the fourteenth century AD King Jogājīt Cauhān was ruler of 2000 villages. In the *paraganā* of Kāmpil there were 360 villages that were given by King Jogājīt to 84 brāhmaṇas. They began to pay taxes to the *bādśāh*. After sometime, because of a famine, the tax-money could not be paid to the ruler. King Akbar sent a tax collector named Mahamūd Khān to Kāmpilya to get the money. The Council of the Province called the 84 *brāhmaṇa*s to their own assembly and spoke harsh words to them. The *brāhmaṇa*s became angry at that and on that occasion weapons were also used. The Assembly of the Province sentenced the *brāhmaṇa*s to death. Afterwards the 84 *brāhmaṇa*s secretly left Kāmpil. Some of them went to stay in a village called Punthar (Puṇyasthal), that is a couple of *koṣa* in the *iśāna* (north-east) direction from the town of Kāmpil. In Kāmpil there is an old well (called *avadhūtī kuiyān*) at which the *caurāsiyā*, eighty-four, *brāhmaṇa*s used to stay. They were born blind but they were still very good cowrie gamblers. They were endowed with such an intuition that they could guess what numbers were thrown by others.

When the news of the death sentence arrived at the King's court, another governor of the province, whose name was Bakhtabuland Khān,was sent to Kāmpil. He started searching the 360 villages, but he could not find any landlords. Then the villagers told him that some of the 84 *brāhmaṇa*s had died and others had left and were so scared that they would not come back. The governor made a proclamation asking anyone who could run the region to come forward. Then he was told that

Lālā Jasavantrāy (Jasū Bhagat), who was the foremost among the *brāhmaṇa*s, could run the region but for fear of the governor he did not want to come forward. So the governor said to his secretary Lālā Rājārām: You and Lālā Jasavantrāy belong to the same *jāti*, so try to convince him and bring him here. Lālā Rājārām convinced Lālā Jasavantrāy to meet the governor. Then the edict of the Kampil district with the signature of the Assembly and the Royal Seal was given to Jasū Bhagatjī, Lālā Jasavantrāy.

Lālā Jasavantrāy used to live in the village of Saksenā Kāyastha Sankisā, that is about 12 *kosa* from Kāmpil to the *āgneya koṇa*, south-west, on the northern banks of the river Kālī. At the door of his house there was a *baḍ vṛkṣa*, a banyan tree. One day the king's army encamped there. That day the owner of an elephant did cut some branches from the banyan to feed his elephant. When Bhagatjī discovered this he got upset. With him there was also a *purohita*, who stayed near Bhagatjī's house. This *purohita* had seven sons who were very arrogant. The eldest noticed the distress of Bhagatjī and sprang on the trunk of the elephant and cut the *mahaut*'s ears. The Royal Army intervened; on the other side there were the *purohita* and his seven sons, Bhagatjī and a well-equipped force. A big fight followed and very many soldiers of the army died. In the end the *purohita*'s side won. Then the army chief himself attacked and after killing the seven sons of the *purohita* and the force of Bhagatjī, looted the houses and went away. In the village and in the house of Bhagatjī sounds of grieving echoed. The *purohita* understood that what had to happen did happen. Bhagatjī turned a deaf ear to everything but he gave all his possessions to the seven young widows, and only wearing two *dhotī* he went away. Distressed, he got to Kāmpil and fell asleep under a tree. In the morning the sun rays made Bhagatjī sweat. A snake saw this and gave shade to the *brāhmaṇa* by expanding its hood. This was seen by a herdsman who was grazing his animals. The astrologer interpreted this to be a very good omen and asked Bhagatjī to become the master of the village. So it is true that if you give one you will receive a hundred. Bhagatjī had shown his kindness to the *purohita*, and so later he was rewarded many times more in Kāmpil. He had two sons: Mādhavadās and Rāīmal. They were both childless. For this reason Bhagatjī consulted the *paṇḍitas* and asked them why he had no grandchildren. They answered that although he had given all his possessions to the seven widows of the sons of the *purohita*, the *ātmā* of the *purohita* was not satisfied yet. There was a way to pacify it: when one of the two wives of his sons was at the eighth month of gestation, then on Monday of any light half fortnight of any month, *khīr pūrī* should be offered to seven *brāhmaṇas*. Also five clothes and the proper *dakṣiṇā* (offer of money) should be given. *Havana* (Brāhmaṇical fire sacrifice) was also to be performed. The remains from the plates of the *brāhmaṇas* in the form of *prasāda* should be given with respect to the pregnant woman and any other fortunate woman. In that way the family succession would be ensured. Bhagatjī to maintain the dignity of his family said: 'Who doesn't follow this rule because of non-belief or greed, will never find happiness, this is the prudent counsel of Jasū Bhagat.'

By Lord's grace the eldest son's wife became pregnant. Then Bhagatjī made all the aforesaid offerings and in this way the progeny flourished. The second son had no offspring yet. He declared among friends that he would also feed five *brāhmaṇas* respectfully and in secret. Afterward he also begot descendants. Nowadays the number of Bhagatjī's dynasty has increased up to nearly two thousand. They live in Kāmpil, Kuṁvarpur, the provinces of Mainpurī, Śāhajahānpur, Badāyūn, Iṭāvā, Karahal, Farrukhābād, Fatehgarh and other places. And they all accept the rule dictated by Bhagatjī. Two other rules were added by his successors. (1) Not to accept any money during marriage (vartonī ke samay); (2) In the district of Sankisā never accept food or water. The progeny of Mādhavadās, the eldest son of Bhagatjī, is called *caudharī* (headman, chieftain). The descendants of Rāīmal, who was the Prime Minister of King Ṭoḍarmal, were called *Kānūngo* (an officer of the revenue department having charge of land records of a district). The author has recorded all this information from the manuscript of the book Dalpati Candrikā.

In Kāmpil there have also been great poets. (1) Māthura Caube Mukaṭimaṇi (*Kavirāja*). Aurangzeb gave him 500 *bīghā* of freehold land that is still in the possession of the family. (2) Puruṣottama, a *brāhmaṇa* of the Gokarṇa *gotra*, who wrote a book entitled *Hanumāndūtattva* in the name of the king of Kamāyū, Bājabahādurcandra. (3) Śukadeva (*Kavirāja*) was a *brāhmaṇa* of the Śuklas of Kānyakubja. He lived at Bigahāpur. These *brāhmaṇas* are also called Miśra. In 1728 he wrote a philosophical book, *Candagrantha*. In 1733 he concluded the *Fājilālīprakāśa*, a treatise on *nāyakabheda*. (4) Ṭoḍarmal Śukla (*mallakavi*) who wrote the *Rasa Candrikā*, a work on *nāyakabheda*. (5) Toṣanidhi Śukla wrote *Ātmaśikṣā* in the name of Caudharī Premrāja of Ḍhilāvalī in 1847, and in 1889 at the request of King Daulatisinh of Rijor he composed the *Daulaticandrikā*. He also wrote other books in Hindi and Sanskrit. (6) Tulasī Rāma, who wrote a book on Vedānta in Sanskrit entitled *Jñānakallolinī*. He also compiled a miscellaneous work of poetry in Hindi. He lived until the age of 29. (7) Navaldāsa Kāyastha. He was a Vaiṣṇava *sādhu*. His main work is *Navaldohāvalī*, but he also compiled other books of miscellaneous poetry.

In Kāmpil there is also a well called Dalathamman *kuṇḍa*. People say that when King Pṛthvīrāja Cauhān was running away, after having abducted the daughter of Jayacanda, the King of Kannauj, and the army of the latter was pursuing him, both the armies stopped at this *kuṇḍa* to quench their thirst. Pṛthvīrāja Cauhān arrived at Soron and defeated the army of King Jayacanda. This event is recorded in *Pṛthvīrājarāso, parva* 61.

Durgadatta Sharma

अथ काम्पिल्लमहात्म्यप्रारम्भः

Kāmpilyamahātmya

मंगलाचरण
Maṅgalācaraṇa

ओं नमोजगदुत्पत्तिभृतिसंहृतिकारिणे ।
ज्ञानविज्ञानरूपाय ब्रह्मणे परमात्मने ॥ १ ॥

I salute *paramātmā* who is the producer, sustainer and transformer of the world, who has the form of both the supreme and the lower knowledge. **[1]**

यस्यास्ते जननी नचापि जनको भृत्यो न वाधीश्वरो
नो मित्रं न चशत्रुरस्ति न सुता पुत्रः कलत्रं नवा ।
न भ्राता भगिनी तथैव न गुरुः शिष्योनवा वर्त्तते
तन्नित्यं परतः परं शिवकरं ब्रह्मद्वयं धीमहि ॥ २ ॥

I meditate on *paramātmā* who has neither mother nor father, neither servant nor lord, neither friend nor enemy, no wife and neither daughter nor son, neither brother nor sister, neither teacher nor disciple; on that non-dual *Brahma* who is always, and beyond the beyond, the wellfarer of all. **[2]**

यत्कृपादृष्टिसंदृष्टः सहस्रांशुरिवापरः ।
लवेनैव भवेन्मर्त्यस्तस्मै श्रीगुरवेनमः ॥ ३ ॥

The man who is seen by one of his merciful glances becomes at once brilliant like the sun; that *sad guru* I salute. **[3]**

सर्वैः कविजनैर्नित्यं स्वकीयमतिपूर्वकम् ।
क्रियते देवसम्बन्धिकीर्त्तनं कीर्त्तिवर्द्धनम् ॥ ४ ॥

All the poets by their intelligence (*buddhi*) make eulogies of their own divinity, bestower of grace. **[4]**

अतोमयापि क्रियते स्वमनोषानुसारतः ।
काम्पिल्लक्षेत्रमाहात्म्यं धर्म्मकामार्थमोक्षदम् ॥ ५ ॥

For this reason, with the knowledge I have, I also make the *mahātmya* of Kāmpilyakṣetra, that grants *dharma, artha, kāma, mokṣa.* **[5]**

पठ्यतां पठ्यतां सम्यक् श्रूयतां श्रूयतां सदा।
दृश्यतां दृश्यतां तूर्णं मम पूर्णः परिश्रमः॥ ६॥

O good man, listen or read this *Kāmpilla Māhātmya* and consider my effort. **[6]**

श्रीमद्भागवतं पुराणमखिलं तद्वन्महाभारतं पाद्मं
शैवमथावलोक्य हरिवंशं वैष्णवं स्कन्दकम्।
यत्काम्पिल्ल महत्त्वसूचकवचः संगृह्य तत्सर्वतः
कुर्वेश्रोतृमनोहरं शुभतरं काम्पिल्लमाहात्म्यकम्॥ ७॥

I compose the excellent and dear *Kāmpilla Māhātmya* on the basis of the quotations referring to Kāmpilya *kṣetra* collected from *Śrimadbhāgavat Purāṇa*, *Mahābhārata*, *Padma Purāṇa*, *Śiva Purāṇa*, *Harivaṁśa Purāṇa*, *Viṣṇu Purāṇa* and *Skanda Purāṇa.* **[7]**

विद्वद्वन्द्योस्मद्गुरुस्ताततातः प्राप्तं किञ्चिच्चेतनं यत्कृपातः।
दुर्गादत्तोभूनिवासात्मजातः काम्पिल्लेऽस्मद्वेश्मदेवापगातः॥ ८॥

I received knowledge from my father who was also my *guru*, honoured by learned scholars; my name is Durgadatta and my house is on the banks of the Gaṅgā, in the town of Kāmpil. **[8]**

केचिन्महाभारतीयाः केचिच्च हरिवंशगाः।
पुराणान्तरतः केचिदुद्धृत्य लिखिता मया॥ ९॥

Some of the *śloka*s of this *Kāmpilla Māhātmya* are from the *Mahābhārata*, some others are from *Harivaṁśa Purāṇa* and other *śloka*s have been collected from other Purāṇas. **[9]**

केचित्कथाप्रसङ्गार्थं श्लोकाः सन्त्यत्र मत्कृताः।
यदवद्यं भवेदत्र सुधियः शोधयन्तु तत्॥ १०॥

Some other *śloka*s introducing the story are composed by me. What might be incorrect can be rectified by the learned scholars. **[10]**

अथ कथाप्रसंगः

Kathāprasaṅgaḥ,
the Beginning of the Story

1

The Talk Between Śiva and Nandin about the Origin of Kālī

व्यास उवाच -

नैमिषे युगसन्ध्यायां यज्ञपूर्णाहुतेः परम्।
सूतं सुखस्थं सम्प्रीचुर्मुनयः शौनकादयः ॥ ११ ॥

सूतपूर्णाहुतिं भुंक्ते केयं काम्पिल्लवासिनी।
तन्माहात्म्यं तथोत्पत्तिं श्रोतुमिच्छामहेवयम्॥ १२ ॥

Vyāsajī said —

In the Naimiṣāraṇya in the time of transition, *sandhi*, between *dvāpara* and *kali yuga*, after the complete ritual oblation, *pūrṇāhuti*, Śaunaka and other *munis* asked Sūtajī:

O Sūtajī, who is that *Kāmpillavāsinī*, She who stays in Kampilla, who enjoys the offerings of *pūrṇāhuti*. We want to hear her *mahātmya* and learn about her origin. **[11-12]**

इति तेषां वचः श्रुत्वा महर्षीणां महार्थवत्।
ओमित्युक्त्वा ततः प्राह हृष्टात्मा रौमहर्षणिः॥ १३॥

वयं क्षितौ धन्यतमा नराणां यतो भवद्भिर्जगतोहिताय।
सम्पृच्छ्यते पुण्यकथाकलापो महात्मभिः संसृतिचक्रमुक्तैः॥ १४ ॥

Having listened to the words of those *maharṣis*, the son of Romaharṣaṇa, Sūtajī, also called Ugraśravā said: "I am lucky in this world because I have been asked by people like you, who attained *mukti*, a question concerning a very sacred story." **[13-14]**

यथानुयोगःक्रियते भवद्भिस्तथैव राज्ञा जनमेजयेन ।
पृष्ठः सम्यग्व्यासशिष्योमहात्मा यो वै वैशम्पायननामधेयः ॥ १५ ॥

O *ṛṣi*, you are asking me this question in the same way that King Janamejaya did with the disciple of Vyāsajī, Vaiśampāyana. **[15]**

यथाह राज्ञेजनमेजयाय कथाकलापं स मुनिप्रधानः ।
तथा शृणुध्वं सुसभाहिताशया यथातथं मद्वचनं मुनीन्द्राः ॥ १६ ॥

And as Vaiśampāyana heard the story from King Janamejaya, in the same way you shall listen to it. **[16]**

एकस्मिन्समये विप्राः स राजा जनमेजयः ।
पृष्ठवान्सर्पसत्रान्ते व्यासशिष्यं महामुनिम् ॥ १७ ॥
केयं काली महाभाग काच काम्पीलवासिनी ।
एतत्तत्त्वं समाचक्ष्व सर्वज्ञोसि मतोमम ॥ १८ ॥

Once King Janamejaya, after performing the *sarpa-yajña*, the sacrifice of the snake, asked Vaiśampāyana: "O Illustrious One, who is this Kālī, and who is this Kāmpilyavāsinī. Please tell me this secret, because I know you are omniscient." **[17-18]**

वैशंपायन उवाच -

साधु पृष्ठं महाराज श्रूयतां वचनंमम ।
एवमेव पुरापृच्छन्नन्दी कैलास ईश्वरम् ॥ १९ ॥
नमस्ते शिख साक्षी त्वं सर्वज्ञस्त्वं जगद्गुरो ।
ब्रूहि मे कथमुत्पन्ना काली काम्पीलवासिनी ॥ २० ॥

Vaiśampāyana said —

O *mahārāja*, you are asking a very good question, in the same way that Nandin asked Śivajī on Mount Kailāsa: "O Śivajī, I bow to you; You are the omniscient witness: please tell me how Kāmpilyavāsinī Kālī came to be." **[19-20]**

शिव उवाच -

नन्द्यतां नन्द्यतां नन्दिन्सन्ति तीर्थाण्यनेकशः ।
कम्पिलासदृशं तीर्थं नास्ति भूमण्डले क्वचित् ॥ २१ ॥

नामनिर्वचनं चास्य शृणुनन्दिन्समाहितः ।
कम्पिनः शरणंलातीत्येतस्मात्कम्पिलाभिधा ॥ २२ ॥

कंकारात्कञ्जजनुषः पिकाराच्च पिनाकिनः ।
लक्ष्मीपतेर्लकाराद्वा संजाता कम्पिलाभिधा ॥ २३ ॥

कम्पिला कथ्यते कैश्चित्कैश्चित्काम्पिल्लमित्युत ।
कैश्चित्काम्पीलमित्येवं काम्पिल्यमिति चापरैः ॥ २४ ॥

Śivajī said —

Be happy, O Nandin! Even if there are many pilgrimage places, *tīrtha*s, on the earth, there is no *tīrtha* comparable to Kāmpila.

O Nandin, now listen to the meaning of the name 'Kāmpila'. Because she gives refuge to the sinner shivering (*kaṁp*) from fear, her name is Kāmpila. The first syllable *kaṁ* comes from *kañj-januṣa* (born from a lotus), Brahmājī; the syllable *pi* derives from the name of Śivajī, Pinākin (armed with the bow or spear, *pināka*); and the syllable *la* from Lakṣmīpati, one of the names of *Bhagavān* Viṣṇu. Thus the name Kāmpila is composed by these three syllables combined together. Some call it Kampila, others call it Kāmpilla or Kāmpīla, whilst it is also known as Kāmpilya by others. **[21-24]**

अथातः सम्प्रवक्ष्यामि कालीमाहात्म्यमुत्तमम् ।
यस्यश्रवणतोनन्दिन्परांनिर्वृतिमाप्स्यसि ॥ २५ ॥

O Nandin, now I will tell you how this Kālīkṣetra has been eulogised; by listening to the eulogy you will attain a deep peace. **[25]**

शुभाशुभानि कर्माणि भवन्ति फलवन्तिहि ।

भूलोकोयं ततः श्रेष्ठः सर्वलोकेषु गीयते ॥ २६ ॥

तत्रापि भारतं वर्षं भारतेपि नवोपराः ।
नवोपरेषु च प्रोक्तं कालीक्षेत्रं परं शुभम् ॥ २७ ॥

This place is the best among all the holy places because it bestows the consequences of both good and bad actions (*karmāṇi*). And, in this perspective, on this earth (*bhūloka*) the best country is Bhāratavarṣa, and in the Bhāratavarṣa the best places are the nine *ūsara*[1] and among these nine *ūsara*, the Kālī *kṣetra* is considered the best. **[26-27]**

भारते यत्कृतं पुण्यं तस्य लक्षगुणं फलम् ।
नवोपरेषु यच्चीर्णं तस्य कोटिगुणंभवेत् ॥ २९ ॥

स्नानं दानं जपो होमो देवतापितृपूजनम् ।
कालीक्षेत्रे कृतं यच्च तदानन्त्याय कल्पते ॥ २९ ॥

O Nandin, the merits, *puṇya*, obtained in Bhāratavarṣa are a hundred thousand times more fruitful than in the rest of the world; in Bhāratavarṣa the nine *ūsara* give a million times the reward of a *puṇya*. But indefinitely greater are the fruits of performing *snāna*, *dāna, japa, homa* both for gods and for ancestors, in the Kālī *kṣetra*. **[28-29]**

नन्द्युवाच -

के ते नवोपराः प्रोक्तावर्षेस्मिन्भारते प्रभो ।
तेषुकाली कुतः श्रेष्ठा तन्ममाचक्ष्व यत्नतः ॥ ३० ॥

Nandin said —

O Lord, in this Bhāratavarṣa, what are the names of the nine *ūsara*, and why is the Kālī *kṣetra* considered the best among them? **[30]**

शिव उवाच -

1. Deserts, saline soil; *tapobhūmi*: a land suitable for asceticism.

रेणुका सूकरः काशी काली कालवटेश्वरौ ।
कालञ्जरोमहाकाली ब्रह्मावर्तोनवोपराः ॥ ३१ ॥

Śivajī said —

(1) Reṇukā, (2) Sūkaraḥ (Soraun), (3) Kāśī, (4) Kālī, (5) Kālaveśvara, (6) Vaṭeśvara, (7) Kālañjara, (8) Mahākāla, (9) Brahmāvartta, these are the nine *ūsara*. **[31]**

नन्दिन्पूर्वमकिञ्चित्त्वे संसृक्षोः परमात्मनः ।
प्रधानं क्षत्रपीठाभ्यां ज्योतिषोनिर्गतं वभौ ॥ ३२ ॥

O Nandin, in the beginning when there was nothing, the *jyotirūpa paramātmā*, the Absolute in its form of light, had the desire to create the manifestation, and the *pradhāna prakṛti* disclosed herself along with the *kṣatra*s and the *pīṭha*s. **[32]**

तदेव त्रिषुलोकेषु महाकालीतिगोयते ।
लक्ष्मीः स्वाहा स्वधा श्रद्धा धीर्ह्रीःक्षुत्तृड्दयाऽव्यया ॥ ३३ ॥

Pradhāna prakṛti itself is famous in the three worlds with the name of Mahākālī. Lakṣmī, Svāhā, Svadhā, Śraddhā, Buddhi, Lajjā, Kṣudhā, Tṛṣā, Dayā, Avyayā are also Her other names. **[32-33]**

सा समन्तात् खमालोक्य ओमित्युक्त्वा ततःस्वयम् ।
आकृष्य त्रिगुणं तस्मात् सप्तमूर्तीः ससर्जह ॥ ३४ ॥

सत्त्वादुद्वावीश्वरीविष्णू श्रीब्रह्माणौ रजोगुणात् ।
तमसस्तु त्रयीशानौ शेषाच्छेषमजी जनत् ॥ ३५ ॥

Having seen the whole space, *prakṛti* pronounced the sound *oṁ*, and by that *jyoti* (light) produced the three qualities, *sattva*, *rajas*, *tamas* along with seven other *mūrti* personifications. From the quality of *sat* were emanated Durgā and Viṣṇu, from *raj* Lakṣmī and Brahmā, and from the quality of *tam* Sarasvatī and Mahādeva. The seventh manifestation was made with the remaining part, giving form to Śeṣa. **[34-35]**

ब्रह्मणे सा त्रयीं दत्वा सम्बोध्याह पृथक्पृथक् ।
ब्रह्मन् विधे विरिंचेऽज त्रयि विद्ये स्वरेऽक्षरे ॥ ३६ ॥

तथैव हरये लक्ष्मीं दत्वा सम्बोधयत्युभौ ।
हरे कृष्ण विभो विष्णो लक्ष्मि श्रीः कमले रमे ॥ ३७ ॥

पश्चाच्छिवाय दत्वोमां तत आमन्त्रयत्युभौ ।
शिव श्रीकण्ठ रुद्रेश उमे गौरि शिवे सति ॥ ३८ ॥

शेषमाह सहस्रास्य अनन्त धरणीधर ।
इत्युक्त्वा तत्क्षणादासीत्साक्षाज्ज्योतिःस्वरूपिणी ॥ ३९ ॥

Then *pradhāna prakṛti* gave Sarasvatī to Brahmājī and addressed him as Brahmā, Virañci, Vidhi, Aja; then She turned to Sarasvatī calling her: Trayī, Vidyeśvarī, Akṣarī. In the same way she coupled Lakṣmī to Viṣṇu and said to him: Hari, Kṛṣṇa, Vibhu, Viṣṇu, and to Lakṣmī, Śrī, Kamalā, Ramā. Thus she joined Umā to Śivajī, saying to Śivajī, Śiva, Śrīkaṇṭha, Rudra, Īśa; and to her, Umā, Gaurī, Śivā, Satī. Then, as she did with the foresaid gods, i.e., giving names that correspond to qualities, she addressed Śeṣa as Śeṣa, Sahsramukha, Ananta, Dharaṇīdhara. After that, *pradhāna prakṛti* in no time became one with the *jyotirūpa paramātmā*. **[36-39]**

तदहूँकृतिध्वनेः पञ्चभूतान्यासन्नदन्नभः ।
वहन्वायुर्दहन्वह्निर्वृहद्वार्यचलामही ॥ ४० ॥

From the echo of the sound *huṁ* uttered by that *prakṛti,* the five elements were sent forth. The ether, *nabha*, joined with the sound, *nāda*, the flowing air, *vāyu*; the burning fire, *agni* is the increasing water, *vāri*; and the immovable earth, *mahī*. **[40]**

एतत्कारणमालोक्य सप्तते शरणंययुः ।
अवाऽवेत्यूचिरे तत्र पुनः सासीद्यथापुरा ॥ ४१ ॥

The seven *mūrti*, Brahmājī, etc., saw all this and took refuge in that *prakṛti*. They started saying, 'Protection, Protection!'. Then She took again the previous form of Devī, abandoning the *jyotirūpa*, form of light. **[41]**

ततस्तांकादयोभ्यर्च्च्य परिक्रम्य प्रणम्यच ।
स्तुत्वा जयजयेत्यक्त्वा तदग्रे ननृतुर्मुदा ॥ ४२ ॥
नृत्यान्ते पुनरूचुस्ते विधाय करसम्पुटम् ।
प्रसीदाम्ब किमाज्ञाप्यं तत्कर्त्तुं प्रोद्यताः स्महे ॥ ४३ ॥

Brahmājī and the other *devatā* offered to that Kālī *pūjā*, adoration, *parikramā*, circumambulation, *praṇāma*, respectful salutation, *stuti*, eulogy, and repeating 'victory, victory' started to dance in front of Her. Then with folded hands they said: 'O Mother we will execute what you order!'. **[42-43]**

महाकाल्युवाच -

श्रूयतां भो ममाज्ञैपा शेष त्वं धरणींधर ।
द्वन्द्वीभूय भवन्तोपि जगत्सृज्याद् भृयाद्धृयात ॥ ४४ ॥
अद्य प्रभृति लोकेषु स्वैश्वर्यीकर्तुमर्हथ ।
अंशेन स्थीयतामत्र ततःस्वैरं निवास्यताम् ॥ ४५ ॥
इत आत्रित्रिक्रोशान्तं क्षेत्रं सर्वमघापहम् ।
इहैवागम्यतामेतच्छरणं वो भविष्यति ॥ ४६ ॥
अहमत्र बसिष्यामि नाम्ना काम्पिल्लवासिनी ।
अम्बेऽन्विकेति मन्त्रेण भोक्ष्ये पूर्णाहुतिं मखे ॥ ४७ ॥
काल्याश्रमः कालिकुण्डं कालिपूः कालिकाव्रतम् ।
कालीमहत्त्वश्रवणं पंचकाली ह मुक्तिदा ॥ ४८ ॥

Mahākālī said —

'O Śeṣa, you shall uphold the earth. And you, Brahmājī, etc., with your wives, will be the cause of creation, maintenance and transformation of the world, assigned respectively to Brahmājī, Viṣṇu and Mahādeva.

You will increase your own glory but a part (*aṁśa*) of you will always stay here. After you will also reside wherever you wish to. The three miles' area all around here is a *kṣetra* that destroys every sin. When you are distressed by any cause, here you will find protection because, with the name Kāmpilyavāsinī, I will have my dwelling place here. Moreover, the *pūrṇāhuti* (the finishing touch of a sacrifice, the complete oblation) offered with the *mantra* starting with 'Ambe, Ambike, Ambālike . . .'[2] will be directly accepted by me. And in this place I will grant *mukti*, with my five forms, *pañcakālīrūpa*, i.e., *Kālī āśrama, Kālī kuṇḍa, Kālī purī, Kālī vrata, Kālī mahātmya.*' **[44-48]**

॥ इति श्री काम्पिल्लमाहात्म्ये शिवनन्दिसम्वादे कालयुत्पत्तिवर्णनो नाम प्रथमोऽध्यायः ॥

Here ends the first chapter of the Kāmpilyamahātmya.

---

2. *Ambe ambike ambālike na mā nayatikaścan* । *sasastyśśvakaḥ subhadrikāṁ kāmpīlavāsinīm* ।। Ambā, Ambikā, Ambālikā were the three daughters of the King of Kāśī. They were kidnapped by Bhīṣma to be married to his step brother Vicitravīrya. Ambā was sent back because she had already a secret relation with Śālva, ruler of the city named Saubha. (Ādi-Parvan 186, 15). Ambikā became the elder widow of Vicitravīrya. She was the mother of Dhṛtarāṣṭra by Vyāsa and grandmother of the Kauravas. Ambālikā was the youngest widow of Vicitravīrya and mother of Pāṇḍu and grandmother of the Pāṇḍavas. Regarding this, it is also to notice the epithet *Tryambaka* referred to Śiva Mahādeva.

2

The Talk Between Śiva and Nandin on the Creation and the Importance of Mantra and Dikśa

शिव उवाच -

काल्यां तपस्यतां नोऽभून्मुक्तीच्छाऽतोयमूषरः ।
इत्युक्त्वा स्वांशतां स्थाप्य लोकान् क्लृप्त्वान्तरास्महे ॥ १ ॥

लोकस्या वयमद्यापि ब्रह्मा स्रजति नित्यशः ।
सृष्टिं पालयते विष्णुस्तत्संहर्त्ता हरोस्म्यहम् ॥ २ ॥

तदेतत् कालचक्राख्यं यत्र सृष्ठिश्चतुर्विधा ।
स्वेदजा अण्डजाश्चैवउद्भिज्जाश्च जरायथुजाः ॥ ३ ॥

स्वेदजाः कृमिदंशाद्याः पक्षिसर्पादयीण्डजाः ।
उद्भिज्जास्तरुगुल्माद्या नृगवाद्या जरायुजाः ॥ ४ ॥

ब्रह्मास्याद्ब्राह्मणा जाता वाहुभ्यां क्षत्रजातयः ।
ऊरुभ्यामूरुजा जाताः पद्भ्यां शूद्रास्ततो भवन् ॥ ५ ॥

अन्तेन्त्यजा मलान्म्लेच्छा इत्येता नरजातयः ।
देशकर्मविभेदेन तद्भेदास्तु सहस्रशः ॥ ६ ॥

Śivajī said —

In that Kālīkṣetra by means of penance, *tapas*, we all got the desire of being released, *mukta*. We called that place *ūsara*; it was established with a portion (*aṁśa*) of us. Then, creating all the other worlds, we started to dwell in them.

So till today we are present in our own worlds and according to the order of Mahākālī, Brahmājī produces the world, Viṣṇu preserves it, whilst I annihilate it.

Where there is the Wheel of Time, *kālacakra*, there are these four kinds of beings: *svedaja, aṇḍaja, udbhija, jarāyuja*. Worms, insects and the like belong to the *svedaja* (sweat-producing) type. Birds and serpents, etc., are called *aṇḍaja* (born from an egg). Trees and plants are *udbhija* (growing from seed). Man and animals are of the *jarāyuja* (born from the womb, viviparous) category.

O Nandin, from the mouth of Brahmājī the *brāhmaṇa*s, from his arms the *kṣatriya*s, from the thighs the *vaiśya*s, and from the feet the *śūdra*s were produced.

In the end the *antyaja*, untouchables, and from impurity the *mleccha*s appeared, who also belong to mankind. Within this there are thousands of intermediary differences in countries (*deśa*) and behaviours (*karmāṇi*). **[1-6]**

नरविप्रक्रियालुज्ञधर्मवित्साधुनिःस्पृहाः ।
एते यथोत्तरं मान्या एभ्यः कालीद्विजोवरः ॥ ७ ॥

कालीस्थब्राह्मणो यत्र तावत् तत्रापि तीर्थता ।
सर्वतीर्थोद्भवं पुण्यं लभते ना तदर्चनात् ॥ ८ ॥

कालीस्थब्राह्मणः सेव्यो मन्त्रो ग्राह्यस्तदास्यतः ।
कालीक्षेत्रेविशेषेण स मन्त्रोऽखिलसिद्धिदः ॥ ९ ॥

Among all the beings man is the best. Among the men *brāhmaṇa*s are the best. Among the *brāhmaṇa*s performing sacrifice, best are the *vidvān* (learned ones); among these, the *dharmajña* (knower of *dharma*). Among the *dharmajña brāhmaṇa*s, the *sādhu* are considered the best; among these the *niṣkāma* (lit. desireless) and among the *niṣkāma brāhmaṇa*s, the ones who reside in the Kālīkṣetra are really the best. Wherever the Kālīkṣetra *brāhmaṇa*s are present, that place becomes a *tīrtha*, because just by merely respecting the *brāhmaṇa*s who dwell in the Kālī *kṣetra*, man attains the meritorious fruit of every *tīrtha*. The Kālī *kṣetra* *brāhmaṇa*s are worthy of praise. Learning the *mantra* uttered by them is proper and especially the *mantra*s which are heard in the Kālīkṣetra are bringers of *siddhi*, complete success, in any activity. **[7-9]**

मन्त्राङ्कास्त्रिगुणीकार्याः स्वनामाक्षरसंयुताः ।
ते चतुर्भिरथो भाज्याः शून्यशेषेन शोभनम् ॥ १० ॥

सुदीक्षा माधवे मासि तथा भाद्रादिसप्तसु ।
निर्जलारामतिथ्योश्च सत्तीर्थे ग्रहणे सदा ॥ ११ ॥

बुधवारः सदा त्याज्यस्तथैव धरणीसुतः ।
रिक्तादितिथयोवर्ज्या भरण्यादीनि भानि च ॥ १२ ॥

अदीक्षिता दस्युतुल्या धर्मकर्मवहिःकृताः ।
तैः सार्द्धं नैव वक्तव्यमुक्त्वान्ते श्रवणं स्पृशेत् ॥ १३ ॥

ब्रह्मा विष्णुः शिवश्चण्डी सोमोऽर्कोऽग्निर्मरुज्जलम् ।
मन्त्रज्ञदक्षिणे कर्णे तिष्ठन्ति नव देवताः ॥ १४ ॥

One should join his name-syllables to the triplicated syllables of the *mantra*, and if no sound remains after dividing the first four syllables that *mantra* should be conceived as inauspicious.

Now I will speak of the right *muhūrta* for taking *dīkṣā*. The best month for that is *vaiśākha* and also all the seven months after *bhādo*. Also *nirjalā ekādaśī* and the *rāmanaumī* are two good days for *dīkṣā*; moreover, it can be taken during any eclipse, both solar and lunar, in an auspicious *tīrtha*.

The *mantra dīkṣā* is to be abandoned on the days of Tuesday and Wednesday, as well as in the days when there is no special recurrence and in days which are prohibited. It is also forbidden to take *dīkṣā* under constellations of bad omen such as *bharaṇī*, etc.

Without *dīkṣā* man is a fallen person, unsuccessful in any

work. With such people the magnificent man should not converse; if it is inevitable, then he should touch his right ear.

Because the nine gods (Brahmājī, Viṣṇu, Mahādeva, Devī, Candramā, Sūrya, Agni, Pavana, Jala) stay in the right ear of the person who knows *mantra*. **[10-14]**

पुण्यभूमौ जपेन्मन्त्रमार्यावर्तस्तु पुण्यभूः ।
अन्तर्वेदी महापुण्या काम्पिल्यं तु जपस्थलम् ॥ १५ ॥

यत्रदेवर्षिसिद्धाद्या जपात् सिद्धिं प्रपेदिरे ।
तत् तत्पदानि पुण्यानि तन्मुख्यः कपिलाश्रमः ॥ १६ ॥

कपिलोऽत्र तपस्तप्त्वा गङ्गासागरमभ्यगात् ।
तत्पदं कथ्यतेऽद्यापि काम्पिल्ये कपिलाकुटी ॥ १७ ॥

कपिलस्य तपोभूमिः सद्यः सिद्धिप्रदा मता ।
दर्शनादेव सा नन्दिन् पुनाति सकुलं नरम् ॥ १८ ॥

O Nandin, repeat the *mantra* in a holy land. Āryāvartta is said to be pure. In it the *antarvedī* (the Gaṅgā-Yamunā Doāb) is very pure. And in the *antarvedī* the foremost place for repeating the *mantra* is Kāmpilyapūra — where *devatā*s, *ṛṣi*, *siddha,* etc., by reciting the *mantra,* acquired the *siddhi*, supernatural capability, complete knowledge. The place where they muttered or meditated on the *mantra* is the purest, and among them the place of the *muni* Kapila is the best indeed. After having performed asceticism here, Kapila *muni* went to Gaṅgāsāgara. His *tapaḥ sthāna*, his place for asceticism, is still today called Kapila *kuṭī*.

Since those times the place of Kapila *muni* is bestower of spiritual success. Nandin, only by visiting it one purifies himself and his family. **[15-18]**

पूर्वं गुरुं परीक्षेत पश्चाद्दीक्षां समाचरेत् ।
सद्गुरोर्लक्षणं नन्दिन् शृणुष्वैकाग्रमानसः ॥ १९ ॥

षट्कर्मा पुत्रवान स्वङ्गो धर्मपत्नीपतिर्गृही ।
दृढव्रती दयायुक्ती ब्राह्मणो गुरुरुत्तमः ॥ २० ॥

Before taking initiation one should inspect the teacher. O Nandin, now listen to the distingushing features of a *guru*. He should perform *adhyāpan*, instruction, and the other six duties of a *brāhmaṇa*. He should have children and an excellent body. Married according to the law of *dharma*, house-holder, steady in fulfilling his vows, compassionate, such a *brāhmaṇa* is said to be a most eminent *guru*.

॥ इति श्री का० मा० मंत्रदीक्षाविधानं नाम द्वितीयोऽध्यायः ॥
Here ends the second chapter of the Kāmpilyamahātmya.

3

The Talk Between Śiva and Nandin on the Tryambakeśa Liṅgam

शिव उवाच -

कांपिल्ये त्रिधनुर्भूमिः सिद्धपीठस्तदन्तरे ।
शत्रुघ्नारोपितं लिङ्गं रामेश्वर इतिस्मृतम् ॥ १ ॥

नन्दिन् पुरा कुवेराय लिङ्गमेकं मयार्पितम् ।
त्र्यम्बकाख्यं यमभ्यर्च्य कुवेरो भूद्धनेश्वरः ॥ २ ॥

अथ तं सगणं जित्वा रावणी लोकरावणः ।
सपुष्पकं त्र्यम्वकेशमादाय स्वपुरं ययौ ॥ ३ ॥

तत्राशोकवने स्थाप्य पूजयामास यत्नतः ।
चण्डीश्वरमितिख्यातं ततः सोऽभूत् त्रिलोकजित् ॥ ४ ॥

वहुकाले व्यतीतेऽथ रामो दशरथात्मजः ।
सानुगं रावणं हत्वा नृपं कृत्वा विभीषणम् ॥ ५ ॥

अशोकवाटिकां गत्वा दृष्टवास्तत्र जानकीम् ।
चण्डीशाख्यं स्थाणुलिङ्गं व्योमयानं च पुष्पकम् ॥ ६ ॥

ततोरामः समादाय सीतां चण्डीश्वरं तथा ।
स्वपुरीमागतःसद्यःपुष्पकस्थः सलक्ष्मणः ॥ ७ ॥

Śivajī said —

O Nandin, in the town of Kāmpilya the *siddhapīṭha* is enclosed in three *dhanuṣa*, twelve *hasta*s, of land. In its middle there is a *śivaliṅgam*, called Rāmeśvara, that was installed by Śatrughna.

O Nandin, I had firstly given to Kubera a *liṅgam*, named Tryambaka; by worshipping it Kubera became lord of wealth and prosperity.

Then in another time Rāvaṇa won Kubera and looted from him the aerial-chariot (*vimāna*) Puṣpaka and the Tryambakeśa *liṅgam*, bringing them to Laṅkā.

After installing it in the Aśoka grove, with the name Caṇḍīśvara, he started to perform its *pūjā*, by which he got the power to control the triple world.

Much later, Śrī Rāmacandrajī defeated Rāvaṇa and gave the kingdom to Vibhīṣaṇa.

In the Aśoka grove he found Sītājī, the Caṇḍīśvara *Śiva-liṅgam* and the Puṣpaka *vimāna.*

So King Rāmacandrajī with Jānakījī, the Caṇḍīśvara *liṅgam* and Lakṣmaṇa sat on the the Puṣpaka *vimāna* and went to Ayodhyā. **[1-7]**

अथो वहुतिथे काले लवणासुरपीडितोः ।
मुनयोराममभ्येत्य व्यसनं स्वं समूचिरे ॥ ८ ॥
राजन्नास्ते मधुवने लवणोनाम दानवः ।
विघ्नं करोति नो नित्यं पूयशोणितकर्दमैः ॥ ९ ॥
ऋते भवन्तं को हन्याल्लवणं तं सुदुर्जयम् ।
तस्मात् प्रसीद भगवञ्छरणागतवत्सल ॥ १० ॥

Some time after that, some *munis*, afflicted by a demon, Lavaṇāsura by name, arrived at the court of Rāmacandrajī and explained their problem.

They said —

O Mahārāja, in the Madhuvan forest there is a *dānava* called Lavaṇāsura. He troubles us with a rain of pus, blood and mud. O Lord, none can kill him but you. O protector, O refuge of the distressed, please kill him! **[8-10]**

शिव उवाच -

इति तेषां वचः श्रुत्वा राघवः करुणार्द्रधीः ।
शत्रुघ्नं प्रेषयामास मुनीनामर्थसिद्धये ॥ ११ ॥

स गत्वा साकम्टषिभिर्हत्वाथ लवणासुरम् ।
तत्रैव वासयामास नगरीं मथुराभिधाम् ॥ १२ ॥

Śivajī said —

O Nandin, Śrī Rāmacandrajī heard the question of the *muni*s and sent Śatrughna to remove the *dānava*. Śatrughna with the sages arrived at the Madhuvan forest, killed Lavaṇāsura and founded the town of Mathurā there. **[11-12]**

ततः कदाचिच्छत्रुघ्नीदिदृक्षूराममग्रजम् ।
राजधानीं स्वपूर्वेषामयोध्यां गन्तुमुद्यतः ॥ १३ ॥

मध्येमार्गं ददर्शाथ पाञ्चालविषये शुभम् ।
कालीक्षेत्रं महापुण्यं मुनिभिर्बहुभिर्युतम् ॥ १४ ॥

तत्र तां स्थापयामास मूर्तिं शत्रुनिषूदनः ।
रामोयामानयामास लङ्कातो रावणान्तकृत् ॥ १५ ॥

काम्पिल्यादुत्तरे भागे जन्हुजादक्षिणे तटे ।
नाम रामेश्वरं कृत्वा पूजयित्वाऽकरोत् स्तुतिम् ॥ १६ ॥

After sometime Śatrughna left that place to reach Ayodhyā, to meet his brother Śrī Rāma. On the road, he crossed the country of Pāñcāla. There he saw a very sacred place called Kālīkṣetra. The *śivaliṅgam* that Rāmacandra had brought from Laṅkā after the defeat of Rāvaṇa, was installed by Śatrughna in that Kālīkṣetra. At the north of Kampil town and at the south of Gaṅgā, he gave to that *śivaliṅgam* the name of Rāmeśvara, and started the worship of it. **[13-16]**

शत्रुघ्न उवाच -

इन्दुर्भाले विन्दुरूपो विभाति शूलं पाणौ क्षेममूलं हि यस्य ।
यो लोकेशो व्योमकेशोऽम्बिकेशो नित्यं सोस्मच्छङ्करः शङ्करोस्तु ॥ १७ ॥

यद्वामाङ्गे शैलकन्या ऽतिधन्या जन्होःकन्याऽस्त्युत्तमाङ्गे यदीये ।
यंसंसेव्येन्द्रोपिनाकी पिनाकी नित्यं० ॥ १८ ॥

यः सन्तुष्टोङ्गानि पुष्टीकरोति रुष्टो भूयः कष्टतामादधाति ।
हृष्टः क्लिष्टानां निहन्त्याश्वनिष्ठं नित्यं० ॥ १९ ॥

भूमीरूपो वारिरूपोऽग्निरूपो योवा देवो वायुरूपः स्वरूपः ।
यः संसारस्यादिमध्यान्तरूपो नित्यं० ॥ २० ॥

यस्माद्भीतो वाति वातः सदैव यस्माद्भीतस्तिग्मरश्मिर्ह्यु देति ।
नित्यं मृत्युर्यद्भयाद्धन्ति जन्तून् नित्यं० ॥ २१ ॥

Śatrughnajī said —

That Śiva who has the crescent moon on the forehead, benefactor of the world, with the *triśūla* in his hand, who is the Lord of the world, sky-haired, *aṁvikeśa* — he will always look after my welfare.

Who has Pārvatī at his left side, and the Gaṅgā flowing from his head; to whom Indra bowed before becoming the king of heaven — he will always look after my welfare.

That Śivajī who gives strength when satisfied and pain when displeased; when he is content he quickly destroys the sufferings of the afflicted — he will always look after my welfare.

The five *tattva* (earth, water, fire, wind, ether) are just some of his forms. He who is the beginning, the middle portion and the end of the whole world, will always look after my welfare.

Because it fears him, the wind always blows and the sun rises; through fear of him, Death destroys every being. He will always look after my welfare. **[17-21]**

शिव उवाच -

एवं मां स्तुत्य शत्रुघ्नः प्रणम्याथ पुनः पुनः ।
प्राचीं दिशं जगामाशु रामदर्शनलालसः ॥ २२ ॥

Śivajī said —

In this way Śatrughna after offering me this eulogy and bowing again and again, moved eastward to meet Śrī Rāmacandrajī. **[22]**

॥ इति श्री का० मा० रामेश्वरप्रष्ठिापनं नाम तृतीयोऽध्यायः ॥

Here ends the third chapter of the Kāmpilyamahātmya.

4

The Talk Between Śiva and Nandin on the Greatness of the Rāmeśvara Temple

शिव उवाच -

रामेशे प्लवगः कश्चिद्दष्टः सर्पेण संस्थितः ।
स मामकैरिहानीतोमद्गणोऽभूद्घटोदरः ॥ १ ॥

Śivajī said —

O Nandin, in the Rāmeśvara temple a monkey was stung by a snake and died. My messengers brought it here, on the Mount Kailāsa, where it became one of my *gaṇa*, named Ghaṭodara. **[1]**

अथान्यं कथयिष्येऽहमितिहासं पुरातनम् ।
नन्दिन् रामेशमाहात्म्यसम्बद्धं भुक्तिमुक्तिदम् ॥ २ ॥

रामेशोपासकः कश्चिद्विप्र आसोज्जितेन्द्रियः ।
उमादत्त इतिख्यातो दुर्भिक्षार्त्तो ययौ पराक् ॥ ३ ॥

गच्छन मार्गेऽस्मरच्छम्भुं रामेशं स पदे पदे ।
हारामेश्वर हा कालि हा काम्पिल्ल विमुक्तिद ॥ ४ ॥

इत्थंगतः स काश्मीरे कालक्षेपं चकार ह ।
कन्दमूलफलाद्यर्थं नित्यमेव वनं ययौ ॥ ५ ॥

एकदाऽसौ वनं गत्वा यावन्निववृते द्विजः ।
तावदग्रे समायातस्तैलिङ्गविषयाधिपः ॥ ६ ॥

स नत्वोवाच विप्रेन्द्रं मामेषा सम्प्रवाधते ।
ब्रह्महत्याऽनिशं ह्यस्याः कथं मुच्येयमुच्यताम् ॥ ७ ॥

O Nandin, I will tell you other stories about the greatness of Rāmeśvara.

There was a *brāhmaṇa*, Umādatta by name, who was a servant of the Rāmeśvara temple. Once because of famine he went westward. While walking along the road he was constantly thinking of Rāmeśvara Śivajī: 'O Rāmeśvara, O Kālī, O Kāmpilya.

He arrived in Kashmir, where he started to get his maintenance. Eating roots and fruits he stayed in the jungle. Once while he was coming from the forest he met a king from Tailaṅga region (Andhra Pradesh).

He saluted with respect Umādatta and said — "O *brāhmaṇa*, for a long time I have been afflicted by the ghost of *brahmahatyā*.[3] How can I get free from this? Please tell me." **[2-7]**

उमादत्त उवाच -

कुत्रत्यस्त्वं कथं प्राप्ता ब्रह्महत्या सुदारुणा ।
इदानीं कुत आयातस्तन्मे ब्रूहि यथातथम् ॥ ८ ॥

Umādatta said —

Where do you come from, and how did you stain yourself with such a crime? **[8]**

राजोवाच -

तैलिङ्गेशः सुवर्मास्मि सर्वशास्त्रास्त्रपारगः ।
न मया समयाचाराः परित्यक्ताः कदाचन ॥ ९ ॥

सोहं कदाचिद्विपिनं गत्वा हत्वा मृगान् वहून् ।
परिश्रान्तस्तु विप्रर्षे निवृत्तः स्वगृहं प्रति ॥ १० ॥

3. The feminine personification of the guiltiness derived from killing a *brāhmaṇa*.

तावन्मार्गे ब्रह्महत्या मामाह नृपते त्वया ।
निहतौ मृगरूपेण रमन्तौ द्विजदम्पती ॥ ११ ॥

इत्युक्त्का मामनुगता निमेषार्द्धं न मुञ्चति ।
न सुखं मे दिवारात्रं ब्रह्मन कुत्रापि भूतले ॥ १२ ॥

स्नातो वहुषु तीर्थेषुगतो वाराणसीं पुरीम् ।
न मां त्यजति दुष्टेयं किं कार्यं ब्रूहि तद्द्विज ॥ १३ ॥

The King said —

I am the King of the Tailanga region, and my name is Suvarmā. I know the secret of every weapon (*astra-śastra*). I have always kept my vows and followed the rules of conduct. Once I went hunting in the forest and after killing many deer I was on my way home. Then the ghost of *brahmahatyā* came to me and said: "You have just killed a *brāhmaṇa* and his wife who were roaming in the jungle in the form of deer." So she did not leave me even for a while and day and night I cannot have a moment of peace. I have visited and bathed in many holy places, included Kāśī, but this ghost never leaves me. O *brāhmaṇa*, what can I do? [9-13]

शिव उवाच -

इत्युक्तस्तं सुवर्माणं पुनः प्रोवाच स द्विजः ।
उमादत्तो महाप्राज्ञो ब्रह्महत्यानिपीडितम् ॥ १४ ॥

मा भयं कुरु राजेन्द्र साक्षात् काम्पिल्लमण्डले ।
शिवे त्रातरि भक्तानां क्व भयं शरणैषिणाम् ॥ १५ ॥

सुवर्मन् नवधा भक्त्या सन्तुष्टोभवति प्रभुः ।
भक्तिमान् यः स पुरुषः शेषाः स्वोदरपूरकाः ॥ १६ ॥

शृणु तां नवधा भक्ति शम्भोः कीर्त्तिः श्रुतिः स्मृतिः ।
सेवार्चनं स्तुतिर्दास्यं सख्यमात्मनिवेदनम् ॥ १७ ॥

य एवं नवधा भक्त्या सेवेत शिवदं शिवम् ।
ब्रह्महत्यादिपापानि नोपसर्पन्ति तं नृप ॥ १८ ॥

Śivajī said —

After listening to the words of the unhappy King Suvarmā, Umādatta said: "Do not fear, King! The devotees who reside in the Rāmeśvara Śivajī temple in the Kāmpilya region never have any kind of fear. O Suvarmā, Śivajī is pleased by the nine-fold devotion: who is endowed with devotion is really a man, all the others are just filling their stomachs. Now listen to what are the nine kinds of devotion: *kīrtan*, singing songs of Śivajī; listening to the stories of Śiva; remembering; service; offering; prayers; the attitude of a servant; friendship with Śiva's devotees, and self-sacrifice.

O King, the man who follows this ninefold devotion to Śivajī, the ghost of the sin of *brahmahatyā* does never even come near him. **[14-18]**

राजन् देवाः सगन्धर्वाः पितरः सिद्धचारणाः ।
देवर्षयश्च दैतेया यक्षरक्षांसि किंनराः ॥ १९ ॥

चैत्रमासे कृष्णपक्षे चतुर्दश्यां झषे रवौ ।
देवापगायामायान्ति रामेश्वरशिवान्तिके ॥ २० ॥

तत्र त्वं गच्छ नृपते जान्हव्यां स्नानमाचर ।
रामेशार्चनतः सद्यो धूतपापो भविष्यसि ॥ २१ ॥

चैत्रकृष्णचतुर्दश्यामुपवासं करोति यः ।
स्नायाच्च जान्हवीतोये रामेशं पूजयेत् तथा ॥ २२ ॥

रात्रौ जागरणं कुर्यान्नामकीर्त्तनमेव च ।
सर्वपापविनिर्मुक्तो न पुनर्जन्म भाग्भवेत् ॥ २३ ॥

दुर्लभं स्वर्णदीतीरे रामेशशिवदर्शनम् ।
तथा नृप चतुर्दश्यामुपवासीति दुर्लभः ॥ २४ ॥

उपवासो जागरणं संनिधौ परमेशितुः ।
अर्चा च शिवलोकस्य नृणां सोपानपद्धतिः ॥ २५ ॥

यथा रामेश्वरी देवः सेतुवन्धे व्यवस्थितः ।
कालीक्षेत्रे तथैवायमुभौ तुल्यफलप्रदौ ॥ २६ ॥

On the fourteenth day (*caturdaśī*) of the black lunar fortnight of the month of *caitra*, with the sun in the constellation of Mīna (Piscis), *devatā*, *gandharva*, *pitara*, wandering *siddha*, *devarṣi*, *daitya*, *rākṣasa*, *kinnara* come to the Rāmeśvara Śivajī from the river Gaṅgā.

O King, go there and after performing an ablution in the Gaṅgā, worship Rāmeśvara Śivajī. Only by doing this will you be cleansed of all sins. Whoever will perform all this on the proper day, and fast and stay awake all night, repeating or singing the names of Śivajī, that man of virtue will never take another birth.

O Lord of men, it is rare for man to take a bath in the Gaṅgā, and also rare it is to get a view of the Rāmeśvara *śivaliṅgam*. And one who observes the vow of *caturdaśī* is even more rare. Staying near the form of Śivajī, being awake and adoring Him are ways by which man will get to the *Śivaloka*, the abode of Śiva.

The Rāmeśvara *śivaliṅgam* in Kampil bestows the same merit as the Rāmeśvara *śivaliṅgam* at Setubandhu (Rāmeśvaram, Tamil Nadu)." **[19-26]**

शिव उवाच -

इत्युक्तस्तेन विप्रेण राजा काम्पिल्यमागतः ।
रामेशः पूजयामास ब्रह्महत्यानिवृत्तये ॥२७ ॥

तत्रासौ दीक्षितो भूत्वा व्रतं कृत्वा यथाविधि ।
विकल्मषः प्रतस्थेऽथ सुवर्मा स्वपुरं प्रति ॥ २८ ॥

इत्थं ये ये समायाताः काल्यां रामेश्वरान्तिके ।
ते ते मुक्तिपदं प्राप्त महापातकिनोपि च ॥ २९ ॥

इति ते कथितं नन्दिन् रामेश्वरकथानकम् ।
श्रुतं हरति पापानि चातुर्वर्ग्यं ददाति च ॥ ३० ॥

Śivajī said —

After listening to the words of Umādatta, King Suvarmā went to Kampil and made the *pūjā* to Rāmeśvara *śivaliṅgam* to destroy the sin of *brahmahatyā*. There he was initiated and observed the vow; by that he cleansed the sin. Then he went to his country. So any sinner who would come to the Kālīkṣetra to see the Rāmeśvara *śivaliṅgam*, will attain *mokṣa*. O Nandin, I told you the story of Rāmeśvara *śivaliṅgam*, by listening to which a man becomes free from every fault and gets the four goals of life, viz., *kāma, artha, dharma, mokṣa*. **[27-30]**

वैशम्पायन उवाच -

इत्युक्त्वाभूद्धरस्तूष्णीं तावद्देवाः समागताः ।
सदाशिवं तदाभ्यर्च्य प्रतिजग्मुर्यथा गतम् ॥ ३१ ॥

Vaiśampāyana said —

Thus spoke Śiva. Then he did not talk. All the *devatā* arrived and after making the *pūjā* to Sadāśiva, they returned to their abodes. **[31]**

॥ *इति श्री का० मा० रामेश्वरमहत्त्ववर्णनं नाम चतुर्थोऽध्यायः* ॥
Here ends the fourth chapter of the Kāmpilyamahātmya.

5

Śiva Curses Gaṅgā and Pārvatī to Take Human Nature

जनमेजय उवाच -

ब्रह्मन्नत्यद्भुतं ह्येतद्रामेश्वरकथानकम्।
प्रकीर्त्तितं भगवता सर्वपापप्रणाशनम्॥ १॥
अथान्यदपि यत् किञ्चित् तीर्थं कालीगतं भवेत्।
तन्ममाचक्ष्व यत्नेन श्रोतुमिच्छामि साम्प्रतम्॥ २ ॥

Janamejaya said —

O *muni*, you have told me the marvellous story of Rāmeśvara Śivajī. Now, if there are some other *tīrtha* in the Kālīkṣetra, please tell me. **[1-2]**

सूत उवाच -

एवमुक्तो महाराज्ञा स वैशम्पायनो मुनिः।
यदाह तच्छृणुध्वं भो ऋषयः प्रीतमानसाः॥ ३॥

Sūta said —

O *ṛṣi*, now listen to the story the *muni* Vaiśampāyana told King Janamejaya in answer to the latter's question. **[3]**

वैशम्पायन उवाच -

यः कम्पिलाख्यपुरतोदिशि चोत्तरस्यां
कालेश्वरः शिव इति प्रथितः पृथिव्याम्।

तस्य प्रभावमखिलं च तदुद्भवं च
सम्यक्समाहितमनाः शृणु कौरवेन्द्र ॥ ४ ॥

Vaiśampāyana said —

O King of the Kurus, listen to the origin and effectiveness of the Kāleśvara *śivaliṅgam*, which is in the northern part of Kampil. **[4]**

शप्तैकदा स्वपतिना गिरिशेन देवी
यद्धेतुना क्षितिपते शृणे तस्य तत्त्वम्।
शम्भुः कदाचन जगाम विरिञ्चिलोकमा-
लोकनार्थमृषभेण सुरर्षभस्य ॥ ५ ॥
ब्रह्माऽऽगतं स्वभवनं गिरिशं निशम्य
त्यक्त्वाऽऽसनं भवनतोवहिराजगाम।
सत्कृत्य कृत्यविदथी बहुमानपूर्वं तुष्ठाव
सून्टतगिरा सकलैर्मुखैः स्वैः ॥ ६ ॥
तस्योपरिस्थमुखतः स्तुबतो
विरिञ्चेर्जातस्तदा खरतरः खरतुल्यनादः।
शम्भुस्तदेव कुपितोस्य शिरो जहार
हास्यं ममायमकरोदिति विभ्रमेण ॥ ७ ॥
पापात्मिका त्वरितमेव नृदेव दैवी
हत्याभिधा मुनिवरैः किल कथ्यते या।
स्थातुं शिवोपरि समुद्यम मङ्क्त कर्त्री दुद्राव
तामथ विलोक्य शिवोप्यधावत्॥ ८ ॥
कैलासमाप प्रथमं त्रिदिवं धरित्रीं
पातालसप्तकमथो स समुद्रशैलान्।
सर्वत्र तद्विधिशिरोहननीत्थहत्यारूपं
ददर्श नरपाल न शर्म लेभे ॥ ९ ॥

O King, lord of the earth, once Śivajī cursed Pārvatī; hear also the reason why it happened. One time Śivajī, riding on his ox, went to visit Brahmā. When Brahmājī knew that Śivajī was arriving at his abode, he ran out of his home and started to sing prayers with all his five heads. On that occasion from the upper head of Brahmā some awful words were pronounced. Śivajī got angry at this mistake of Brahmā, and cut off that head. O King, the ghost of *brahmahatyā* came running to take possession of Śivajī, and he ran away. He first went to Mount Kailāsa, then from the sky he got to the earth, through the seven *pātāla* (hells), into the ocean, then he turned to the mountains, but in every place he could not find peace because of the ghost of *brahmahatyā*. **[5-9]**

एवं पुनः पुनरितस्तत एव धावँल्लक्ष्मीपते-
निर्लयमाशु गतो गिरीशः ।
द्रृष्टवा स तत्र भगवन्तममोघलीलं स्वीयं
जगाद चरितं सकलं यथाऽऽसीत् ॥ १० ॥
विष्णुस्ततो भगवतो गिरिशस्य सर्वं
वृत्तं निशम्य समुवाच नृराज हत्याम् ।
गौरीपतिं पतितगामिनि पुण्यपूरं दूरं
दुरात्मसु विहाय च याहि याहि ॥ ११ ॥
किं नो विभेषि दुरितोपशमाय दुष्टे
यद्दर्शनस्मरणकीर्त्तनवन्दनानि ।
जानासि नैव मदनारि मघौघहारि
यन्नाम काममनुसृत्य गृणन्ति मर्त्याः ॥ १२ ॥
यो योगिभिर्मुनिवरैरसुरैः सुरैश्च सिद्धैः समाधिगतनिर्मलवृत्तिचित्तैः ।
नित्यः परादपिपरः पुरुषः पुराणः संध्यायते शिवतरः शिवदः सदैव ॥ १३ ॥

Running here and there Girīśa arrived at *Vaikuṇṭha*. There he met with Śrī Bhagavān Viṣṇu and explained his condition.

O King! Bhagavān Viṣṇu heard all the story and then spoke to the ghost of *brahmahatyā*: "O vile! Why you do not fear? Don't you know that this is Śivajī, by whose sight, memory, name, and by bowing at whose feet all the sins are destroyed? Men get every desire accomplished by repeating his name. He is the object of the contemplation of *yogī*, *daitya*, *devatā*, and *siddha*, steady in the *samādhi* with their mind completely purified. He is Śivajī, invariable, beyond the beyond, *purāṇapuruṣa*, the form of welfare, who always gives happiness." **[10-13]**

वैशम्पायन उवाच -

इत्थं समाकर्ण्य बचो मुरारेः पुरारिमूलादथ सद्य एव ।
जगाम पारीक्षित भीतभीता सा ब्रह्महत्याऽखिलपापिसङ्घे ॥ १४ ॥

शिवोपि कैलासगिरिं समागतस्ततः परं क्रोध वशंगतो विधिः ।
किमद्य कर्त्तव्यमतः परंमयाऽनयापि कार्यं नहिं साधितं मम ॥ १५ ॥

विचिन्त्य चैवं विदधौ विचक्षणः क्षणादतिक्रोधपरां नगाङ्गजाम् ।
तथैव जन्होस्तनयां विधाय च द्वयोर्विचित्रं चरितं ददर्श सः ॥ १६ ॥

ततस्त्रपाहीनतरे दिवानिशं नृशंसवत् क्रोधपरीतमानसे ।
अयुध्यतां ते विगतस्मृती यथा निवारयामास तदा सदाशिवः ॥ १७ ॥

तमप्यनादृत्य पुनस्तथैवते विवादशीले नगजा च जन्हुजा ।
वभूवतुस्तत् प्रसमीक्ष्य शङ्करःशशाप गङ्गां गिरिजां च भूपते ॥ १८ ॥

सुरस्वभावः सुतरां समुज्झितो मनुष्यभावो विशदीकृतो यतः ।
अतः परित्यज्य सुरेन्द्रविष्टपं विनष्टबुद्धी धरणीं गमिष्यतः ॥ १९ ॥

गङ्गा भवित्री नृपशान्तनोः स्त्री नगाङ्गजा च द्रुपदस्य पुत्री ।
निशम्य तच्छापमुभे भयार्ते नरेन्द्र तत्पादतले निपेततुः ॥ २० ॥

Vaiśampāyana said —

O son of Parīkṣit (Janamejaya)! When the ghost of *brahmahatyā* heard the speech of Murāri, she got scared and left Śivajī. She went to possess another sinner. Then Śivajī went to Kailāsa. Thereafter Brahmā got angry and started to think: "What should I do now? I got no justice from this *brahmahatyā*."

Out of revenge he planned of sowing discord between Pārvatī and Gaṅgājī, so that they started fighting violently. They went on fighting day and night, both being overcome by anger. Then Śivajī stopped them.

But not respecting the order of Śivajī they went on wrangling. Then Śivajī cast a spell on them.

"Gaṅgā, Girījā, you shall both leave the *daivī* (divine) nature and get a *mānava* (human) nature, so that you will have to go from the *devaloka* to the *manuṣyaloka*.

Gaṅgā will be the wife of King Śāntanu and Pārvatī will be the daughter of King Drupada." O King, when the two goddesses heard the malediction, struck with fear, they fell at the feet of Śivajī. **[14-20]**

गङ्गागौर्यावूचतुः

शापान्तः क्रियतां स्वामिन् दीनयोर्दीनवत्सल ।
देवदेव दयासिन्धो प्रणतार्त्तिप्रणाशन ॥ २१ ॥

नावयोर्मातुरुदराज्जनिः स्याद्धरणीतले ।
पाणिग्राहश्च स भवेद्यस्त्वया सदृशोनरः ॥ २२ ॥

The two implored in many ways to the god of gods, destroyer of the pains of his devotees, to cancel the curse. "May our birth on the earth not happen from a maternal womb. And may our husband be like you." **[21-22]**

वैशम्पायन उवाच -

एवमुक्तोऽसिसंहृष्टः प्रोवाच भगवान्भवः ।
श्रूयतामेकभावेन गङ्गे गौरि वचो मम ॥ २३ ॥

गङ्गेऽहं तव तुष्ट्यर्थं प्रतीपतनुसम्भवः ।
शान्तनुर्नाम नृपतिर्भविष्यामि धरातले ॥ २४ ॥

तत्र त्वं मामनुप्राप्य पतिं प्रेमपरिप्लुता ।
अष्टौ पुत्रान्समुत्पाद्य पुनः कैलासमाप्स्यसि ॥ २५ ॥

गिरिजे त्वं ममादेशान्निवसान्तर्हिता सतो ।
पाञ्चालदेशे काम्पिल्ले नाम्ना काम्पीलवासिनी ॥ २६ ॥

तत्र त्वामर्चयिष्यन्ति मुनयोऽमलमानसाः ।
अम्बेम्बिकेतिमन्त्रेण भुङ्क्ष्व पूर्णाहुतिं मखे ॥ २७ ॥

द्वापरे समनु प्राप्ते तृतीययुगपर्यये ।
द्रुपदोनाम राजर्षिश्चन्द्रवंशसमुद्भवः ॥ २८ ॥

भविष्यति स पुत्रार्थं जान्हवीदक्षिणे तटे ।
करिष्यति महायज्ञं तदा त्वं प्रकटीभव ॥ २९ ॥

नाम्ना कालीति विख्याता कृष्णेति द्रौपदीति च ।
तत्र त्वामर्जुनोभूत्वा तनयः पाण्डुभूपतेः ॥ ३० ॥

भित्त्वा लक्ष्यं वरिष्यामि काम्पिल्ले राजसंसदि ।
यद्भालल्लोचनमिह हृद्गतं तत् मम ॥ ३१ ॥

Vaiśampāyana said —

Śivajī answered: "O Gaṅgā, O Gaurī! Listen to my talk. To make you happy I will become the son of King Pratīpa, Śāntanu. So that you will get me in the form of Śāntanu, and after giving birth to eight sons you will come to Kailāsa. O Pārvatī, you will reside in secret in the country of Pañcāla, in the town of Kāmpilya, with the name of Kāmpilyavāsinī. There the *munis* will perform your sacrifice and you will enjoy the *pūrṇāhuti* by the *mantra* starting with — *ambe ambike ambālike*. In the third era called *dvāpara yuga* there will be a king of the *candravaṁśa*, lunar dynasty. In order to have children he will perform a *yajña* on the right bank of the Gaṅgā; from that *yajña* you will appear. You will be called Kṛṣṇā, Kālī, Draupadī. Then I will be the son of King Pāṇḍu, Arjuna. In his heart there will be my third eye." **[23-31]**

वैशम्पायन उवाच -

इत्युत्तकासीद्धरस्तूष्णीं तदाराजर्षिसत्तम ।
जन्हुजा गिरिजा चैव नरलोकमवापतुः ॥ ३२ ॥

एतस्मिन्नेव काले तु प्रतीपः क्षत्रियर्षभः ।
तपस्तेपे सुतस्यार्थे सभार्यः कुरुनन्दन ॥ ३३ ॥

तयोः समभवत् पुत्री वृद्धयोः स महाभिषः ।
शान्तस्य जज्ञे सन्तानस्तस्मादासीत् स शान्तनुः ॥ ३४ ॥

स राजा शान्तनुर्धीमान देवराजर्षिसत्कृतः ।
धर्मात्मा सर्वलोकेषु सत्यवागितिविश्रुतः ॥ ३५ ॥

दमो दानं क्षमा बुद्धिर्ह्रीर्धृतिस्तेज उत्तमम्।
नित्यान्यासन महासतत्त्वे शान्तनौ पुरुषर्षभे ॥ ३६ ॥

Vaiśampāyana said —

After saying that Śivajī stayed silent. Gaṅgā and Girījā reached the world of men. On that occasion, King Pratīpa was engaged in asceticism in order to get a son. The aged queen had for her son that Mahābhiṣa who had been a glorious king in his previous life and capable of changing old people into youths merely by the touch of his hand. He was called Śāntanu[4] because he was born from a *śāntā*, i.e., old woman. He was very intelligent and regulated in character; respected by *devatā* and *rājarṣi*. He was well known in the three worlds as a truthful man. Control of the faculties, charity, forgiveness, knowledge, aversion to bad activities, forbearance and strength were all qualities he possessed. **[32-36]**

स एवंगुणसम्पन्नो धर्मार्थकुशलो नृपः।
वभूव मृगयाशीलः सततं बनगोचरः ॥ ३७ ॥

स मृगान् महिषांश्चैव विनिघ्ननाजसत्तमः।
गङ्गामनुचचारैकः सिद्धचारणसेविताम् ॥ ३८ ॥

तस्य रूपगुणोपेता गङ्गा स्त्रीरूपधारिणी।
उत्तीयं सलिलात् तस्माल्लोभनीयतमाकृतिः ॥ ३९ ॥

मानुषं विग्रहं कृत्वा श्रीमन्तं वरबर्णिनी।
भाग्योपनतकामस्य भार्या चोपनताऽभवत् ॥ ४० ॥

रममाणस्तया सार्द्धं यथाकामं नरेश्वरः।
अष्ठावजनयत् पुत्रांस्तस्याममरसंनिभान् ॥ ४१ ॥

अष्टमे त्वथ संजाते कुमारे जन्हुनन्दिनी।
शापावसाने नृपते निजधाम जगाम सा ॥ ४२ ॥

Skilful in *dharma* and *arthaśāstra*, King Śāntanu always used

4. He had two wives. One was Gaṅgā by whom Bhīṣma was born and the other one was Satyavatī, mother of Citrāṅgada and Vicitravīrya.

to go hunting in the forest. Once whilst hunting alone, he reached the bank of the Gaṅgā. There a wonderful woman endowed with all qualities came out from the water. Gaṅgā became Śāntanu's wife. They had eight sons. When the eighth son was born, Bhīṣma, the curse given by Śivajī was completed and Gaṅgā set-off for her place, the Kailāsa.

॥ इति श्री का० मा० गङ्गागिरिजाशापोनाम पञ्चमोऽध्यायः॥

Here ends the fifth chapter of the Kāmpilyamahātmya.

6

The Story of Droṇācārya and Aśvatthāmā[5]

वैशम्पायन उवाच -

अथ सा गिरिजा राजन् भर्तुरादेशकारिणी ।
संजज्ञे यज्ञसेनस्य बेदीमध्यात् सुमध्यमा ॥ १ ॥

धृष्टद्युम्नेन सहिता द्रोणान्तकरणेन हि ।
तद्यज्ञकुण्डमद्याऽपि द्रौपदीकुण्डमुच्यते ॥ २ ॥

Vaiśampāyana said —

Then much later Pārvatī, faithful to the order of her husband, and Dhṛṣṭadyumna, the killer of Droṇa, appeared from the sacrifice pool, *yajña-kuṇḍa*, of King Drupada. That *yajña-kuṇḍa* is still called Draupadī *kuṇḍa*. **[1-2]**

जनमेजय उवाच -

मुने द्रुपदपुत्रस्य धृष्ठद्युम्नस्य पावकात् ।
द्रौपद्याश्च समुत्पत्तिं पुनर्मेवद विस्तरात् ॥ ३ ॥

द्रोणश्च द्रुपदश्चैव सखायौ केन हेतुना ।
वभूवतुः पुनर्भिन्नौ कथा तच्चापि कीर्तय ॥ ४ ॥

Janamejaya said —

O *muni*, Dhṛṣṭadyumna and Draupadī appeared from the

5. The stories from this chapter up to the twenty-seventh are from *Mahābharata*, Adi-Parvan.

fire. Explain again in detail this point to me. Why was there an argument between Droṇa and Drupada, who used to be friends when they were young? **[3-4]**

वैशम्पायन उवाच -

गङ्गाद्वारं प्रति महान् वभूव भगवानृपिः ।
भरद्वाज इति ख्यातः सततं संशितव्रतः ॥ ५ ॥

सोभिषेक्तुं गतो गङ्गां पूर्वमेवागतां नदीम् ।
ददर्शाप्सरसं साक्षाद्घृताचीमाप्लुतामृषिः ॥ ६ ॥

तस्यास्तदा नदीतीरे वसनं पर्यवर्तत ।
व्यपकृष्टाम्वरां द्रृष्ट्वा तामृषिश्चकमे ततः ॥ ७ ॥

तस्यां संसक्तमनसोभरद्वाजस्य धीमतः ।
चिरस्य रेतश्चस्कन्द तद्रृषिर्द्रोण आदधे ॥ ८ ॥

ततः समभवद्द्रोणः कुमारस्तस्य धीमतः ।
अध्यगीष्ठ स वेदांश्च वेदाङ्गानि च सर्वशः ॥ ९ ॥

Vaiśampāyana said —

The *maharṣi* Bharadvāja used to stay at the northern door of Kapilanagara. Once he went to the Gaṅgā to bathe. There he saw the *apsarā*, nymph, Dr̥tācī. She was bathing without clothes and at that sight the *r̥ṣi* started to desire her. With the mind charmed by the *apsarā* the semen, for so long restrained, was discharged. That semen was collected by the *r̥ṣi* into a *droṇa* (a kind of sacrifical vessel). From that vessel was born Droṇācārya, who learnt the *Veda* and the *Vedāṅga*. **[5-9]**

भरद्वाजस्य तु सखा पृषतोनाम पार्थिवः ।
तस्यापि द्रुपदी नाम तदा समभवत् सुतः ॥ १० ॥

स नित्यमाश्रमं गत्वा द्रोणेन सह पाषतः ।
चिक्रीडाध्ययनं चैव चकार क्षत्रियर्षभः ॥ ११ ॥

अग्निवेशं महाभागं भरद्वाजः प्रतापवान ।
प्रत्यपादयदाग्नेयमस्त्रमग्निसुतं नृप ॥ १२ ॥

पुनर्द्रोणोऽग्निवेशस्य महर्षेरन्तिके नृप ।
अस्त्रार्थमगमत पूर्वंधनुर्वेदचिकीर्षया ॥ १३ ॥

ब्रह्मचारी विनीतात्मा जटिलो वहुलाः समाः ।
अवसत स चिरं तत्र गुरुशुश्रूषणेरतः ॥ १४ ॥

ततोग्निवेशः सुप्रीतो मुनिर्भरतसत्तम ।
भारद्वाजं तदाग्नेयं महास्त्रं प्रत्यपादयत् ॥ १५ ॥

पाञ्चाल्यो राजपुत्रश्च यज्ञसेनो महावलः ।
इष्वस्त्रहेतोर्न्यवसत्तस्मिन्नेव गुरौ तदा ॥ १६ ॥

स तु द्रोणसखा चासीदुपकारी प्रियंकरः ।
स तेन सह सङ्गम्य वर्त्तयन् सुचिरं प्रभो ॥ १७ ॥

अब्रवीदिति तं द्रोणं बचनं प्रीतिवर्द्धनम् ।
अहं प्रियतमः पुत्रः पितुर्द्रोण महात्मनः ॥ १८ ॥

अभिषेच्यति मां राज्ये स पाञ्चाल्यो यदा तदा ।
त्वद्भोग्यं भविता तात सखे सत्येन ते शपे ॥ १९ ॥

मम भोगाश्च वित्तं च त्वदधीनं सुखानि च ।
एवमुक्त्वाथ बब्राज कृतास्त्रःपूजितोमुना ॥ २० ॥

Bharadvāja was friend of the king of Kāmpilya, Pṛṣata, whose son, Drupada, had just been born in those days. He used to go everyday to the *āśrama* of Bharadvāja to study and play with Droṇācārya. O King, the son of fire, the *ṛṣi* Agniveśa had learnt from Bharadvāja the science of the *āgneyāstra*, a formidable weapon. Then Droṇācārya went to the *ṛṣi* Agniveśa to learn the *dhanurvidyā*. And he stayed there for much time. When Agniveśa was happy with the disciple, he gave him the *āgneyāstra*. And Drupada also went to learn the *dhanurvidyā* at the hermitage of Agniveśa. There King Drupada and Droṇācārya became very good friends and spent much time together. Drupada used to say to Droṇācārya that he was the beloved of his father. He said: "When he will leave the kingdom to me then all the kingdom will be yours. Friend, I swear this is true. My enjoyment, richness and happiness will be subject to your authority." After their training the two went back to their respective houses. **[10-20]**

ततस्तु पृषतेऽतीते स राजा द्रुपदोभवत् ।
भरद्वाजोपि भगवानारुरोह दिवं तदा ॥ २१ ॥

तत्रैव निवसन् द्रोणस्तपस्तेपे महातपाः ।
स शुश्राव महात्मानं जामदग्न्यं परन्तपम् ॥ २२ ॥

ब्राह्मणेभ्यो महाराज दित्सन्तं वसु सर्वशः ।
ततो द्रोणोवृतः शिष्यैरुपागच्छद्भृगूद्वहम् ॥ २३ ॥

अथ तं सर्वमुत्सृज्य बनं जिगमिषुं तदा ।
जामदग्न्यं महात्मानं भरद्वाजात्मजीब्रवीत् ॥ २४ ॥

भरद्वाजात्समुत्पन्नं न मातुरुदरोद्भवम् ।
आगतं वित्तकामं मां विद्धि द्रोणं द्विजोत्तमम् ॥ २५ ॥

Then King Pṛṣata died and the kingdom passed under the power of Drupada. And on the other side also the *maharṣi* Bharadvāja went to *Vaikuṇṭha*, the abode of Śrī Viṣṇu. Droṇācārya continued to practice asceticism in that very place. He learnt that Paraśurāma was giving all his property to the *brāhmaṇa*s. So Droṇācārya with all his disciples went to Mount Mahendra, where Bhṛgūdvāja Paraśurāma stayed. By that time Paraśurāmajī had already given away all his possessions and was going into the forest. But Droṇācārya said: "O *muni*, I am the son of Bharadvāja, not born from a womb; My name is Droṇācārya and I came to take some wealth from you." **[21-25]**

राम उवाच -

शरीरमात्रमेवाद्य ममेदमवशेषितम् ।
अस्त्राणिच महार्हाणि शस्त्राणि विविधानि च ॥ २६ ॥

अस्त्राणि वा शरीरं वा वरयैतन्मयोद्यतम् ।
एवमुक्तस्तु रामेण भारद्वाजोब्रवीद्वचः ॥ २७ ॥

अस्त्राणि मे समग्राणि ससंहाराणि भार्गव ।
सप्रयोगरहस्यानिदातुमर्हस्यशेषतः ॥ २८ ॥

Paraśurāmajī said —

Now only my body and my weapons are left because all the

rest I have already given. So if you like ask my body or my weapons, whatever you choose I will give. Droṇācārya answered: "O Bhārgava give to me all the arms and weapons." **[26-28]**

वैशम्पायन उवाच -

तथेत्युक्त्वा ततस्तस्मै प्रादादस्त्राणि भार्गवः ।
प्रतिगृह्य ततो द्रोणः कृतकृत्यस्तदाऽभवत् ॥ २९ ॥

ततः पितृनियोगाच्च पुत्रलोभाच्च गौतमीम् ।
नातिकेशीं महाप्रज्ञामुपयेमे महाव्रताम् ॥ ३० ॥

अलभद्गौतमी पुत्रमश्वत्थामानमौरसम् ।
भीमविक्रमकर्माणमादित्यसमतेजसम् ॥ ३१ ॥

पुत्रेण तेन प्रीतोभूद्द्रोणो राजर्षिसत्तम ।
यथा द्रोणेन सुप्रीतो भरद्वाजो भवत् पुरा ॥ ३२ ॥

Vaiśampāyana said —

Paraśurāmajī said 'so be it' and gave immediately all the weapons and arms to Droṇācārya. He accepted them all and felt obliged.

Then, following the order of his father and wanting progeny, Droṇācārya married the daughter of the son of Gautama (Śaradvat). He had a son called Aśvatthāmā. He was capable of terrible actions and fiery like the sun. As Bharadvāja had been happy to beget Droṇācārya, so Droṇācārya was very happy to beget Aśvatthāmā. **[29-32]**

गोक्षीरं पिवतो द्रृष्ट्वा धनिनस्तत्र पुत्रकान् ।
अश्वत्थामाऽरुदद्बालस्तद्द्रोणं मोहमादधे ॥ ३३ ॥

न स्नातकोऽवसीदेत वर्तमानः स्वकर्मसु ।
इतिसञ्चिन्त्य मनसा तं देशं बहुशोभ्रमन् ॥ ३४ ॥

विशुद्धमिच्छन् नृपते धर्मोपेतं प्रतिग्रहम् ।
अन्तादन्तं परिक्रम्य नाध्यगच्छत् पयस्विनीम् ॥ ३५ ॥

अथ पिष्टोदकेनैनं लोभयन्ति कुमारकाः ।
पीत्वा पिष्टरसं बालः क्षीरं पीतं मयापि च ॥ ३६ ॥

ननर्त्तोत्थाय कौरव्य हृष्टो वाल्याद्विमोहितः ।
तं द्रष्ट्वा नृत्यमानं तु वालैः परिवृतं सुतम् ॥ ३७ ॥

हास्यतामुपसम्पन्नं कश्मलं द्रोणमाविशत् ।
द्रोणं धिगस्त्वधनिनं यो धनं नाधिगच्छति ॥ ३८ ॥

पिष्टोदकं सुतो यस्य पीत्वा क्षीरस्य तृष्णया ।
नृत्यति स्म मुदा युक्तः क्षीरं पीतं मयाप्युत ॥ ३९ ॥

इति संभाषतां तेषां श्रुत्वा वाचं नरर्षभ ।
आत्मानमात्मना गर्हन मनसेदं व्यचिन्तयत् ॥ ४० ॥

अपि चाहं पुरा बिपैर्वर्जितोगार्हतो बसे ।
परोपसेवां पापिष्ठां न च कुर्यां धनेप्सया ॥ ४१ ॥

इति मत्वा प्रियं पुत्रं द्रोण आदाय भूपते ।
पूर्वस्नेहानुरागित्वात् सदारो द्रुपदं गतः ॥ ४२ ॥

अभिषिक्तं तु तं श्रुत्वा कृतार्थोस्मीति चिन्तयन् ।
प्रियं सखायं सुप्रीतो राज्यस्थं समुपागमत् ॥ ४३ ॥

संस्मरन् सङ्गमं चैव वचनं चैव तस्य तत् ।
अब्रवीत् पुरुषव्याघ्र सखायं विद्धि मामिति ॥ ४४ ॥

उपस्थितस्तु द्रुपदं सखिवच्चाथ सङ्गतः ।
स तं निराकारमिव प्रहसन्निदमब्रवीत् ॥ ४५ ॥

Seeing the sons of the rich people drinking milk, Aśvatthāmā cried for having some. Droṇācārya had no cow and regretted not having one. To accomplish the duty of *gṛhastha dharma*, i.e., to fulfil any shortage of the family, Droṇācārya toured all across the country looking for a milk cow but he could not find it. O King, Aśvatthāmā's insistence on asking for milk made Droṇācārya take a decision. He went to the court of King Drupada. Remembering Drupada's love and statement (all my kingdom will be subject to you), Droṇācārya said to Drupada: "O King, I consider you a friend of mine." But whereas the *brāhmaṇa* had a friendly attitude toward the king, Drupada with disrespect started to deride Droṇācārya. **[33-45]**

अकृतेयं तव प्रज्ञा ब्रह्मन् नातिसमंजसा ।
यदात्थ मां त्वं प्रसभं सखा तेहमिति द्विज ॥ ४६ ॥

सङ्गतानीह जीर्यन्ति कालेन परिजीर्यतः ।
सौहृदं मे त्वया ह्यासीत् पूर्वं सामर्थ्यबन्धनम् ॥ ४७ ॥

नाश्रोत्रियः श्रोत्रियस्य नारथी रथिनः सखा ।
नाऽराजा पार्थिवस्यापि सखिपूर्वं किमिष्यते ॥ ४८ ॥

न ह्यनाढ्यः सखाऽऽढ्यस्य नाविद्वान् विदुषः सखा ।
न शूरस्य सखा क्लीवः सखिपूर्वं किमिष्यते ॥ ४९ ॥

साम्याद्धि सख्यं भवति वैषम्यान्नोपपद्यते ।
न सख्यमजरं लोके कस्यचिज्जातु विद्यते ॥ ५० ॥

नाह राज्ञामुदीर्णानामेवंभूतैर्नरैः क्वचित् ।
सख्यं भवति मन्दात्मन् श्रियाहीनैर्धनच्युतैः ॥ ५१ ॥

अहं त्वया नजानामि राज्यार्थे सम्विदं कृताम् ।
एकरात्रं तु ते ब्रह्मन् काम दास्यामि भोजनम् ॥ ५२ ॥

"*Brāhmaṇa*, your idea of to be a friend of mine shows that your intelligence is corrupted. By the passing of time in this world, friendship also is ruined. Our friendship was brought about by the then situation. As a *śrotraya* (those *brāhmaṇa*s in whose family the *Veda* is recited from ten generations) not versed in the *Veda*, a king without the kingdom, the poverty of the rich, the stupidity of the learned and the cowardice of the valiant friend cannot exist, how can you consider me your friend? By being of the same rank friendship can be possible, not by dissimilarity. And any friendship with anyone is not everlasting. Fool! Has any friendship ever happened between great kings and poor people like you? I don't remember any agreement with you about the kingdom. O *brāhmaṇa*, I will give you food only for one night, no more." **[46-52]**

वैशम्पायन उवाच -

एवमुक्तस्तदा द्रोणः सदारः प्रस्थितस्ततः ।
तां प्रतिज्ञां प्रतिज्ञाय यां कर्ता नचिरादिव ॥ ५३ ॥

स विनिश्चित्य मनसा पाञ्चाल्यं प्रति बुद्धिमान ।
जगाम कुरुमुख्यानां नगरं नागसाहूयम् ॥ ५४ ॥

तस्मै पौत्रान् समादाय वसूनि विविधानि च ।
प्राप्ताय प्रददौ भीष्मः शिष्यान् द्रोणाय धीमते ॥ ५५ ॥

द्रोणः शिष्यांस्ततः पार्थानिदं वचनमब्रवीत ।
समानीय तु तान् शिष्यान् द्रुपदस्याऽसुखाय वै ॥ ५६ ॥

आचार्यवेतनं किञ्चिद्धृदि यद्वर्ततेमम ।
कृतास्त्रैस्तत् प्रदेयं स्यात् तद्वतं वदताऽनघाः ॥ ५७ ॥

तच्छ्रुत्वा कौरवेयास्ते तूष्णीमासन् विशाम्पते ।
अर्जुनस्तु ततः सर्वं प्रतिजज्ञे परन्तप ॥ ५८ ॥

ततोर्जुनं मूर्ध्नि तदा द्रोण आघ्राय तं मुहुः ।
प्रीतिपूर्वं परिष्वज्य प्ररुरोद तमाह च ॥ ५९ ॥

प्रयतिष्ये तथा कंर्त्तु यथा नान्योधनुर्द्धरः ।
त्वत्समो भविता लोके सत्यमेतद्ब्रवीमि ते ॥ ६० ॥

Vaiśampāyana said —

O King, as soon as Droṇācārya heard that he went away. He made a promise to himself: to make up for that wrong as soon as possible. He went to Hastināpura. There Bhīṣma Pitāmaha offered to him much wealth and made him the teacher of his nephews, the Kauravas and the Pāṇḍavas. Droṇācārya told them the humiliation he had met with Drupada; he said: "O disciples, will you give the promised *dakṣiṇā* to the teacher, once you got the teaching?" All stayed silent. Only Arjuna agreed. Then Droṇācārya embraced Arjuna and crying said: "I will do my best to make you an archer such as none ever will be on earth." **[53-60]**

॥ *इति श्री का० मा० द्रोणार्जुनप्रतिज्ञानं नाम षष्ठोऽध्यायः* ॥
Here ends the sixth chapter of the Kāmpilyamahātmya.

7

The Fight Between Droṇācārya and King Drupada

वैशम्पायन उवाच -

पाण्डवान्धार्तराष्ट्रांश्च कृतास्त्रान् प्रसमीक्ष्य सः ।
गुर्वर्थदक्षिणाकालं द्रोणः प्राप्तममन्यत ॥ १ ॥

ततः शिष्यान्समानीय आचार्योर्थमचोदयत् ।
द्रोणः सर्वानशेषेण दक्षिणार्थं महीपते ॥ २ ॥

पञ्चालराजं द्रुपदं गृहीत्वा रणमूर्द्धनि ।
पर्यानयत भद्रंवः सास्यात् परमदक्षिणा ॥ ३ ॥

तथेत्युक्त्वातु ते सर्वे रथैस्तूर्णं प्रहारिणः ।
आचार्यधनदानार्थं द्रोणेन सहिता ययुः ॥ ४ ॥

ततोभिजग्मुः पञ्चालान् निघ्नन्तस्ते नरर्षभाः ।
ममृदुस्तस्य नगरं द्रुपदस्य महौजसः ॥ ५ ॥

दुर्योधनश्च कर्णश्च युयुत्सुश्च महाबलः ।
दुःशासनो विकर्णश्च जलसन्धः सुलोचनः ॥ ६ ॥

एते चान्ये च वहवः कुमारा बहुविक्रमाः ।
अहंपूर्वमहं पूर्वमित्येवं क्षत्रियर्षभाः ॥ ७ ॥

ततो वररथारूढाः कुमाराः सादिभिः सह ।
प्रविश्य नगरं सर्वे राजमार्गमुपाययुः ॥ ८ ॥

Vaiśampāyana said —

O King, seeing the Pāṇḍavas and the Kauravas well educated, Droṇācārya thought the right time for the *guru-dakṣiṇā* (a fee given to a spiritual preceptor) had come. So he called all the disciples and said: "Go and catch the king of Kāmpilya, Drupada: that will be my *guru-dakṣiṇā*." The disciples sat on their chariots and with Droṇācārya they went to Kampil. Duryodhana, Karṇa, Yuyutsu, Duḥśāsana, Vikarṇa, Jalasaṅgha, Sulocana, and others started to devastate the country of Pañcāla, crying out: we will fight with the Prince! Through the main road the princes entered into the town. **[1-8]**

तस्मिन् काले तु पाञ्चालः श्रुत्वा द्रष्ट्वा च तद्बलम् ।
भ्रातृभिः सहिता राजस्त्वरया निर्ययौ गृहात् ॥ ९ ॥

ततस्तु कृतसंनाहो यज्ञसेनो महीपतिः ।
ददर्श शरवर्षाणि मुञ्चन्तः कौरवान् रणे ॥ १० ॥

ततो रथेन शुभ्रेण समासाद्य तु कौरवान् ।
यज्ञसेनः शरान् घोरान् व वर्ष युधि दुर्जयः ॥ ११ ॥

पूर्वमेव तु संमन्त्र्य पार्थो द्रोणमथाब्रवीत् ।
दर्पोद्रिकात् कुमाराणामाचार्यं विप्रसत्तमम् ॥ १२ ॥

एषां पराक्रमस्यान्ते वयं कुर्याम साहसम् ।
एतैरशक्यः पाञ्चाल्यो ग्रहीतुं रणमूर्द्धनि ॥ १३ ॥

एवमुत्त्कातु कौन्तेयो भ्रातृभिः सहितोनघः ।
अर्द्धक्रोशे तु नगरादतिष्ठद्बहिरेव सः ॥ १४ ॥

When King Drupada saw the army coming, he quickly jumped on his chariot with all his relatives and fled. A shower of arrows fell and King Drupada also shot his arrows. Arjuna noticing the elation of the Kauravas said to Droṇācārya: "We will fight after the Kauravas; King Drupada cannot be won by them. Thus he and his four brothers stopped half a *kosa* out of the town." **[9-14]**

द्रुपदः कौरवान् द्रष्ट्वा प्राधावत समन्ततः ।
महता शरजालेन मोहयन् कौरवीं चमूम् ॥ १५ ॥

समुद्यतं रथैनैकमाशुकारिणमाहवे ।
अनेकमिव संत्रासान्मेनिरे तत्र कौरवाः ॥ १६ ॥

ततः शङ्खाश्च भेर्यश्च मृदङ्गाश्च सहस्रशः ।
प्रावाद्यन्त महाराज पञ्चालानां निवेशने ॥ १७ ॥

सिंहनादश्च संजज्ञे पञ्चालानां महात्मनाम् ।
धनुर्ज्यातलशब्दश्च संस्पृश्य गगनं महान् ॥ १८ ॥

दुर्योधनो विकर्णश्च सुवाहुर्दीर्घलोचनः ।
दुःशासनश्च संक्रुद्धः शरवर्षैरवाकिरन् ॥ १९ ॥

सीतिविद्धो महेष्वासो द्रुपदो युधिदुर्जयः ।
व्यधमत् तान्यनीकानि तत्क्षणादेव भारत ॥ २० ॥

दुर्योधनं विकर्णं च कर्णं चापि महाबलम् ।
नानानृपसुतान् वीरान् सैन्यानि विविधा न च ॥ २१ ॥

अलातचक्रवत सर्वं चरन् बाणैरतर्पयत् ।
द्रुपदस्यशरा घोरा विचेरुः सर्वतोदिशम ॥ २२ ॥

ततस्तु नागराः सर्वे मुसलैर्यष्टिभिस्तथा ।
अभ्यवर्षन्त कौरव्यान्वर्षमाणा घना इव
सबालवृद्धास्ते पौराः कौरवानभ्ययुस्तदा ॥ २३ ॥

श्रुत्वा सुतुमुलं युद्धं कौरवा भरतर्षभ ।
द्रवन्तिस्म नदन्तिस्म क्रोशन्तः पाण्डवान् प्रति ॥ २४ ॥

King Drupada succeeded in puzzling the Kauravas. With a mesh of arrows and moving rapidly hither and thither, King Drupada looked like many people to the frightened Kauravas. Then the army of Pañcāla started to play thousands of conches and battle-drums. The war-cries and the sound of the bows of the warriors of Pañcāla filled the sky. Duryodhana, Vikarṇa, Subāhu, Dīrghalocana and Duḥśāsana reacted angrily to the enemy's arrows. On that occasion King Drupada scattered in an instant the armies of Duryodhana, Vikarṇa, Karṇa and other princes. Like a glowing fire King Drupada was showering arrows all around himself. Then all the inhabitants of the town started to kill the Kauravas with sticks and stones. The action was so bloody that the Kauravas ran away crying to where the Pāṇḍavas had stopped. **[15-24]**

पाण्डवास्तु स्वनं श्रुत्वा आर्त्तानां लोमहर्षणम् ।
अभिवाद्य ततो द्रोणं रथानारुरुहुस्तदा ॥ २५ ॥

युधिष्ठिरं निवार्याशु मायुध्यस्वेति पाण्डवम् ।
माद्रेयौ चक्ररक्षौच फाल्गुनश्च तदाकरोत् ॥ २६ ॥

सेनाग्रगो भीमसेनस्तदाभूद्गदयो सह ।
तदा शत्रुस्वनं श्रुत्वा भ्रातृभिः सहितोनघः ॥ २७ ॥

आयाज्जवेन कौन्तेयो रथेनानादयन् दिशः ।
पञ्चालानां ततः सेनामुद्धूतार्णवनिस्वनाम् ॥ २८ ॥

The Pāṇḍavas heard the cries of distress and after saluting their *guru* Droṇācārya, they got on their chariots. Arjuna said to Yudhiṣṭhira: "Don't go to fight." He placed Nakula and Sahadeva at each side and Bhīma, wielder of the club, in the front. **[25- 28]**

भीसेनो महाबाहुर्दण्डपाणिरिवान्तकः ।
प्रविवेश महासेनां मकरः सागरं यथा ॥ २९ ॥

स्वयमभ्यद्रवद्भीमो नागानीकं गदाधरः ।
तद्युद्धकुशलः पार्थो बाहुवीर्येण चातुलः ॥ ३० ॥

अहनत् कुञ्जरानीकं गदया कालरूपधृत् ।
ते गजा गिरिसङ्काशाः क्षरन्तो रुधिरं बहु ॥ ३१ ॥

भीमसेनस्य गदया भिन्नमस्तकपिण्डकाः ।
पतन्तिस्म तदा भूमौ वज्राघातादिवाचलाः ॥ ३२ ॥

गजानश्वान् रथांश्चैव पातयामास पाण्डवः ।
पदातीन् रथिनश्चैव न्यवधीदर्जुनाग्रजः ॥ ३३ ॥

गोपाल इव दण्डेन राजन् पशुगणान् वने ।
चालयन् रथनागांश्च संचचाल वृकोदरः ॥ ३४ ॥

Fearless like the god of death, Yamarāja, they entered the town, sweeping aside the army of Pañcāla as a crocodile swims through the sea. They attacked with elephants because they were very skilful in that kind of fighting. The elephants struck by the death-like Bhīma, as mountains struck by lightning, fell on the ground with a lot of bloodshed.

Bhīmasena destroyed all the troops, elephants, horses and chariots. As the cow-herder drives the animals with a stick, so Bhīma scattered the entire the army of Pañcāla. **[29-34]**

॥ इतिश्री का० मा० द्रुपदकौरवयुद्धं नाम सप्तमोऽध्यायः ॥

Here ends the seventh chapter of the Kāmpilyamahātmya.

8

Intervening of Arjuna and Capture of Drupada

वैशम्पायन उवाच -

भारद्वाजप्रियं कर्तुमुद्यतः फाल्गुनस्तदा ।
पार्षतं शरजालेन क्षिपन्नागात् स पांडवः ॥ १ ॥

हयौघांश्च रथौघांश्च गजौघांश्च समन्ततः ।
पातयामास समरे युगान्ताग्निरिव ज्वलन् ॥ २ ॥

ततस्ते हन्यमानावै पंचालाः सृञ्जयास्तथा ।
शरैर्नानाविधै स्तूर्णं पार्थं संछाद्य सर्वशः ॥ ३ ॥

सिंहनादं मुखैः कृत्वा समयुध्यन्त पाण्डवम् ।
सिंहनादं ततः श्रुत्वा नामृष्यत् पाकशासनिः ॥ ४ ॥

ततः किरीटी सहसा पञ्चालान् समरेऽद्रवत् ।
छादयन्निषुजालेन महता मोहयन्निव ॥ ५ ॥

शीघ्रमभ्यस्यतो वाणान् संदधानस्य चानिशम् ।
नान्तरं ददृशे लोकः कौन्तेयस्य यशस्विनः ॥ ६ ॥

सिंहनादश्च संजज्ञे साधुशव्देन मिश्रितः ।
ततः पाञ्चालराजस्तु तदा सत्यजिता सह ॥ ७ ॥

Vaiśampāyana said —

Shooting thousands of arrows Arjuna attacked King Drupada, and like the fire at the end of time he destroyed all the horses, elephants and chariots. Then the Pañcāla army and the brave Sṛñjaya, screaming challenging cries, rained arrows on Arjuna so that he could not bear it anymore. He retorted against the Pañcāla army, showering uncountable arrows upon them. The army was confounded. No one could see when he nocked the arrows to the bowstring and when he shot them. The Kauravas were celebrating with war cries and exclamations such as 'Excellent' and 'Hurrah!'.

Again Drupada with his son Satyajīta ran against Arjuna, as Indra did against Śaṁvaradaitya. **[1-7]**

त्वणमाणोभिदुद्राव महेन्द्रं शम्वरो यथा ।
महता शरवर्षेण पार्थः पाञ्चालमावृणोत् ॥ ८ ॥

ततो हलहलाशब्द आसीत् पांचालके वले ।
जिघृक्षति महासिंहे गजानाभिव यूथपम् ॥ ९ ॥

दृष्ट्वा पार्थं तदाऽऽयान्तं सत्यजित् सत्यविक्रमः ।
पांचालं वै परिप्रेप्सुर्द्धनञ्जयमथाद्रवत् ॥ १० ॥

ततस्त्वर्जुन पांचालौ युद्धाय समुपस्थितौ ।
व्यक्षोभयेतां तौ सैन्यमिन्द्रवैजोचनाविव ॥ ११ ॥

ततः सत्यजितं पार्थो दशभिर्मर्मभेदिभिः ।
विव्याध बलवद्गाढं तदद्भुतमिवाभवत् ॥ १२ ॥

ततः शरशतैः पार्थं पांचालः शीघ्रमार्दयत् ।
पार्थस्तु शरवर्षेणच्छाद्यमानोमहारथः ॥ १३ ॥

वेगं चक्रे महावेगो धनुर्ज्यामवमृज्य च ।
ततः सत्यजितश्चापं छित्वा राजानमभ्ययात् ॥ १४ ॥

अथान्यद्धनुरादाय सत्यजिद्वेगवत्तरम् ।
साश्वं ससूतं सरथं पार्थ विव्याध सत्वरः ॥ १५ ॥

स तन्नममृषे पार्थः पांचालेनार्दितो युधि ।
ततस्तस्य विनाशात्र्थं सत्वरं व्यसृजच्छरान् ॥ १६ ॥

हयान् ध्वजं धनुर्मुष्टिमुभौ तौ पार्स्निसारथी ।
स तथा भिद्यमानेषु कार्मुकेषु पुनः पुनः ॥ १७ ॥

Like a strong lion attacking the king of the elephants Arjuna moved forward to catch King Drupada. Sounds of fear echoed throug the army of Pañcāla. Satyajīta ran against Arjuna in order to save King Drupada. A fierce battle broke out between Arjuna and Satyajīta. To the ten arrows shot by Arjuna, Satyajīta replied with a hundred. Then Arjuna with a rapid movement snapped Satyajīta's bow and rushed against Drupada. But Satyajīta quickly got another bow and went on shooting arrows against Arjuna and his horses, charioteer and chariot. Arjuna answered destroying the horse, the ensign, the bow, the chariot and the charioteer of Satyajīta. Satyajīta no longer wanted to fight. **[8-17]**

हयेषु विनियुक्तेषु विमुखोऽभवदाहवे ।
स सत्यजितमालोक्य तदा विमुखमाहवे ॥ १८ ॥

वेगेन महता राजन्नभ्यवर्षत पाण्डवम् ।
तदा चक्रे महद्युद्धमर्जुना जयतां वाः ॥ १९ ॥

तस्य पार्थो धनुश्छित्वा ध्वजं चोर्व्यामपातयत् ।
पञ्चभिस्तस्य विव्याध हयान् सूतं च सायकैः ॥ २० ॥

तत उत्सृज्य तच्चापमाददानं शरावरम् ।
खड्गमुद्यम्य कौन्तेयः सिंहनादमथाकरोत् ॥ २१ ॥

पांचालस्य रथस्येषामाप्लुत्य सहसापतत् ।
पाञ्चालरथमास्थाय अवित्रस्तो धनञ्जयः ॥ २२ ॥

विक्षोभ्याम्भोनिधिं पार्थस्तं नागमिव सोग्रहीत् ।
ततस्तु सर्वे पाञ्चाला द्रवन्तिस्म दिशो दश ॥ २३ ॥

दर्शयन् सर्वसैन्यानां स बाह्वोर्बलमात्मनः ।
सिंहनादस्वनं कृत्वा निर्जगाम धनञ्जयः ॥ २४ ॥

आयान्तमर्जुनं दृष्ट्वा कुमाराः सहितास्तदा ।
ममृदुस्तस्य नगरं द्रुपदस्य महात्मनः ॥ २५ ॥

O King, when Drupada noticed that Satyajīta was tired by the battle, he went in front of Arjuna. Then Arjuna broke the bow and dropped the standard of Drupada. With five arrows he killed the four horses and the charioteer. King Drupada wanted to get another bow, but Arjuna holding a sword jumped from his chariot onto the chariot of the king. With a frightful cry he terrorised the army of Pañcāla which was huge like the sea, and grasped King Drupada like a snake-coil. All the army fled.

O King, showing the strength of his arms and crying loudly, Arjuna came out through the army of Pañcāla. When Bhīma and the other princes saw Arjuna coming, they started to plunder and pillage the town of Kāmpilya. **[18-25]**

अर्जुन उवाच -

सम्बन्धी कुरुवीराणां द्रुपदो राजसत्तमः ।
मावधीस्तद्बलं भीम गुरुदानं प्रदीयताम् ॥ २६ ॥

Then Arjuna said —

"O Bhīma, King Drupada is a relative of the Kauravas, for this reason don't kill his army. Let us give the *guru-dakṣiṇā*." **[26]**

वैशम्पायन उवाच -

भीमसेनस्तदा राजन्नर्जुनेन निवारितः ।
अतृप्ती युद्धधर्मेषु न्यवर्त्तत महाबलः ॥ २७ ॥

ते यज्ञसेनं द्रुपदं गृहीत्वा रणमूर्द्धनि ।
उपाजह्रुः महामात्यं द्रोणाय भरतर्षभ ॥ २८ ॥

भग्नदर्पंहृतधनं तं तथा वंशमागतम् ।
स वैरं मनसा ध्यात्वा द्रोणो द्रुपदमब्रवीत् ॥ २९ ॥

विमृद्य तरसा राष्ट्रं पुरं ते मृदितं मया ।
प्राप्य जीवं रिपुवशं सखिपूर्वं किमिष्यते ॥ ३० ॥

एव मुक्त्वा प्रहस्यैवं किंचित् स पुनरब्रवीत् ।
माभैः प्राणभयाद्वीर ब्राह्मणाः क्षमिणो वयम् ॥ ३१ ॥

आश्रमे क्रीडितं यत्तु त्वया वाल्ये मया सह ।
तेन सम्वर्द्धितः स्नेहः प्रीतिश्च क्षत्रियर्षभ ॥ ३२ ॥

प्रार्थयेऽहं त्वया सख्यं पुनरेव नराधिप ।
वरं ददामि ते राजन् राज्यस्यार्द्धमवाप्नुहि ॥ ३३ ॥

अराजा किल नो राज्ञः सखा भवितुमर्हति ।
अतः प्रयतितं राज्ये यज्ञसेन मया तव ॥ ३४ ॥

राजासि दक्षिणे कूले भागीरथ्याऽहमुत्तरे ।
सखायं मां विजानीहि पांचाल यदि मन्यसे ॥ ३५ ॥

Vaiśampāyana said —

O King, Bhīmasena was not satisfied by the battle but he stopped, heeding the words of Arjuna. The princes with the counsellors offered Drupada to Droṇācārya. Seeing Drupada humiliated and subjugated by the enemy, Droṇācārya reminded him of the previous hostility: "O Drupada, I have conquered your kingdom, then looted your town, and now your life is under my power. Now tell me what about our friendship?" Smiling for a while Droṇācārya said: "Do not fear for your life, because I am a readily-forgiving *brāhmaṇa*. In childhood we used to play together and for this you are very dear to me. O King, I want to hold a friendly disposition towards you again, and I am going to give you a gift. Take half of the kingdom. I have conquered your kingdom only because you had said earlier that I was not a king and I could not be friend with a king such as you. The southern bank of Gaṅgā will be your kingdom and the northern bank will be my kingdom. O King of Pañcāla, if you like we can be friends again now." **[27-35]**

द्रुपद उवाच -

अनारश्चर्यमिदं ब्रह्मन् विक्रान्तेषु महात्मसु ।
प्रीये त्वयाहं त्वत्तश्च प्रीतिमिच्छामि शाश्वतीम् ॥ ३६ ॥

Drupada said —

"O *brāhmaṇa*, no wonder that you have showed a valiance such as to defeat a king. I am proud of you and I always want to be a friend of yours." **[36]**

वैशम्पायन उवाच -

एवमुक्तः स तं द्रोणोमोक्षयामास भारत ।
सत्कृत्य चैनं प्रीतात्मा राज्यार्द्धं प्रत्यपादयत् ॥ ३७ ॥

माकन्दीमथ गङ्गायास्तीरे जनपदाऽयुताम् ।
सोध्यावसद्दीनमनाः काम्पिल्यं च पुरोत्तमम् ॥ ३८ ॥

दक्षिणांश्चैव पांचालान् यावच्चर्मन्वती नदी ।
आहिच्छत्रं च विषयं द्रोणः समभिपद्यत ॥ ३९ ॥

द्रोणेन चैवं द्रुपदः परिभूतोथ पालितः ।
क्षात्रेण च वलेनास्य नापश्यत् स पराजयम् ॥ ४० ॥

हीनं विदित्वा चात्मानं ब्राह्मेण स वलेन तु ।
पुत्रजन्मपरोप्सन् वै पृथिवीमन्वसंचरत् ॥ ४१ ॥

असत्कारः स तु महान् मुहूर्त्तमपि तस्य तु ।
नापैति हृदथाद्राजन् दुर्मनाः स कृशोभवत् ॥ ४२ ॥

Vaiśampāyana said —

O Bhārata (Janamejaya), when Droṇācārya heard this he let King Drupada go free and he also respectfully gave him half of the kingdom. King Drupada, with devout heart, began to live on the right bank of Gaṅgā, in the deserted Mākandī, "Mistinī"[6], and in Kampil. He was the king of the country between the southern bank of the Gaṅgā and the northern bank of the river Cambala, the South Pañcāla. Droṇācārya was king of Ahicchatra and the northern Pañcāla.

O King, Drupada being defeated and forgiven by Droṇācārya, understood that Droṇācārya would never be defeated by a *kṣatriya* because in front of the power of a *brāhmaṇa* the strength of a *kṣatriya* is annihilated. He started to harbour evil thoughts: to get such a *brāhmaṇa*-like son able to revenge the indignity he had suffered. As he was continuously brooding on hatred he became sad and weak. **[36-42]**

॥ *इतिश्री का० मा० द्रुपदपराजयोनामाष्टमोऽध्यायः* ॥

Here ends the eighth chapter of the Kāmpilyamahātmya.

6. This place is at about five *kosa* in the west direction from Kampil. There is evidence of an ancient settlement there.

9

King Drupada Thinks up a Revenge and Birth of Dṛṣṭadyumna and Draupadī

वैशम्पायन उवाच -

अमर्षी द्रुपदोराजा कर्मसिद्धान् द्विजर्षभान् ।
अन्विच्छन् परिचक्राम ब्राह्मणावसथान् बहून् ॥ १ ॥

पुत्रजन्म परीप्सन् वै शोकोपहतचेतनः ।
नास्ति श्रेष्ठमपत्थं म इति नित्यमचिन्तयत् ॥ २ ॥

जातान् पुत्रान् स निर्वदाद्धिग्वन्धूनिति चाब्रवीत् ।
निश्वासपग्मश्चासीद्द्रोणं प्रतिचिकीर्षया ॥ ३ ॥

प्रभावं विनयं शिक्षां द्रोणस्य चरितानि च ।
क्षात्रेण च वलेनास्य चिन्तयन्नाध्यगच्छत ॥ ४ ॥

प्रतिकर्तुं नृपश्रेष्ठा यतमानोपि भारत ।
अभितः सोथदल्माषीं जाह्नवीं च परिभ्रमन् ॥ ५ ॥

ब्राह्मणावसथं पुण्यमाससाद महीपतिः ।
यत्र नास्नातकः कश्चिन्न चासीदव्रती द्विजः ॥ ६ ॥

Vaiśampāyana said —

O King, the angry King Drupada searched in many *āśrama* for some *brāhmaṇa* capable of performing *karmasiddha*, a perfect sacrifice, in order to get a son. He always thought that he did not have a very good son. He used to reproach his other sons including Satyajīta. And the heavy feeling of the revenge got by Droṇācārya was growing day by day.

Seeing Droṇācārya's influence, politeness, and moral conduct King Drupada could not even bear the verdict of Droṇācārya. At that time, wandering between Gaṅgā and Yamunā, he arrived at a place where all the *brāhmaṇa*s were instructed in the *Veda*. **[1-6]**

तत्रैव च महाभागः सोपश्यत् संशितव्रतौ ।
याजोपयाजौ ब्रह्मर्षी शाम्यन्तौ परमेष्ठिनौ ॥ ७ ॥

संहिताध्ययने युक्तौ गोत्रतश्चापि काश्यपौ ।
कानीनौ युक्तरूपौ तौ ब्राह्मणावृषिसत्तमौ ॥ ८ ॥

स तावामन्त्रयामास सर्वकामैरतन्द्रितः ।
बुध्वा वय तयोस्तत्र कनीयांसमुपह्वरे ॥ ९ ॥

पादशुश्रूषणे युक्तः प्रियवाक् सर्वकामदः ।
अर्चयि यथान्यायमुपयाजमुवाच सः ॥ १० ॥

येन मे कर्मणा ब्रह्मन् पुत्रःस्याद्द्रोणमृत्यवे ।
उपयाज कृते तस्मिन् गवां दास्यामि तेऽर्बुदम् ॥ ११ ॥

यद्वा तेऽन्यन्द्विजश्रेष्ठ मनसः सुप्रियं भवेत् ।
सर्वं तत् ते प्रदाताहं नहि मेत्रास्ति संशयः ॥ १२ ॥

इत्युक्तो नाहमित्येवं तमृषिः प्रत्यभाषत ।
आराधयिष्यन् द्रुपदः स तं पर्यचरत् पुनः ॥ १३ ॥

ततः सम्वत्सरस्यान्ते द्रुपदं स द्विजोत्तमः ।
उपयाजोऽब्रवीत् काले राजन् मधुरया गिरा ॥ १४ ॥

ज्येष्ठो भ्राता ममागृह्णाद्विचरन् गहने वने ।
अपरिज्ञातशौचायां भूमौ निपतितं फलम् ॥ १५ ॥

तदपश्यमहं भ्रातुरसाम्प्रतमनुव्रजन् ।
विमर्शं सङ्करादाने नायं कुर्यात् कथंचन ॥ १६ ॥

दृष्ट्वा फलस्य नापश्यद्दोषान् पापानुबन्धकान् ।
विविनक्ति न शौचं यः सोन्यत्रापि कथं भवेत ॥ १७ ॥

सहिताध्ययनं कुर्वन् वसन् गुरुकुले च यः ।
भैक्षमुच्छिष्टमन्येषां भुङ्क्ते स्म च यदा तदा ॥ १८ ॥

कीर्तयन् गुणमन्नानामघृणो च पुनः पुनः ।
तं वे फलार्थिनं मन्ये भ्रातरं तर्कचक्षुषा ॥ १९ ॥

In that place King Drupada met two *ṛṣi* Yāja and Upayāja. Both of them had got to a high status and calmness of mind. They were always absorbed in reading the *Veda*. They belonged to the *gotra* of Kāśyapa and, like Karṇa, they were born from a young girl; because of this they also knew how to perform abominable functions. Knowing about their ascetic power, King Drupada humbly took the youngest *ṛṣi*, Upayāja, aside and said: "O Upayāja, please perform a rite for me so that a son will be born who will kill Droṇācārya. I will give you a *dakṣiṇā* of one thousand million cows. And whatever you like I will give you; I don't have any problem in doing that."

Upayāja listened to the king's talk and answered: "I will never do what you are asking!" Nevertheless King Drupada continued to serve that sage for one year. Consequently Upayāja, pleased by the favours of King Drupada, said: "Once my older brother Yāja and I were in the forest. There he picked up a fallen fruit from the impure ground. I noticed that he doesn't discriminate between pure and impure. One who doesn't mind about the purity of a fallen fruit can do other impure tasks. When we were at the *āśrama* of the teacher he was asking insistently for the leftovers from the food of the other students. I mean that Yāja likes wealth, this I have seen by myself. O king, go to him, he will perform the sacrifice you ask." **[7-19]**

तं वे गच्छस्व नृपते स त्वां सयाजयिष्यति ।
जुगुप्समानो नृपतिर्मनसेदं विचिन्तयन् ॥ २० ॥

उपयाजवचःश्रुत्वा याजस्याश्रममभ्यगात् ।
अभिसम्पूज्य पूजार्हमथ याजमुवाच सः ॥ २१ ॥

अयुतानि ददान्यष्टौ गवां याजय मां विभो ।
द्रोणवैराभिसंतप्तं प्रह्लादयितुमर्हसि ॥ २२ ॥

स हि ब्रह्मविदां श्रेष्ठो ब्रह्मास्त्रे चाप्यनुत्तमः ।
तस्माद्द्रोणः पराजैष्ट मां वै स सखिविग्रहे ॥ २३ ॥

ततो नास्ति क्षत्रियोऽस्यांपृथिव्यां कश्चिदग्रणीः ।
कौरवाचार्यमुख्यस्य भारद्वाजस्य धीमतः ॥ २४ ॥

द्रोणस्य शरजालानि प्राणिदेहहराणि च ।
षडरत्नि धनुर्यस्य दृश्यते परमं महत् ॥ २५ ॥

स हि ब्राह्मणवेषेण क्षात्रं वेगमसंशयम् ।
प्रतिहन्ति महेष्वासो भारद्वाजो महामनाः ॥ २६ ॥

क्षत्रोच्छेदायविहितोजामदग्न्य इवापरः ।
तस्य ह्यस्त्रवलं घोरमप्रधृष्यं नरैर्भुवि ॥ २७ ॥

ब्राह्मं संधारयंस्तेजो हुताहुतिरिवानलः ।
समेत्य स दहत्याजौ क्षात्रधर्मपुरःसरः ॥२८ ॥

ब्रह्मक्षत्रे च विहिते ब्राह्म तेजो विशिष्यते ।
सोऽहंक्षात्राद्बलाद्धीनी ब्राह्म तेजः प्रपेदिवान् ॥ २९ ॥

द्रोणाद्विशिष्टमासाद्य भवन्तं ब्रह्मवित्तमम् ।
द्रोणान्तकमहं पुत्रं लभेयं युधि दुजयम ॥ ३० ॥

As soon as King Drupada heard this malevolent advice he went immediately to meet Yāja. "O Yāja, I give you now a present of 80000 cows, and I will give one thousand million as *dakṣiṇā* if you accomplish a sacrifice, *yajña*, for me. Release me from the smart of my enemy Droṇācārya's wrong. He is most excellent in both the *brahma-vidyā* (metaphysical knowledge) and the *astra-vidyā* (the art of using weapons, archery) — for this reason he could defeat me. On this earth there is no *kṣatriya* more valiant than him. The arrows of the teacher of the Kauravas, Droṇācārya, bear destruction for all creatures. Moreover his bow is of six *aratni* (the distance between the elbow and the fist is one *aratni*). Droṇācārya is destroyer of the *kṣatriya*, like a Paraśurāma disguised in the dress of *brāhmaṇa.* The power of his weapons cannot be withstood by anyone. Like a blazing fire he reduces to ash his enemies in battle. Droṇācārya possesses the *tejas* (glow, brillance) of both the *brāhmaṇa* and the *kṣatriya* —

for this reason he is excellent. But in you there is only the *brahmatejas* and for that you can be better than Droṇa, because by acting like a *kṣatriya*, he has lost the perfection of *brahmatejas*. I have just the power of *kṣatriya* and so I am inferior to Droṇa; for this reason I have come for protection to you. With your help I will beget a valiant son who will destroy Droṇācārya. O Yāja, now carry out my task. I will give you a *dakṣiṇā* of one thousand million cows." **[20-30]**

तत्कर्म कुरु मे याज वितराम्यर्वुदं गवाम् ।
त्थेत्युक्त्वा तु तं याजी याज्यार्थमुपकल्पयत् ॥ ३१ ॥

गुर्वर्थ इति चाकाममुपयाजमचोदयत् ।
याजो द्रोणविनाशाय प्रतिजज्ञे तथा च सः ॥ ३२ ॥

ततस्तस्य नरेन्द्रस्य उपयाजो महातपाः ।
आचरव्यौ कर्म वैतानं तदा पुत्रफलाय वै ॥ ३३ ॥

स च पुत्रो महावीर्यो महातेजा महाबलः ।
इष्येत यद्विधी राजन् भविता ते तथा सुतः ॥ ३४ ॥

भारद्वाजस्य हन्तारं सोऽभिसन्धाय भूपतिः ।
आजहे तत् तथा सर्वं द्रुपदः कर्मसिद्धये ॥ ३५ ॥

यातस्तु हवनस्यान्ते देवीमाज्ञापयत् तदा ।
प्रेहि मां राज्ञि पृषति मिथुनं त्वामुपस्थितम् ॥ ३६ ॥

After listening to King Drupada, Yāja agreed to perform the *yajña*, and he decided what was required for that. Upayāja was not prepared to do that *yajña*, but Yāja told him that the *dakṣiṇā* was very valuable so that he also made the promise to destroy Droṇācārya. Then Upayāja gave the dispositions for the *yajña* by which King Drupada would get a son. "O King, as you want you will get a very valiant son." With the thought of "a son who will kill Droṇācārya" King Drupada collected all the necessary materials for the sacrifice. Then at the end of the *havana* (rite), Yāja said to Drupada's Queen: "O Queen, come here and you will have a boy and a girl." **[31-36]**

राज्ञ्युवाच -

अवलिप्तं मुखं ब्रह्मन् दिव्यान् गन्धान् विभर्मि च ।
सुतार्थे नोपलव्धास्मि तिष्ठ याज ममप्रिये ॥ ३७ ॥

The Queen said that her mouth was not pure because of betel and other flavoured things so that she could not come in the place of the *yajña*. She told them, "O *brāhmaṇa*, wait a while." **[37]**

याजउवाच -

याजेन श्रपितं हव्यमुपयाजाभिमन्त्रितम् ।
कथं कामं न सन्दध्यात् सा त्वं विप्रेहि तिष्ठ वा ॥ ३८ ॥

Again Yāja said —

Listen O Queen, the food prepared by me and the offering purified by the *mantra* of my brother are not to be compared with human intercourse and also the rite cannot stand for much time, so whether you come or not, from our power now one son and one daughter will be born. **[38]**

वैशम्पायन उवाच -

एवमुवक्त्वातु याजेन हुते हविषि संस्कृते ।
उत्तस्थौ पावकात् तस्मात् कुमारो देवसंनिभः ॥ ३९ ॥

ज्वालावर्णो घोररूपः किरीटं वर्म चोत्तमम् ।
विभ्रत् सखड्गः सशरो धनुष्मान् विनदन् मुहुः ॥ ४० ॥

सोऽध्यारोद्रथवरं तेन च प्रययौ तदा ।
ततः प्रणेदुः पञ्चालाः प्रहृष्टाः साधुसाध्विति ॥ ४१ ॥

हर्षाविष्टास्ततश्चैतान् नेयं सेहे वसुन्धरा ।
भयापहो राजपुत्रः पञ्चालानां यशस्करः ॥ ४२ ॥

राज्ञः शोकापहो जात एष द्रोणवधाय वै ।
इत्युवाच महद् भूतमदृश्यं खेचरं तदा ॥ ४३ ॥

कुमारी चापि पाञ्चाली वेदीमध्यात् समुत्थिता ।
सुभगा दर्शनीयाङ्गी स्वसितायतलोचना ॥ ४४ ॥

श्यामा पद्मपलाशाक्षी नीलकुञ्चितमूर्द्धजा ।
ताम्रतुङ्गनखी सुभ्रूश्चारुपीनपयोधरा ॥ ४५ ॥

मानुषं विग्रहं कृत्वा साक्षादमरबर्णिनी ।
नीलोत्पलसमो गन्धो यस्यः क्रोशात् प्रधावति ॥ ४६ ॥

या विभर्ति परं रूपं यस्य नास्त्युपमा भुवि ।
देवदानवयक्षाणामीप्सिता देवरूपिणी ॥ ४७ ॥

तां चापि जातां सुश्रोणीं वागुवाचा शरीरिणी ।
सर्वयोषिद्वरा कृष्ण निनोषुः क्षत्रियान क्षयम् ॥ ४८ ॥

सुरकार्यमियं काले करिष्यति सुमध्यमा ।
अस्या हेतोः कौरवाणां महदुत्पत्स्यते भयम् ॥ ४९ ॥

तच्छ्रुत्वा सर्वपाञ्चालाः प्रणेदुः सिहसङ्घवत् ।
नचैतान् हषसम्पूर्णानियं सेहे वसुन्धरा ॥ ५० ॥

Vaiśampāyana said —

After saying that Yāja offered the oblation to the fire, and from that *yajña-kuṇḍa* a boy appeared like a god. With a fearful form like a burning fire, wearing the crown, the armour, the bow and arrows, and the sword he roared terribly. He sat on a chariot and went. The delighted residents of Pañcāla, seeing him, started to shout with joy. It seemed that the earth could not contain the happiness of so many men. Then a voice from the sky said that this son of the king will increase the glory of Pañcāla, will relieve the grief of King Drupada and will destroy Droṇācārya. After that a girl appeared from the same *yajña-kuṇḍa*. She was very beautiful with big eyes. Her complexion was dark and her eyes were red like the lotus; her nails were long, the eyebrows were fine and her breasts full. She was really the manifestation of the Devī herself. Her body had the perfume of the blue lotus that could be smelt from one *kosa* away. On this earth there was no beauty that could be compared with her; *devatā*, *daitya*, *yakṣa* fell in love with her. Also when she appeared a celestial voice boomed: "This girl will destroy the *kṣatriyas*. At the proper time she will accomplish the task of the gods. The Kauravas will have to suffer great fear because of this girl." All Pañcāla reverberated with applause and war cries. It seemed that the earth could not bear the load of the jubilation of Pañcāla. **[39-50]**

तौ दृष्ट्वा पार्षती याजं प्रपेदे वै सुतार्थिनी ।
न वै मदन्यां जननीं जानीयातामिमाविति ॥ ५१ ॥

तथेत्युवाच तां याजो राज्ञः प्रियचिकीर्षया ।
तयोश्च नामनी चक्रुर्द्विजाः सम्पूर्णमानसाः ॥ ५२ ॥

धृष्टत्वादत्यमर्षित्वाद् द्युम्नोद् द्युत्सम्भवादपि ।
धृष्टद्युम्नः कुमारोयं द्रुपदस्य भविष्यति ॥ ५३ ॥

कृष्णेत्येवाब्रुवन् कृष्णां कृष्णाऽभूत् सापि वर्णतः ।
एवं तन्मिथुनं जज्ञे द्रुपदस्य महात्मनः ॥ ५४ ॥

धृष्टद्युम्नं तु पाञ्चाल्यमानीय स्वं निवेशनम् ।
उपाकरोदस्त्रहेतोर्भारद्वाजः प्रतापवान् ॥ ५५ ॥

अक्षोभणीयं दैवं हि भावि मत्वा महामतिः ।
तथा तत् कृतवान् द्रोण आत्मकीर्त्यनुरक्षणात् ॥ ५६ ॥

The Queen, seeing the two, Dhṛṣṭadyumna and Draupadī, said to Yāja that she accepted the burden to be the mother of the two celestial creatures. "So be it", Yāja said. Then the *brāhmaṇa* named the two children. Because he had been imagined in mind, *dṛṣṭa*, and endowed with splendour and power, *dyumna*, the boy was called Dhṛṣṭadyumna. And the girl was called Kṛṣṇā, because of her dark complexion. O King, in this way Dhṛṣṭadyumna and Draupadī were born from the *yajña* of King Drupada. Then Droṇācārya, submitting to Fate, accepted Dhṛṣṭadyumna as a disciple. **[51-56]**

॥ *इतिश्री का० मा० द्रौपदीसम्भवोनाभ नवमोऽध्यायः* ॥

Here ends the ninth chapter of the Kāmpilyamahātmya.

10

Preparations for the *Svayaṁvara* of Draupadī

THE story of the meeting of the Pāṇḍavas and the *gandharvarāja* Aṅgārārpaṇa.

वैशम्पायन उवाच -

यज्ञसेनस्य कामस्तु पाण्डवाय किरीटिने ।
कृष्णां दद्यामिति सदा न चैतद्विवृणोतिसः ॥ १ ॥

सोन्वेषमाणः कौन्तेयं पाञ्चाल्यो जनमेजय ।
दृढं धनुरनानाम्यं कारयामास भारत ॥ २ ॥

यन्त्रंवैहायसं चापि कारयामास कृत्रिमम् ।
तेन यन्त्रेण समितं राजा लक्ष्यंचकार सः ॥ ३ ॥

इदं सज्यं धनुः कृत्वा सज्जैरेभिश्च सायकैः ।
अतीत्य लक्ष्यं यो वेद्धा स लव्धा मत्सुतामिमाम् ॥ ४ ॥

इति स द्रुपदो राजा स्वयम्वरमघोषयत् ।
तच्छ्रुत्वा पार्थिवाः सर्वे समीयस्तत्र भारत ॥ ५ ॥

दुर्योधनपुरोगाश्च सकर्णाः कुरवो नृप ।
ब्राह्मणाश्च महाभाग देशेभ्यः समुपागमन् ॥ ६ ॥

Vaiśampāyana said —

O King, King Drupada wanted to marry his daughter Kṛṣṇā, Draupadī, to Arjuna. But he did not talk about that to anyone. So he made a bow so stiff that none could bend it. Then he fixed it high in the sky, with a golden fish as a target;[7] right below it he placed a *yantra*, a propeller quickly whirling so that it could disturb, or even stop, the archer. Then he made a proclamation by drum-beat: "Who so ever will pierce the target with this bow and these five arrows standing on the whirling *yantra*, he will obtain my daughter." When all the kings, and Karṇa, Duryodhana and the other Kauravas heard this, they came there. Also many *brāhmaṇa* arrived there from different countries. **[1-6]**

ततस्ते नरशार्दूला भ्रातरः पंच पाण्डवाः ।
प्रययुर्द्रौपदीं द्रष्टुं तं च देशं महोत्सवम् ॥ ७ ॥
ते प्रयाता नरव्याघ्राः सहमात्रा परंतपाः ।
राज्ञा दक्षिणपंचालान् द्रुपदेनाभिरक्षितान् ॥ ८ ॥
समैरुदङ्मुखैमर्गैर्यथोद्दिष्टं परंतपाः ।
ते त्वगच्छन्नहीरात्रात् तीर्थं सोमाश्रयायणम्+ ॥ ९ ॥
मातरं ते पुरस्कृत्य प्रतस्थुः कौरवर्षभ ।
आसेदुःपुरुषव्याघ्रा गङ्गायां पाण्डुनन्दनाः ॥ १० ॥
उल्मुकं तु समुद्यम्य तेषामग्रेधनंजयः ।
प्रकाशार्थं ययौ तत्र रक्षार्थं च महाबलः ॥ ११ ॥
तत्र गङ्गाजले रम्ये विविक्ते क्रीडयन् स्त्रियः ।
ईर्ष्युर्गन्धर्वराजो वै जलक्रीडामुपागतः ॥ १२ ॥
शब्दं तेषां स शुश्राव नदीं समुपसर्पताम् ।
तेन शब्देन चाविष्टश्चुक्रोध वलवद्वली ॥ १३ ॥
स दृष्ट्वा पाण्डवांस्तत्र सह मात्रा परन्तपान ।
विस्फारयन् धनुर्घोरमिदं वचनमब्रवीत् ॥ १४ ॥

And also the Pāṇḍavas with their mother moved to southern Pañcāla; they also wanted to see Draupadī's beauty. So (heading north) they arrived in the night at Rudāyan. O King

7. *Lakṣya*; even if in the original work it is only written *lakṣya*, in the *BhP.*, *SkandaP* (10, 83, 19) and the Ādi-Parvan of the *Bharatsāra* (10, 5) it is clearly written 'golden fish', *suvarṇa matsya*.

of the Kurus (Janamejaya), first of all was proceeding Arjuna who had some burning sticks in his hands because of darkness, followed by Kuntī and the others; in this way they got to the banks of Gaṅgā. There, the *gandharvarāja* Aṅgārārpaṇa was playing in the water with his women.[8] He got very angry when he heard the sound of the five Pāṇḍavas coming. And when he saw the five Pāṇḍavas with their mother Kuntī he took up his frightening bow and said: **[7-14]**

सन्ध्या संरज्यते घोरा पूर्वरात्र्यागमेषु या ।
अशीतिभिर्लवैर्हीनं तन्मुहूर्तं प्रचक्षते ॥ १५ ॥

विहितं कामचाराणां यक्षगन्धर्वरक्षसाम् ।
शेषमन्यन्मनुष्याणां कर्मचारेषु वै स्मृतम् ॥ १६ ॥

लोभात् प्रचारं चरतस्तासु वेलासु वै नरान् ।
उपक्रान्ता निगृह्णीमो राक्षसैः सह वालिशान् ॥ १७ ॥

अतो रात्रो प्राप्नुवतो जलं ब्रह्मविदो जनाः ।
गर्हयन्ति नरान् सर्वान् बलस्थान् नृपतीनपि ॥ १८ ॥

आरात् तिष्ठत मा मह्यं समीपमुपसर्पत ।
कस्मान्मां नाभिजानीत प्राप्तं भागीरथीजलम ॥ १९ ॥

अङ्गारपर्णं गन्धर्वं वित्त मां स्वबलाश्रयम् ।
अहं हि मानी चेर्ष्युश्च कुबेरस्य प्रियः सखा ॥ २० ॥

अङ्गारपर्ण मित्येवं ख्यातं चेदं वनं मम ।
अनुगङ्गं चरन् कामांश्चित्रं यत्र रमाम्यहम् ॥ २१ ॥

न कौणपाः शृङ्गिणो वा न देवा न च दानवाः ।
इदं समुपसर्पन्ति तत् किं समुपसर्पथ ॥ २२ ॥

"When the night comes, only up to 80 *lava*, equal to 40 *pala*, (a period corresponding to few minutes after sunset) a man can wander around. The rest of the night is the roaming time for *yakṣa*, *gandharva* and *rākṣasa*. I punish with my stick those greedy people who come here in the night. For

8. The tale of the *gandharva* Citraratha who fought against Arjuna is described in *Mbh.*, Ādi-Parvan, *adhyāya* 169, *śloka* 79.

this reason the learned men speak ill of those who wander in the night time. Stay far from me! Don't come near! Don't you know, I am the *gandharva* Aṅgārārpaṇa, a very good friend of Kubera. This forest is also well known with my proper name, Aṅgārārpaṇa. I like to wander here and there along the banks of the Gaṅgā. In this place even *rākṣasa*, *śṛṅgī devatā* (gods who are engaged in the 'heroic' practice, *vīra sādhaka*) and also *daitya* do not come. How did you dare to approach?" **[15-22]**

अर्जुन उवाच -

समुद्रे हिमवत्पार्श्वे नद्यामस्यां च दुर्मते ।
रात्रावहनि सन्ध्यायां कस्य गुप्तः परिग्रहः ॥ २३ ॥

भुक्तो वाऽप्यथवाऽभुक्तो रात्रावहनि खेचर ।
न कालनियमो ह्यस्ति गङ्गां प्राप्य सरिद्वराम् ॥ २४ ॥

वयं च शक्तिसम्पन्ना अकाले त्वामधृष्णुम ।
अशक्ता हि रणे क्रूर युष्मानर्चन्ति मानवाः ॥ २५ ॥

पुरा हिमवतश्चैषा हेमशृङ्गाद्विनिःसृता ।
गङ्गा गत्वा समुद्राम्भः सप्तधा समपद्यत ॥ २६ ॥

गङ्गां च यमुनां चैव प्लक्षजातां सरस्वतीम् ।
रथस्थां सरयूं चैव गोमतीं गण्डकीं तथा ॥ २७ ॥

अपर्युषितपापास्ते नदीः सप्त पिबन्ति ये ।
इयं भूत्वा चैकवप्राशुचिराकाशगा पुनः ॥ २८ ॥

देवेषु गङ्गा गन्धर्व प्राप्नोत्यलकनन्दताम् ।
तथा पितॄन् वैतरणी दुस्तरा पापकर्मभिः ॥ २९ ॥

असम्बाधा देवनदी स्वर्गसम्पादनी शुभा ।
कथमिच्छसि तां रोद्धुं नैष धर्मः सनातनः ॥ ३० ॥

अनिवार्यमसम्बाधं तव वाचा कथं वयम् ।
न स्पृशेम यथाकामं पुण्यं भागीरथीजलम् ॥ ३१ ॥

Arjuna said —

O fool, whose women stay hidden in the ocean, in the

Himālaya, and along the Gaṅgā. It may be day or night, and twilight also, on the banks of Gaṅgā there is no rule about time. We are able for this; we came to disturb you in this improper time. Do you consider those who are not capable good people? This Gaṅgā comes from Himālaya, divides herself in seven streams, that flow into the ocean: Gaṅgā, Yamunā, Plakṣjātā-Sarasvatī, Rathasthā, Saryū, Gomatī, Gaṇḍakī. The man who drinks their water gets rid of any sin. O *gandharva*, this Gaṅgā comes from the sky and she is called Alakanandā in the *devaloka*, the world of gods. In the *yamaloka*, the world of death, she is called Vaitaraṇī. None can put any restriction on Her, but you are impeding us, and this is against the *dharma*. Do you think we are going to abstain from the water of Gaṅgā only because you are stopping us? **[23-31]**

वैशम्पायन उवाच -

अङ्गारपर्णस्तच्छुत्वा क्रुद्ध आनम्य कार्मुकम् ।
मुमोच वाणान् निशितानहीनाशीविषानिव ॥ ३२ ॥

उल्मुकं भ्रामयंस्तूर्णं पाण्डवश्चर्म चोत्तमम् ।
व्यपोहत शरास्तस्य सर्वानेव धनञ्जयः ॥ ३३ ॥

Vaiśampāyana said —

O Janamejaya, the *gandharva* immediatly shot a snake-like arrow, but Arjuna drew his weapon. **[32-33]**

अर्जुन उवाच -

विभीषिका वैगन्धर्व नास्त्रज्ञेषु प्रयुज्यते ।
अस्त्रज्ञेषु प्रयुक्तेयं फेनवत् प्रविलीयते ॥ ३४ ॥

मानुषानतिगन्धर्वान् सर्वान् गन्धर्व लक्षये ।
तस्मादस्त्रेण दिव्येन योत्स्येहंत्न तु मायया ॥ ३५ ॥

पुरास्त्रमिदमाग्नेयं प्रादात् किल वृहस्पतिः ।
भरद्वाजाय गन्धर्व गुरुर्मान्यः शतक्रतोः ॥ ३६ ॥

भरद्वाजादग्निवेश्यअग्निवेश्याद्गुरुर्मम ।
साध्विमं मह्यददद् द्रोणो ब्राह्मणसत्तमः ॥ ३७ ॥

Arjuna said —

O *gandharva*, it is impossible to scare those who know the secrets of weapons. I have experienced myself that man is more valiant than the *gandharva*. So I will not fight with you; I will just throw this weapon. This *āgneyāstra*, fiery weapon, was given by the *guru* of Indra, Bṛhaspati, to Bharadvāja. Bharadvāja gave it to Agniveśa, and he gave it to Droṇācārya who gave it to me. **[34-37]**

वैशम्पायन उवाच -

इत्युक्त्वा पाण्डवः क्रुद्धो गन्धर्वाय मुमोच ह ।
प्रदीप्तमस्त्रमाग्नेयं ददाहास्य रथं तु तत् ॥ ३८ ॥

विरथं विप्लुतं तं तु स गन्धर्वं महाबलः ।
अस्त्रतेजः प्रमूढं च प्रपतन्तमवाङ्मुखम् ॥ ३९ ॥

शिरोरुहेषु जग्राह माल्यवत्सु धनञ्जयः ।
भ्रातॄन्प्रति चकर्षाथ सोऽस्त्रपातादचेतसम् ॥ ४० ॥

युधिष्ठिरं तस्य भार्या प्रपेदे शरणार्थिनी ।
नाम्ना कुम्भीनसी राजन् पतिप्राणमभीप्सती ॥ ४१ ॥

Vaiśampāyana said —

O King, after saying that Arjuna threw the *āgneyāstra* and burnt the *gandharva*'s chariot. He seized the unconscious *gandharva* by the hair and dragged him toward his brothers. Then his woman, the *gandharvī* Kumbhīnasī, went to implore King Yudhiṣṭhira. **[38-41]**

गन्धर्व्युवाच -

त्रायस्व मां महाभाग पतिं चेमं विमुञ्च मे ।
गन्धर्वी शरणं प्राप्ता नाम्ना कुम्भीनसी प्रभो ॥ ४२ ॥

Gandharvī said —

O lord, please let my husband go free, I pray you. **[42]**

युधिष्ठिर उवाच -

युद्धे जितं यशोहीनं स्त्रीनाथमपराक्रमम्।
को निहन्याद्रिपुं तात मुञ्चेमं रिपुसूदन ॥ ४३ ॥

Yudhiṣṭhira said —

O Arjuna, one should not kill the enemy defeated in battle if he is also the only protector of his wife; now let him go. **[43]**

अर्जुन उवाच -

जीवितं प्रतिपद्यस्व गच्छ गन्धर्व माशुचः।
प्रदिशत्यभयं तेऽद्य कुरुराजो युधिष्ठरः ॥ ४४ ॥

Arjuna said —

O *gandharva*, do not be sad, King Yudhiṣṭhira is giving you the gift of his protection. **[44]**

गन्धर्व उवाच -

जितोऽहं पूर्वकं नाम मुञ्चाम्यङ्गारपर्णताम्।
न च श्लाघे वलेनाङ्ग न नाम्ना जनसंसदि ॥ ४५ ॥

अस्त्राग्निना विचित्रीयं दग्धो मे रथ उत्तमः।
सोहं चित्ररथो भूत्वा नाम्ना दग्धरथोऽभवम् ॥ ४६ ॥

साध्विमं लब्धवान् लाभं योऽहं दिव्यास्त्रधारिणम्।
गान्धर्व्या माययेच्छामि संयोजयितुमर्जुनम् ॥ ४७ ॥

सम्भृता चैव विद्येयं तपसेह मया पुरा।
निवेदयिष्ये तामद्य प्राणदाय महात्मने ॥ ४८ ॥

संस्तम्भयित्वा तरसा जितं शरणभोगतम्।
यो रिपुं योजयेत् प्राणेः कल्याणं किं न सोर्हति ॥ ४९ ॥

चाक्षुषीनाम विद्येयं यां सीमाय ददौ मनुः।
ददौ स विश्वावसवे मम विश्वावसुर्ददौ ॥ ५० ॥

सेयं कापुरुषं प्राप्ता गुरुदत्ता प्रणश्यति ।
आगमोऽस्या मया प्रोक्तो वीर्यं चापि निबोध मे ॥ ५१ ॥

यच्चक्षुषा द्रष्टुमिच्छेत् त्रिषु लोकेषु किञ्चन ।
तत् पश्येद्यादृशं चेच्छेत् तादृशं द्रष्टुमर्हति ॥ ५२ ॥

एकपादेन षण्मासान् स्थितो विद्यां लभेदिमाम् ।
अनुनेष्याम्यहं विद्यां स्वयं तुभ्यं व्रतेऽकृते ॥ ५३ ॥

विद्यया त्वनया राजन् वयं नृभ्यो विशेषिताः ।
अविशिष्टाश्च देवानामनुभावप्रदर्शिनः ॥ ५४ ॥

Gandharva said —

O Arjuna, after being defeated by you I will drop my own name (Aṅgārārpaṇa), because in the council I will not get any respect from that. My chariot was burnt by your *āgneyāstra*, so I will change my name Citraratha (excellent, bright chariot) to Dagdharatha (burnt chariot). Because I have benefitted a lot, I want to give Arjuna the divine weapon bearer, the *vidyā* of *gandharva*. As you told me before about your *āgneyāstra*, now listen to me. I got this knowledge by hard work. For this reason I ask Arjuna, the holder of my life: that hero who after defeating his enemy grants the gift of life, what is he not able to obtain? This knowledge called *cakṣusī* was given by Manu to Candramā. Candramā gave it to the *gandharva* Viśvavasu, through whom I got it. This knowledge cannot be kept by an unworthy man. I told you already about its origin, now listen to its powers. Whatever you want to see in the three worlds you will be able to see by this *vidyā*. Having stood for six months on one leg a human being is able to get this knowledge. But I am giving it to you without any effort, take it! O Arjuna, by possessing this knowledge we (*gandharva*s) are outstanding humans and we become influential like gods. **[45-54]**

गन्धर्वजानामश्वानामहं पुरुषसत्तम ।
भ्रातृभ्यस्तव तुभ्यं च पृथग्दाता शतं शतम् ॥ ५५ ॥

देवगन्धर्ववाहास्ते दिव्यवर्णा मनोजवाः ।
क्षीणाक्षीणा भवन्त्येते न हीयन्ते च रंहसः ॥ ५६ ॥

पुरा कृतं महेन्द्रस्य बज्रं बृत्रनिवर्हणम् ।
दशधा शतधा चैव तच्छीर्णं वृत्रमूर्द्धनि ॥ ५७ ॥

ततो भागीकृतो देवैर्वज्रभाग उपास्यते ।
लोके यशोधनं किञ्चित् सेव वज्रतनुः स्मृता ॥ ५८ ॥

वज्रपाणिर्ब्रह्मणः स्यात क्षत्रं वज्ररथं स्मृतम् ।
वैश्या वै दानवज्राश्च कर्मवज्रा यवीयसः ॥ ५९ ॥

क्षत्रवज्रस्य भागेन अवध्या वाजिनः स्मृताः ।
रथाङ्ग वडवा सूते शूराश्चाश्वेषु ये मताः ॥ ६० ॥

कामवर्णाः कामजवाः कामतः समुपस्थिताः ।
इति गन्धर्वजाः कामं पूरयिष्यन्ति मे हयाः ॥ ६१ ॥

O best among men, moreover, I give to you five brothers 500 horses that were born in the *gandharvaloka*. These horses are to be ridden only by gods or *gandharva*. They are very beautiful and fast and will never become old and never become tired. In order to kill the *asura* Vṛtra, the *vajra* of Indra was made but when it hit the head of Vṛtra it broke into hundred pieces. Then the gods collected all the pieces. All the things which are excellent in the world are fragments of the *vajra*. The *brāhmaṇa*s perform sacrifice, the warriors ride on chariots, the *vaiśya* trade and the *śūdra* labour. The chariot of the warrior will stay as long as the horses are not killed, because the horse is the main part of the chariot, not the flag or anything like that. My horses are well-built and they move according to your will; by this your tasks will be fulfilled. **[55- 61]**

अर्जुन उवाच -

यदि प्रीतेन ते दत्तं संशये जीवितस्य वा ।
विद्याधनं श्रुतं वापि न तद् गन्धर्व रोचये ॥ ६२ ॥

Arjuna said —

O *gandharva*, you are happy because of the gift of life, but I will not accept whatever you give. **[62]**

गन्धर्व उवाच -

संयोगो वै प्रीतिकरो महत्सु प्रीति दृश्यते ।
जीवितस्य प्रदानेन प्रीतो विद्यां ददामि ते ॥ ६३ ॥

त्वत्तोप्यहं ग्रहीष्यामि अस्त्रमाग्नेयमुत्तमम् ।
तथैव योग्यं वीभत्सो चिराय भरतर्षभ ॥ ६४ ॥

Gandharva said —

O Arjuna, if you by chance are in company of good people your love will grow. I am so happy that I got my life back that I want to give you my *vidyā*. And to mantain our long-lasting friendship, I will accept the *āgneyāstra*. **[63-64]**

अर्जुन उवाच -

त्वत्तोस्त्रेण बृणोम्यश्वान् संयोगः शश्वतोस्तु नौ ।
सखे तद् ब्रूहि गन्धर्व युष्मभ्यो यद् भयं भवेत् ॥ ६५ ॥

Arjuna said —

O friend, after giving the weapon I will take from you the horses; from this our friendship will increase. **[65]**

॥ *इति श्री का० मा० गन्धर्वार्जुनसम्वादो नाम दशमोऽध्यायः* ॥
Here ends the tenth chapter of the Kāmpilyamahātmya.

11

The Gandharva Counsels Arjuna to Take the Ṛṣi Dhaumya as the Purohita of the Pāṇḍavas

अर्जुन उवाच -

कारणं ब्रूहि गन्धर्व कि तद् येन स्म धर्षिताः ।
यान्तो वेदविदः सर्वे सन्तो रात्र्यामनिन्दिताः ॥ १ ॥

Arjuna said —

Why did you threaten virtuous people like us, who were walking on the path in the night? **[1]**

गन्धर्व उवाच -

अनग्नयोऽनाहुतयो न च विप्रपुरस्कृताः ।
यूयं ततो धर्षिताः स्थ मया वै पाण्डुनन्दनाः ॥ २ ॥

दिव्यात्मानो महात्मानः सर्वे शस्त्रभृतांवराः ।
भवन्तो भ्रातरः शूराः सर्वे सुचरितव्रताः ॥ ३ ॥

उत्तमां च मनोबुद्धिं भवतां भावितात्मनाम् ।
जानन्नपि च वः पार्थ कृतवानस्मि धर्षणाम् ॥ ४ ॥

स्त्रीसकाशे च कौरव्य न पुमान् क्षन्तुमर्हति ।
धर्षणामात्मनः पश्यन् बाहुद्रविणमाश्रितः ॥ ५ ॥

नक्तं च बलमस्माकं भूय एवाभिवर्द्धते ।
यतस्ततो मां कौन्तेय सदारं मन्युराविशत् ॥ ६ ॥

सोहं त्वयेह विजितः सङ्ख्ये तापत्यवर्द्धन ।
येन तेनेह विधिना कीर्त्यमानं निवोध मे ॥ ७ ॥

ब्रह्मचर्यं परोधर्मः स चापि नियतस्त्वयि ।
यस्मात् तस्मादहं पार्थ रणेऽस्मिन् विजितस्त्वया ॥ ८ ॥

यस्तु स्यात् क्षत्रियः कश्चित् कामवृत्तः परन्तप ।
नक्तं च युधि युद्ध्येत न स जीवेत् कदाचन ॥ ९ ॥

Gandharva said —

You are all without fire and also without *purohita*, priest, guide; for this reason I threatened you. You have divine form, and are great heroes, well armed, faithful to the vows. You have an excellent mind; even if I knew all this I threatened you. The reason for this is that the man who stays with women cannot tolerate those who disrespect him, and my strength in the night increases by being with a woman; so I became angry. And now listen to the reason why you have defeated me. In the world, being *brahmacarya* is the highest *dharma*, and you are always keeping *brahmacarya*: only because of this you could defeat me. The lustful warrior who fights with me in the night will never be able to win. **[2-9]**

यस्तु स्यात् कामवृत्तोपि पार्थ ब्रह्मपुरस्कृतः ।
जयेन्नक्तंचरान् सर्वान् स पुरोहितधूर्गतः ॥ १० ॥

तस्मात् तापत्य यत् किंचिन्नृणां श्रेय इहेप्सितम् ।
तस्मिन् कर्मणि योक्तव्या दान्तात्मानः पुरोहिताः ॥ ११ ॥

वदे षडङ्गे निरताः शुचयः सत्यवादिनः ।
धर्मात्मानः कृतात्मानः स्युर्नृपाणां पुरोहिताः ॥ १२ ॥

जयश्च नियतो राज्ञः स्वर्गश्च तदनन्तरम् ।
यस्य स्याद्धर्म विद्वाग्मी पुरोधाः शीलवान् शुचिः ॥ १३ ॥

लभ्यं लब्धमलब्धंवा लब्धं वा परिरक्षितुम् ।
पुरोहितं प्रकुर्वीत राजा गुणसमन्वितम् ॥ १४ ॥

पुरोहितमते तिष्ठेद्य इच्छेद् भूतिमात्मनः ।
प्राप्तं वसुमतीं सर्वां सर्वशः सागराम्बराम् ॥ १५ ॥

न हि केवलशौर्येण तापत्याभिजनेन च ।
जयेद् ब्राह्मणःकश्चिद्भूमिं भूमिपतिः क्वचित् ॥ १६ ॥

तस्मादेवं विजानीहि कुरूणां वंशवर्द्धन ।
ब्राह्मणप्रमुखं राज्यं शक्यं पालयितुं चिरम् ॥ १७ ॥

And the warrior, even if he is full of desire but in company of a *purohita,* can defeat me. So a king who aspires to success should keep a priest with him. The priest should be well versed in the scriptures, with moral principles, pure, truthful, and one who has subdued the senses. When the *purohita* is pious, wise and virtuous, the king becomes unconquerable and after death he will ascend to the sky. To obtain what he does not have and to protect what is already in his possession, the king should always keep an experienced *purohita.* The king who wants prosperity, who wants to conquer the land, he should follow the advice of his priest. O Tāpatya (Arjuna), without a *purohita* belonging to the Sūryavaṁśa, the solar dynasty started from Tapatī, a king cannot get anything by just being brave and noble. Therefore, a good priest is the cause of a stable kingdom. **[10-17]**

अर्जुन उवाच -

अस्माकमनुरूपो वै यः स्याद्गन्धर्व वेदवित् ।
पुरोहितस्तमाचक्ष्व सर्वं हि विदितं तव ॥ १८ ॥

Arjuna said —

O *gandharva*, please tell me the right priest for us, because there is nothing we can conceal from you. **[18]**

गन्धर्व उवाच -

यवीयान् देवलस्यैष वने भ्राता तपस्यति ।
धौम्य उत्कोचके तीर्थे तं वृणुध्वं यदीच्छथ ॥ १९ ॥

Gandharva said —

The younger brother of the *ṛṣi* Devala, Dhaumya by name,

is performing *tapas* in the *tīrtha* of Utkocaka, near here. You should take him as your *purohita*. **[19]**

वैशम्पायन उवाच -

ततोऽर्जुनोऽस्त्रमाग्नेयं प्रददौ तद्यथाविधि ।
गन्धर्वाय तदा प्रीतो वचनं चेदमब्रवीत् ॥ २० ॥

त्वय्येव तावत् तिष्ठन्तु हया गन्धर्वसत्तम ।
कार्यकाले ग्रहीष्यामः स्वस्ति तेऽस्त्विति चाब्रवीत् ॥ २१ ॥

तेऽन्योन्यमभिसंपूज्य गन्धर्वः पाण्डवाश्च ह ।
रम्याद्भागीरथीतीराद्यथाकामं प्रतस्थिरे ॥ २२ ॥

तत उत्कोचकं तीर्थं गत्वा धौम्याश्रमं तु ते ।
तं बव्रुः पाण्डवा धौम्यं पौरोहित्याय भारत ॥ २३ ॥

तान् धौम्यः प्रतिजग्राह सर्ववेदविदांवरः ।
वन्येन फलमूलेन पौरोहित्येन चैव हि ॥ २४ ॥

ते समाशंसिरे लब्धां श्रियं राज्यं च पाण्डवाः ।
ब्राह्मणं तं पुरस्कृत पांचाली च स्वयंवरे ॥ २५ ॥

पुरोहितेन तेनाथ गुरुणा सङ्गतस्तदा ।
नाथवन्तमिवात्मानं मेनिरे भरतर्षभाः ॥ २६ ॥

स हि वेदार्थतत्त्वज्ञस्तेषां गुरुरुदारधीः ।
तेन धर्मविदा पार्था याज धर्मविदःकृताः ॥ २७ ॥

वोरांस्तु स हि तान् मेने प्राप्तराज्या स्वधर्मतः ।
बुद्धिवीर्यबलोत्साहैर्युक्तान् देवानिव द्विजः ॥ २८ ॥

कृतस्वस्त्ययनास्ते न ततस्ते मनुजाधिपाः ।
मेनिरे सहिता गन्तुं पाञ्चाल्यास्तं स्वयम्वरम् ॥ २९ ॥

ते तु दृष्ट्वा पुरं तच्च स्कन्धावारं च पाण्डवाः ।
कुम्भकारस्य शालायां निवासं चक्रिरे तदा ॥ ३० ॥

तत्र भैक्षं समाजहुर्ब्राह्मणीं बृत्तिमा स्थिताः ।
तान् संप्राप्तस्तथा वीरान् जज्ञिरे न नराः क्वचित ॥ ३१ ॥

Vaiśampāyana said —

Then Arjuna, after giving the *āgneyāstra* to the *gandharva,* said: "Now you keep the horses, we will ask for them at the right time." Then the Pāṇḍava, after meeting the *gandharva*, left the banks of Gaṅgā. They went to the *āśrama* of the *ṛṣi* Dhaumya and spoke to him about becoming their priest. After welcoming them with fruits and root-vegetables, Dhaumya agreed to become their priest. By this the Pāṇḍava's hope of kingdom, wealth and of meeting Draupadī became stronger because now they had a protector, a *guru*. Also Dhaumya considered them as his disciples. And after seeing their heroism, intelligence and enthusiasm he knew that they would surely get their kingdom. Then the Pāṇḍavas, with the permission of Dhaumya, went to Draupadī's *svayaṁvara*. There they stopped at the house of a potter, at 'Bhargān', to look at the city of Kāmpilya and at the camps of the many kings. There they started to beg for *bhikṣā*, charity, in the form of *brāhmaṇa*, so that no one would recognise them. **[20-31]**

॥ इति श्री का० मा० धौम्यपुरोहितकरणं नामैकादशोऽध्यायः॥

Here ends the eleventh chapter of the Kāmpilyamahātmya.

12

The *Svayaṁvara* Tournament

वैशम्पायन उवाच -

ततोर्चिता राजगणा द्रुपदेन महात्मना ।
उपोपविष्ठा मञ्चेषु द्रष्टुकामाः स्वयंवरम ॥ १ ॥

ततः पौरजनाः सर्वे सागरोद्धूतनिस्वनाः ।
शिशुमारशिरः प्राप्य न्यविशंस्ते स्म भूमिपाः ॥ २ ॥

प्रागुत्तरेण नगराद्भूमिभागे समे शुभे ।
समाजवाटः शुशुभे भवनैर्वहुभिर्वृतः ॥ ३ ॥

प्राकारपतिखोपेतो द्वारतोरणमण्डितः ।
वितानेन विचित्रेण सर्वतः समलङ्कृतः ॥ ४ ॥

तूर्यौघशतसङ्कीर्णः पराघ्यार्गुरुधूपितः ।
चन्दनोदकसिक्तश्च माल्यदामोपशोभितः ॥ ५ ॥

कैलासशिखिरप्रख्यैर्नभस्तलविलेखिभि ।
सर्वतः सम्बृतः शुभ्रैः प्रासादैः सुकृतोच्छ्र्यैः ॥ ६ ॥

सुवर्णजालसम्वीतैर्मणिकुट्टिमभूषणैः ।
सुखारोहणसोपानैर्महासनपरिच्छदैः ॥ ७ ॥

स्त्रग्दामसमवच्छन्नैरगुरूत्तमधूपितैः ।
हंसांशुवर्णैबहुभिरायोजनसुगन्धिभिः ॥ ८ ॥

असंबाधशतद्वारैः शयनासनशोभितैः ।
बहुधातुपिनद्धाङ्गैर्हिमवच्छिखरैरिव ॥ ९ ॥

तत्र नानाप्रकारेषु विमानेषु स्वलङ्कृताः ।
स्पर्द्धमाना इवान्योन्यं निषेदुः सर्वपार्थिवाः ॥ १० ॥

तत्रोपविष्टान् ददृशुर्महासत्त्वपराक्रमान् ।
राजसिंहान् महाभागान् कृष्णागुरुविभूषितान् ॥ ११ ॥

महाप्रसादान् ब्रह्मण्यान् स्वराष्ट्रपरिरक्षिणः ।
प्रियान् सर्वस्य लोकस्य स्वकृतैः कर्मभिः शुभैः ॥ १२ ॥

मंचेषु च परार्घ्येषु पौरजानपदा जनाः ।
कृष्णादर्शनसिद्ध्यर्थं सर्वतः समुपाविशन् ॥ १३ ॥

ब्राह्मणैस्ते च सहिताःपाण्डवाः समुपाविशन् ।
ऋद्धिं पाञ्चालराजस्य पश्यन्तस्तामनुत्तमाम् ॥ १४ ॥

Vaiśampāyana said —

Then, after receiving the welcome by Drupada, all the kings sat on chairs to watch the *svayaṁvara* tournament. And the inhabitants of the city gathered at the north-eastern corner with screams of joy. The place where the tournament was held was outside the city in the north-east direction. It was enclosed all around and some buntings of green leaves were hung at every door. The place was adorned with canopies. Many instruments were playing and the air was perfumed with precious incenses. Sandalwood-water was sprinkled and garlands of flower were hung everywhere. There were golden hammocks embellished with jems, mounted on very high little balconies, *aṭā*. The balconies were accessible by steps. The *aṭā* were full of seats and flowers. They were shining like the sky and scented with excellent perfumes; there were huge doors, and many bedsteads, the walls, adorned with precious metals and painted with colours, appeared like a peak of the Himālayas. In the special place for the *vimāna*[9] of the kings, every king was sitting with the spirit of competition. They were like lions among kings. They had besmeared their body with black aloe. They were very gentle, devoted to the *brāhmaṇas*, protectors of their kingdom and loved by everyone. Then the great people of the Pañcāla

9. A car or a chariot self-moving and carrying its occupants through the air.

arrived, eager to see Draupadī. And also the Pāṇḍavas came to see the 'Lakṣmī' of the kingdom of Drupada, and sat with the other *brāhmaṇas*. **[1-14]**

ततः समाजी ववृधे स राजन् दिवसान् बहून् ।
रत्नप्रदानबहुलः शोभितो नटनर्तकैः ॥ १५ ॥

वर्द्धमाने समाजेतु रमणीयेऽन्हि षोडशे ।
आप्लुताङ्गी सुवसना सर्वाभरणभूषिता ॥ १६ ॥

मालां च समुपादाय काञ्चनीं समलङ्कृताम् ।
अवतीर्णा ततो रङ्गं द्रौपदी भरतर्षभ ॥ १७ ॥

पुरोहितः सोमकानां मन्त्रविद् ब्राह्मणः शुचिः ।
परिस्तीर्य जुहावाग्निमाज्येन विधिवत् तदा ॥ १८ ॥

स तर्पयित्वा ज्वलनं ब्राह्मणान् स्वस्ति वाच्य च ।
वारयामास सर्वाणि वादित्राणि समन्ततः ॥ १९ ॥

निःशब्दे तु कृते तस्मिन् धृष्टद्युम्नो विशाम्पते ।
कृष्णामादाय विधिवन्मेघदुन्दुभिनिःस्वनः ॥ २० ॥

रङ्गमध्ये ततस्तत्र मेघगम्भीरया गिरा ।
वाक्यमुच्चैर्जगादेदं श्लक्ष्णमर्थवदुत्तमम् ॥ २१ ॥

O King, that reunion lasted many days, with many gifts and dances. Then on the sixteenth day after taking ablution, wearing beautiful clothes and a golden collar, Draupadī arrived. The royal priest made the appropriate offerings, and made the *brāhmaṇas* recite the favourable *mantras*. All the instruments were hushed. Then when all the assembly were silent Dhṛṣṭadyumna entered with Draupadī, and spoke aloud: **[15-21**]

इदं धनुर्लक्ष्यमिमे च वाणाः शृण्वन्तु मे भूपतयः समेताः ।
छिद्रेण यन्त्रस्य समर्पयध्वं शरैः शितैर्व्योमचरैर्दशार्द्धैः ॥ २२ ॥

एतन्महत् कर्म करोति यो वै कुलेन रूपेण वलेन युक्तः ।
तस्याद्य भार्या भगिनी ममेय कृष्णा भवित्री न मृषा ब्रवीमि ॥ २३ ॥

तानेवमुक्त्वा द्रुपदस्य पुत्रः पश्चादिदं तां भगिनीमुवाच ।
नाम्ना च गोत्रेण च कर्मणा च संकीर्तयन् भूमिपतीन् समेतान् ॥ २४ ॥

"O kings, — pointing with his finger — this is the bow, that is the target and these are the five arrows. That noble person who, standing in the centre of this whirling machine, will pierce with these five arrows the target, will have Draupadī as his wife." After saying this to the kings he started to tell Draupadī the names, the qualities and the feats of every suitor. **[22-24]**

॥ इतिश्री का० मा० धृष्टद्युम्न वाक्यंनाम द्वादशोऽध्यायः ॥

Here ends the twelfth chapter of the Kāmpilyamahātmya.

13

Kings Who Attended the *Svayaṁvara*

धृष्टद्युम्न उवाच -

दुर्योधनो दुर्विषहो दुर्मुखो दुःप्रधर्षणः ।
विविंशतिर्विकर्णश्च सहो दुःशासनस्तथा ॥ १ ॥

युयुत्सुर्वायुवेगश्च सुवर्चाः कनकध्वजः ।
उग्रायुधो वलाकी च करकायुर्विरोचनः ॥ २ ॥

कुण्डकश्चित्रसेनश्च सुवर्चाः कनकध्वजः ।
नन्दकी वाहुशाली च तुहुण्डो विकटस्तथा ॥ ३ ॥

एते चान्ये च बहवो धार्तराष्ट्रा महाबलाः ।
कर्णेन सहिता वीरास्त्वदर्थं समुपागताः ॥ ४ ॥

असङ्ख्याता महात्मानः पार्थिवाः क्षत्रियर्षभाः ।
शकुनिः सौवलश्चैव वृषकोथ वृहद्बलः ॥ ५ ॥

एते गान्धारराजस्य सुताः सर्वे समागताः ।
अश्वत्थामा च भोजश्च सर्वशस्त्रभृतांवरौ ॥ ६ ॥

समवेतौ महात्मानौ त्वदर्थेसमलङ्कृतौ ।
वृहन्तो मणिमांश्चैव दण्डधारश्च पार्थिवः ॥ ७ ॥

सहदेवजयत्सेनौ मेघसन्धिश्च पार्थिवः ।
विराटः सह पुत्राभ्यां शङ्खेनैवोत्तरेण च ॥ ८ ॥

बार्द्धक्षेमिः सुशर्मा च सेनाविन्दुश्च पार्थिवः ।
सुकेतुः सह पुत्रेण सुनाम्ना च सुवर्चसा ॥ ९ ॥

सुचित्रः सुकुमारश्च वृकः सत्यधृतिस्तथा ।
सूर्यध्वजो रोचमानो नीलश्चित्रायुधस्तथा ॥ १० ॥

अंशुमांश्चेकितानश्च श्रेणिमांश्च महाबलः ।
समुद्रसेनपुत्रश्च चन्द्रसेनः प्रतापवान् ॥ ११ ॥

जलसन्धः पिता पुत्रौ विदण्डो दण्ड एव च ।
पौण्ड्रको वासुदेवश्च भगदत्तश्स्च वीर्यवान् ॥ १२ ॥

कालिङ्गस्ताम्रलिप्तश्च पत्तनाधिपतिस्तथा ।
मद्रराजस्तथा शल्यः सहपुत्रो महारथः ॥ १३ ॥

रुक्नाङ्गदेन वीरेण तथा रुक्नरथेन च ।
कौरवाः सोमदत्तश्च पुत्राश्चास्य महारथाः ॥ १४ ॥

समवेतास्त्रयः शूरा भूरिर्भूरिश्रवाः शलः ।
सुदक्षिणश्च काम्बोजो दृढधन्वा च पौरवः ॥ १५ ॥

वृहद्बलः सुषेणश्च शिविरौशीनरस्तथां ।
पटच्चरनिहन्ता च करूषाधिपतिस्तथा ॥ १६ ॥

सङ्कर्षणो वासुदेवो रौक्मिणेयश्च वीर्यवान् ।
साम्बश्च चारुदेष्णश्च प्राद्युम्निः सगदस्तथा ॥ १७ ॥

अक्रूरः सात्यकिश्चैव उद्धवश्च महामतिः ।
कृतवर्मा च हार्दिक्यः पृथुर्विपृथुरेव च ॥ १८ ॥

विदूरथश्च कङ्कश्च शङ्कुश्च सगवेषणः ।
आशावहोऽनिरुद्धश्च समीकः सारिमेजयः ॥ १९ ॥

वीरो वातपतिश्चैव झिल्ली पिण्डारकस्तथा ।
उशीनरश्च विक्रान्तो वृष्णयस्ते प्रकीर्तिताः ॥ २० ॥

भगीरथो वृहत्क्षत्रः सैन्धवश्च जयद्रथः ।
वृहद्रथो वाल्हिकश्च श्रुतायुश्च महारथः ॥ २१ ॥

उलूकः कैतवो राजा चित्राङ्गदशुभाङ्गदौ ।
वत्सराजश्च मतिमान् कोशलाधिपतिस्तथा ।
शिशुपालश्च विक्रान्तो जरासन्धस्तथैव च ॥ २२ ॥

एते चान्ये च वहवो नानाजनपदेश्वराः ।
त्वदर्थमागता भद्रे क्षत्रियाः प्रथिता भुवि ॥ २३ ॥

एते भेत्स्यन्ति विक्रान्तास्त्वदर्थं लक्ष्यमुत्तमम् ।
विध्येत य इदं लक्ष्यं वरयेथाः शुभेऽद्य तम् ॥ २४ ॥

Dhṛṣṭadyumna said —

O noble lady, together with Karṇa are Dhṛtarāṣṭra's sons, Duryodhana, Durmukha, Duḥpragharṣaṇa, Vikarṇa, Saha, Duḥśāsana, Yuyutsu, Vāyuvega, Bhīmavega, Bhīmarava, Ugrāyudha, Valāki, Karavāyu, Virocana, Kuṇḍaka, Citrasena, Suvarcā, Kanakadhvaja, Nandaka, Vāhuśālī, Tuhuṇḍa, and Vikaṭa. They all have come with the purpose of marrying you.

The sons of King Suvala of Kandhāra: Śakuni, Vṛṣaka, Bṛhadvala. Aśvatthāmā, Bhoja, Bṛhanta, Maṇimān. The sons of Jarāsaṅgha. Daṇḍadhara, Sahadeva, Jayatsena, Meghasandhi. Virāṭa and his sons: Śaṅkha, Uttara, Vṛddhakṣema. The sons of Yādava: Suśarmā, King Senabindu, Suketu, and his sons, Sunāma and Suvarcā.

Sucitra, Sukumāra, Vṛka, Satyadhṛti (Yādava), Sūryadhvaja, Rocamān (Candelā), Nīla (the king of Maisūra, Mysore), Citrayudha (the king of Sinhapura). Anśumān, Cekitān (Yādava), Śreṇimān (from Kāśī), the son of Samudrasena (from Baṅga) Candrasena. Jalasaṅgha and his sons Daṇḍa and Vidaṇḍa; Vāsudeva Pauṇḍraka (Puṇḍīrā), the King of Assam Bhagadatta. Tāmralipta (from Kaliṅga), the king of Paṭṭan, the King Śalya from Madrās. His sons Rukmāṅgada and Rukmaratha. Somadatta (Kaurava). His sons Bhūri, Bhūriśravā, Śala, Sudakṣiṇa (Kamboha), Dṛḍhadhanvā (Paurava). The king of Ayodhyā Bṛhadbala, Suṣeṇa (Karṇa's son), Śivi from Uśīnara, the King of Karūṣa Dantavaktra. The Yādavas were: Baladevajī, Śrī Kṛṣṇa, Pradyumna, Sāṁva, Cārudeṣṇa (Pradyumna's brother), Aniruddha, Gada (brother of Baladevajī), Akrūra, Sātyaki, Uddhava, Kṛtavarmā, Pṛthu, Vipṛthu (Akrūra's first cousin); Vidūratha, Kaṅka (Vasudeva's brother), Gaveṣaṇa, Āśāvaha (Vasudeva's son), Aniruddha (another), Śamīka (Vasudeva's brother), Arimejaya (Akrūra's brother), Vīra (Vasudeva's nephew), Vātapati (Satyabhāmā's brother), Jhillī, Piṇḍāraka Uśīnara (Baladeva's brother).

Bhagīratha, Bṛhatkṣatra (King of the Niṣāda), Jayadratha (husband of the sister of King Duryodhana of Sindh), Bṛhadratha, Śrutāyu. Ulūka (Śakuni's son), Citrāṅgada, Subhāṅgada, Vatsarāja, Kośalarāja, Śiśupāla (Candelā), Jarāsaṅgha. These and other kings, like Janaka, the Yavanarāja, etc., have come here for you. You will accept as your husband the one who will be able to pierce the target. **[1-24]**

॥ इतिश्री का० मा० राजनामकीर्तनं नाम त्रयोदशोऽध्यायः ॥

Here ends the thirteenth chapter of the Kāmpilyamahātmya.

14

Draupadī's Refusal for Karṇa

वैशम्पायन उवाच -

तेऽलङ्कृताः कुण्डलिनोयुवानः परस्पर स्पर्द्धमाना नरेन्द्राः ।
अस्त्रं वलं चात्मनि मन्यमानाः सर्वे समुत्पेतुरुदायुधास्ते ॥ १ ॥

रूपेण वीर्येण कुलेन चैव शीलेन वित्तेन च यौवनेन ॥
समिद्धदर्पा मदवेगभिन्ना मत्ता यथा हैमवता गजेन्द्राः ॥ २ ॥

परस्परं स्पर्द्धया प्रेक्षमाणाः सङ्कल्पजेनाभिपरिप्लुताङ्गाः ।
कृष्णा ममैवेत्यभिभाषमाणा नृपासनेभ्यः सहसोदतिष्ठन् ॥ ३ ॥

ते क्षत्रिया रङ्गगताः समेता जिगीषमाणा द्रुपदात्मजां ताम् ।
चकासिरे पर्वतराजकन्यामुमा यथा देवगणाः समेताः ॥ ४ ॥

कन्दर्पदर्पाभिनिपीडिताङ्गा कृष्णागतैस्ते हृदयैर्नरेन्द्राः ।
रङ्गावतीर्णा द्रुपदात्मजार्थं द्वेषं प्रचक्रुः सुहृदोपि तत्र ॥ ५ ॥

अथाऽऽययुर्देवगणा विमानैरुद्रादित्या वसवोऽथाश्विनौ च ।
साध्याश्च सर्वे मरुतस्तथैव यमं पुरस्कृत्य धनेश्वरं च ॥ ६ ॥

दैत्याः सुपर्णाश्च महोरगाश्च देवर्षयो गुह्यकाश्चारणाश्च ।
विश्वावसुर्नारदपर्वतौ च गन्धर्वमुख्याश्च सहाप्सरोभिः ॥ ७ ॥

Vaiśampāyana said —

O King, all the kings present on that occasion were giving each other looks of envy, and hoping it was their turn they all sprang to their feet. They were complete with every quality: beauty, strength, moral conduct, good lineage, wealth, intoxicated with youth, strong like lions from the

Himālaya, pervaded by the spirit of Eros. Everyone was thinking: "I will marry Draupadī." The scene was so magnificent it was reminiscent of the marriage of Pārvatī: the kings like the gods and Draupadī like Pārvatī; the five Pāṇḍavas like the five forms of Śiva. Distressed by the desire for Draupadī even those who were friends in the beginning became hostile to each other.

Then also the gods arrived there with their flying chariots: there was Yamarāja and Kubera, the eleven Rudras, the twelve Ādityas, the eight Vasus, the two Aśvinikumāra, the sixtyfour Sādhyas and the fortynine Pavanas. Also *daitya*, Garuḍa, *nāga*, *devarṣi*, *guhyaka*, *cāraṇa*, *apsarā*, Viśvavasu, Nārada, Parvata and other *gandharava* arrived. **[1-7]**

हलायुधस्तत्र जनार्दनश्च वृष्ण्यन्धकाश्चैव यथाप्रधानम् ।
प्रेक्षांस्मचक्रुर्यदुपुङ्गवास्ते स्थिताश्च कृष्णस्य मते महान्तः ॥ ८ ॥

द्रृष्ट्वा तु तान् मत्तगजेन्द्ररूपान् पञ्चाभिपद्मानिव वारणेन्द्रान् ।
भस्मावृताङ्गानिव हव्यवाहान् कृष्णः प्रदध्यौ यदुवीरमुख्यः ॥ ९ ॥

शशंस रामाय युधिष्ठिरं स भीम सजिष्णुं च यमौ च वीरौ ।
शनैः शनैस्तान् प्रसमीक्ष्य रामो जनार्दनं प्रीतमना ददर्श ह ॥ १० ॥

अन्ये तु वीरा नृपपुत्रपौत्राः कृष्णागतैर्नैत्रमनःस्वभावैः ।
व्यावच्छमाना दद्रशुर्न तान् वै संदष्टदन्तच्छदताम्रनेत्राः ॥ ११ ॥

तथैव पार्थाः पृथुवाहवस्ते वीरौ यमौ चैव महानुभावौ ।
तां द्रौपदीं वीक्ष्य तदा स्म सर्वे कन्दर्पवाणाभिहता बभूवुः ॥ १२ ॥

देवर्षिगन्धर्व समाकुलं तत् सुपर्णनागासुरद्धिजुष्टम् ।
दिव्येन गन्धेन समाकुलं च दिव्यैश्च पुष्पैरवकीर्यमाणम् ॥ १३ ॥

महास्वनैर्दुन्दुभिनादितैश्च वभूव तत् सङ्कुलमन्तरिक्षम् ।
विमानसम्वाधमभूत् समन्तात् सवेणुवीणापणवानुनादम् ॥ १४ ॥

Under the view of Śrī Kṛṣṇa, no one of the Yādavas could hit the target. Śrī Kṛṣṇa recognised the Pāṇḍavas in their disguise of *brāhmaṇa*s, like a fire covered with ashes. He told this to Baladeva, and Baladeva looking at them and started to become happy and looked back at Śrī Kṛṣṇa. All the kings were looking at Draupadī so that they did not recognise the Pāṇḍavas. Overcome with desire they also started to stare at Draupadī. There the sky was full with *vimāna* and a rain of perfumed flowers was falling and the *deva* were playing drums and other instruments. **[8-14]**

ततस्तु तेराजगणाः क्रमेण कृष्णानिमित्तं कृतविक्रमाश्च ।
सकर्णदुर्योधनशल्यशाल्वद्रौणायनिक्राथसुनीथवक्त्राः ॥ १५ ॥

कलिङ्गवङ्गाधिपपाण्ड्यपौण्ड्रा विदेहराजो यवनाधिपश्च ।
अन्ये च नाना नृपपुत्रपौत्रा राष्ट्राधिपाः पङ्कजपत्रनेत्राः ॥ १६ ॥

किरीटहाराङ्गदचक्रवालैर्विभूषिताङ्गाः पृथुवाहवस्ते ।
अनुक्रमं विक्रमसत्त्वयुक्ता बलेन वीर्येण च नर्दमानाः ॥ १७ ॥

तत् कार्मुकं संहननीपपन्नं सज्यं न शेकुर्मनसापि कर्तुम् ।
ते विक्रमन्तः स्फुरता दृढेन विक्षिप्यमाणा धनुषा नरेन्द्राः ॥ १८ ॥

विचेष्टमाना धरणीतलस्था यथावलं शैक्ष्यगुणक्रमाश्च ।
गतौजसः स्रस्तकिरीटहारा विनिः श्वसन्तः शमयांवभूवुः ॥ १९ ॥

हाहाकृतं तद्धनुषा दृढेन विस्रस्तहाराङ्गदचक्रवालम् ।
कृष्णानिमित्तं विनिवृत्तकामं राज्ञां तदा मण्डलमार्तमासीत् ॥ २० ॥

सर्वान् नृपांस्तान् प्रसमीक्ष्य कर्णो धनुर्द्धराणां प्रवरो जगाम ।
उद्धृत्य तूर्णं धनुरुद्यतं तत् सज्यं चकाराशु युयोज वाणान् ॥ २१ ॥

दृष्ट्वा सूतं मेनिरे पाण्डुपुत्रा भित्त्वा नीतं लक्ष्यवरं धरायाम् ।
धनुर्द्धरारागकृतप्रतिज्ञमत्यग्निसोमार्कमथार्कपुत्रम् ॥ २२ ॥

दृष्ट्वा तु तं द्रौपदी वाक्यमुच्चैर्जगाद नाहं वरयामि सूतम् ।
सामर्षहासं प्रसमीक्ष्य सूर्यं तत्याज कर्णः स्फुरितं धनुस्तत् ॥ २३ ॥

Then Duryodhana, Śālva, Śalya, Aśvatthāmā, Krātha, Śiśupāla, Dantavaktra, and the kings of Kaliṅga, Vaṅga, Pāṇḍya, Pauṇḍra, Videha; the king of Yavana and several other princes, adorned with crowns, earrings and other accessories, full of pride, went to take up the bow, but they were unable to bend it. After letting it fall down with a fluttering sound, they started to pant. Among the royal spectators there were sounds of hilarity. Then seeing all the frustrated kings, Karṇa took up the bow and nocked an arrow to the bowstring. When the Pāṇḍavas saw that, they thought that he was going to hit the target, because the power of Karṇa was greater than the fire, the moon and the sun. But seeing him Draupadī in a crying voice said: "I will never marry the charioteer's son." Then Karṇa, angry and derided, looked to the sun and dashed the bow down. **[15-23]**

एवं तेषु निवृत्तेषु क्षत्रियेषु परंतप ।
चेदीनामधिपो वीरो वलवानन्तकोपमः ॥ २४ ॥

दमघोषसुतो धीरः शिशुपालो महामतिः ।
धनुरादायमानस्तु जानुभ्यामगमन्महीम् ॥ २५ ॥

ततो राजा महावीर्यो जरासन्धो महाबलः ।
धनुषोभ्याशमागत्य तस्थौ गिरिरिवाचलः ॥ २६ ॥

धनुषा पीड्यमानस्तु जानुभ्यामगमन्महीम् ।
तत उत्थाय राजा स स्वराष्ट्रमभिजग्मिवान् ॥ २७ ॥

ततः शल्यो महावीरो मद्रराजो महाबलः ।
धनुरारोप्यमाणस्तु जानुभ्यामगमन्महीम् ॥ २८ ॥

King Śiśupāla Candelā also went to hold the bow but he also let it fall to the ground choking down his frustration. Jarāsaṅgha also tried but fell; after getting up, he went home. Also Śalya went but fell in the same way. **[24-28]**

॥ इति श्री का० मा० राजपरामुङ्खीभवन नाम चतुर्दशोऽध्यायः॥

Here ends the fourteenth chapter of the Kāmpilyamahātmya.

15

Arjuna Pierces the Target

वैशम्पायन उवाच -

यदा निवृत्ता राजानो धनुषः सज्यकारणात्।
अथोदतिष्ठद्विप्राणां मध्याज्जिष्णुरुदारधीः ॥ १ ॥

उदक्रोशंस्तदा विप्रा विधुन्वन्तोऽजिनानि च।
दृष्ट्वा संप्रस्थितं पार्थमिन्द्रकेतुसमप्रभम् ॥ २ ॥

केचिदासन् विमनसः केचिदासन् मुदान्विताः।
आहुःपरस्परं केचिन्निपुणा बुद्धिजीविनः ॥ ३ ॥

यत् कर्णशल्यप्रमुखैः क्षत्रियैर्लोकविश्रुतैः।
नानतं बलवद्भिर्हि धनुर्वेदपरायणैः ॥ ४ ॥

तत् कथं त्वकृतास्त्रेण प्राणतो दुवलायसा।
वटुमात्रेण शक्यं हि सज्यं कर्तुं धनुर्द्विजाः ॥ ५ ॥

अवहास्या भविष्यन्ति ब्रह्मणाः सर्वराजसु।
कर्मण्यस्मिन्नसंसिद्धे चापल्यादपरीक्षिते ॥ ६ ॥

यद्येष दर्पाद्धर्षाद्वाप्यथ ब्राह्मणचापलात्।
प्रस्थिती धनुरायन्तुं वार्यतां साधु मागमत् ॥ ७ ॥

केचिदाहुर्युवा श्रीमान् नागराजकरोपमः।
पीनस्कन्धो महावाहुर्धैर्येण हिमवानिव ॥ ८ ॥

सिंहखेलगतिः श्रीमान् मत्तनागेन्द्रविक्रमः।
संभाव्यमस्मिन् कर्मेदमुत्साहेनानुमीयते ॥ ९ ॥

शक्तिरस्य महोत्साहा नह्यशक्तः स्वयं व्रजेत्।
न च तद्विद्यते किंचित् कर्म लोकेषु यद् भवेत् ॥ १० ॥

ब्राह्मणानामसाध्यं हि नृषु संस्थानचारिषु ।
नावहास्या भविष्यामो न च लाघवमाश्रिताः ॥ ११ ॥

न च विद्विष्टतां लोके गमिष्यामो महीक्षिताम् ।
अब्भक्षा वायुभक्षाश्च फलाहारा दृढव्रताः ॥ १२ ॥

दुर्बला अपि विप्रा हि वलीयांसः स्वतेजसा ।
ब्राह्मणो नावमन्तव्यः सदसद्वा समाचरन् ॥ १३ ॥

सुखं दुःखं महद्ध्रस्वं कर्म यत् समुपागतम् ।
जामदग्न्येन रामेण क्षत्रिया निहता युधि ॥ १४ ॥

पीतः समुद्रोऽगस्त्येन अगाधी ब्रह्मतेजसा ।
तस्माद्ब्रुवन्तु सर्वेऽत्र वटुरेष धनुर्महान् ॥ १५ ॥

आरोपयतु शीघ्रं वै तथेत्यूचुर्द्विजर्षभाः ।
एवं तेषां विलपतां विप्राणां विविधा गिरः ॥ १६ ॥

अर्जुनो धनुषोऽभ्याशे तस्थौ गिरिरिवाचलः ।
स तद्धनुः परिक्रम्य प्रदक्षिणमथाकरोत् ॥ १७ ॥

प्रणम्य शिरसा देवमीशानं वरदं प्रभुम् ।
कृष्णं च मनसा ध्यात्वा जगृहेऽथार्जुनो धनुः ॥ १८ ॥

Vaiśampāyana said —

O King, when all the kings tried without success to bend the bow, from the assembly of the *brāhmaṇa* Arjuna rose up. The other *brāhmaṇa* started to roar and shake their deer-skins when they saw him going near the bow. Among them some were disappointed but others were enthusiastic. The two factions started to quarrel. One said — "the bow was not moved by Karṇa and other valiant kings, how could a weak son of *brāhmaṇa* bend it? If he is not able to accomplish it, the *kṣatriya* will laugh at us. This boy is confused by his pride and restlessness. Stop him!" Others were saying: "No, he is young and his shoulders are square and broad; he moves like the king of elephants; his arms are long. He has the endurance of the Himālayas. He walks with the gait of the lion or of the passionate elephant. By his enthusiasm it is seen that he will succeed. If he was not competent, he would not go there. In the world there is nothing impossible for a *brāhmaṇa*. There will be no derision, nor littleness; neither will the *kṣatriya* laugh at us. Also a *brāhmaṇa* who takes only fruit, water and air can be very strong. One should not insult whatever someone has chosen to do. Paraśurāma defeated all the *kṣatriya*, Agastya drank all the ocean: that could be possible only by the *brahmatejas*." Thus all the *brāhmaṇa* consented to let the young man try to bend the bow. Hearing all these voices of the *brāhmaṇa*, Arjuna had reached the central place and was standing still beside the bow. After making the *parikramā* (the ritual circuambulation) of the bow and bowing his head to the boon-giver Śiva, he concentrated on Śrī Kṛṣṇa and lifted up the bow. **[1-18]**

यत् पार्थिवे रूक्मसुनीथवक्त्रै राधेयदुर्योधनशल्यशाल्वेः ।
तदा धनुर्वेदपरैर्नृसिंहैः कृतं न सज्यं महतोपि यत्नात् ॥ १९ ॥

तदर्जुनो वीर्यवतां सदर्पस्तदैन्द्रिरिन्द्रावरजप्रभावः ।
सज्यं च चक्रे निमिषान्तरेण शरांश्च जग्राह दशार्द्धसङ्ख्यान् ॥ २० ॥

विव्याघ लक्ष्यं निपपात तच्च छिद्रेण भूमौ सहसातिविद्धम् ।
ततोन्तरिक्षे च वभूव नादः समाजमध्ये च महान निनादः ॥ २१ ॥

The same bow that could not be lifted even with great efforts by Rukma, Śiśupāla, Dantavaktra, Karṇa, Duryodhana, Śalya, was lifted in one second by Arjuna. He nocked the arrow to the string and lo he pierced the target which fell to the ground. From the sky and from the whole audience a strong shout of joy arose. Indra showered flowers on Arjuna. **[19-21]**

पुष्पाणि दिव्यानि ववर्ष देवः पार्थस्य मूर्ध्नि द्विषतां निहन्तुः ।
चैलानि विव्यधुस्तत्र ब्राह्मणाश्च सहस्त्रशः ॥ २२ ॥

विलक्षितास्ततश्चक्रुर्हाहाकारांश्च सर्वशः ।
न्यपतंस्तत्र नभसः समन्तात् पुष्पवृष्टयः ॥ २३ ॥

शताङ्गानि च तूर्याणि वादकाः समवादयन् ।
सूतमागधसङ्घाश्चाप्यस्तुवंस्तत्र सुस्वराः ॥ २४ ॥

तं द्रष्ट्वा द्रुपदः प्रीतो वभूव रिपुसूदनः ।
सह सैन्येन पार्थस्य साहाय्यार्थमियेष सः ॥ २५ ॥

The jubilant *brāhmaṇa*s were celebrating, by throwing their clothes into the air. Those people who could not hit the target were grieving with loud lamentations. A rain of flowers fell from the sky on the whole assembly. Many instruments started to play and poets and bards sang eulogies. King Drupada with his army went toward Arjuna. **[22-25]**

तस्मिंस्तु शब्दे महति प्रवृद्धे युधिष्ठिरो धर्मभृतां वरिष्ठः ।
आवासमेवोप जगाम शीघ्रं सार्द्धं यमाभ्यां पुरुषोत्तमाभ्याम् ॥ २६ ॥
विद्धं तु लक्ष्यं प्रसमीक्ष्य कृष्णा पार्थं च शक्रप्रतिमं निरीक्ष्य ।
आदाय शुक्लाम्बरमाल्यदाम जगाम कुन्तीसुतमुत्स्मयन्ती ॥ २७ ॥
स तां समादाय विजित्य रङ्गे द्विजातिभिस्तैरभिपूज्यमानः ।
रङ्गान्निराक्रामदचिन्त्यकर्मा पत्न्या तया चाप्यनुगम्यमानः ॥ २८ ॥

At that deafening noise Dharmarāja, Nakula and Sahadeva went to their dwelling. And Draupadī, having seen the *lakṣyavedha*, smiling went to offer the *jayamālā* to Arjuna. Arjuna with Draupadī and all the *brāhmaṇa* left the arena. **[26-28]**

॥ इति श्री का० मा० लक्ष्यबेधोनामपञ्चदशोध्यायः ॥

Here ends the fifteenth chapter of the Kāmpilyamahātmya.

16

The Kings Unacceptance of the *Brāhmaṇa*'s Victory

वैशम्पायन उवाच -

तस्मै दित्सति कन्यां तु ब्राह्मणाय तदा नृपे ।
कोप आसीन्महीपानामालोक्यान्योन्य मन्तिकात् ॥ १ ॥

Vaiśampāyana said —

O King, seeing King Drupada give his daughter to that *brāhmaṇa*, the kings became angry. **[1]**

राजानऊचुः -

अस्मानयमतिक्रम्य तृणीकृत्य च सङ्गतान् ।
दातुमिच्छति विप्राय द्रौपदीं योषितां वराम् ॥ २ ॥

अवरोप्येह वृक्षं तु फलकाले निपात्यते ।
निहन्मैनं दुरात्मानं योयमस्मान् न मन्यते ॥ ३ ॥

नह्यर्हत्येष संमानं नामि बृद्धक्रमं गुणैः ।
हन्मैनं सह पुत्रेण दुराचारं नृपद्विषम् ॥ ४ ॥

अयं हि सर्वानाहूय सत्कृत्य च नराधिपान् ।
गुणवद्भोजयित्वान्नं ततः पश्चान्न मन्यंते ॥ ५ ॥

अस्मिन् राजसमावाये देवानामिव संनये ।
किमयं सदृशं कश्चिन्नृपतिं नैव दृष्टवान् ॥ ६ ॥

न च विप्रेष्वधीकारो विद्यते वरणं प्रति ।
स्वयम्वरः क्षत्रियाणामितीयं शाश्वतो श्रुतिः ॥ ७ ॥

अथवा यदि कन्येयं न च कञ्चिद्वुभूषति ।
अग्नावेनां परिक्षिप्य याम राष्ट्राणि पार्थिवाः ॥ ८ ॥

ब्राह्मणो यदि चापल्याल्लोभाद्वा कृतवानिदम् ।
विप्रियं पार्थिवेन्द्राणां नैष वध्यः कदाचन ॥ ९ ॥

ब्राह्मणार्थं च नो राज्यं जीवितं हि वसूनि च ।
पुत्रपौत्रं च यच्चान्यदस्माकं विद्यते धनम् ॥ १० ॥

अवमानभयाच्चैव स्वधर्मस्य च रक्षणात् ।
स्वयम्वराणामन्येषां माभूदेवम्विधा गतिः ॥ ११ ॥

Those kings were speaking among themselves: "King Drupada is indifferent to us, he wants to give his daughter to that *brāhmaṇa*. He is cutting the full-grown tree to get the fruit: he is not worthy of our respect. We should ignore his old age, we should kill him and his son. Firstly he invited us and made us welcome and offered us food, but then he offends us. He did not like any of us so he gave his daughter to that *brāhmaṇa*. *Svayaṁvara*[10] is the right of the *kṣatriya* and not of the *brāhmaṇa*. And if this girl will not marry any of the kings, she should be thrown in the fire. But even if the *brāhmaṇa* has offended us with his behaviour, he will not be killed. Because our kingdom, lives and wealth rely on the *brāhmaṇa*. We have to do something so that this situation will not happen again in other *svayaṁvara*." **[2-11]**

वैशम्पायन उवाच -

इत्युक्त्वा राजशार्दूला हृष्टाः परिघवाहवः ।
द्रुपदं तु जिघांसन्तः सायुधाः समुपाद्रवन् ॥ १२ ॥

तान गृहीतशरावापान् क्रुद्धानापततो बहून् ।
द्रुपदो वीक्ष्य सन्त्रासाद् ब्राह्मणन् शरणंगतः ॥ १३ ॥

वेगेनापततस्तांस्तु प्रभिन्नानिव वारणान् ।
पाण्डुपुत्रौ महेष्वासौ प्रतियातावरिंदमौ ॥ १४ ॥

---

10. Self-choosing; the election of a husband by a princess or daughter of a *kṣatriya*.

Vaiśampāyana said —

Saying that, the kings with their weapons in hand ran against Drupada to kill him. Drupada saw them and ran away among the *brāhmaṇa*. Arjuna and Bhīmasena went in front of those kings. **[12-14]**

ततः समुत्पेतुरुदायुधास्ते महीक्षितो बद्धगोधाङ्गुलित्राः ।
जिघांसमानाः कुरुराजपुत्रावमर्षयन्तोर्जुनभीमसेनौ ॥ १५ ॥

ततस्तु भीमोद्भुतभीमकर्मा महाबलोवज्रसमानसारः ।
उत्पाठ्य दोर्भ्यां द्रुममेकवीरो निष्पत्रयामास यथा गजेन्द्रः ॥ १६ ॥

तं वृक्षमादाय रिपुप्रमाथी दण्डीव दण्डं पितृराज उग्रम् ।
तस्थौ समीपे पुरुषर्षभस्य पार्थस्य पार्थः पृथुदीर्घबाहुः ॥ १७ ॥

तत् प्रेक्ष्य कर्मातिमनुष्यबुद्धिर्जिष्णुः स हि भ्रातुरचिन्त्यकर्मा ।
विसिस्मिये चापि भयं विहाय तस्थौ धनुर्गृह्य महेन्द्रकर्मा ॥ १८ ॥

तत् प्रेक्ष्य कर्मातिमनुष्यबुद्धिर्जिष्णोः सहभ्रातुरचिन्त्यकर्मा ।
दामोदरो भ्रातरमुग्रवीर्यं हलायुधं वाक्यमिदं वभाषे ॥ १९ ॥

य एष सिंहर्षभखेलगामी महद्धनुः कर्षति तालमात्रम् ।
एषोर्जुनो नात्र विचार्यमस्ति यद्यस्मि सङ्कर्षण वासुदेवः ॥ २० ॥

यस्त्वेष वृक्षं सहसावभज्य राज्ञां निकारे सहसा प्रवृत्तः ।
वृकोदरान्नान्य इहैतदद्य कर्त्तुं समर्थः समरे पृथिव्याम् ॥ २१ ॥

योसौ पुरस्तात् कमलायताक्षस्तनुर्महासिंहगतिर्विनीतः ।
गौरः प्रलम्बोज्ज्वलचारुघोणो विनिःसृतः सोच्युत धर्मराजः ॥ २२ ॥

यौ तौ कुमाराविव कार्तिकेयौ द्वावाश्विनेयाविति मे वितर्कः ।
मुक्ता हि तस्माद्यतुवेश्मदाहान्मया श्रुताः पाण्डुसुताः पृथा च ॥ २३ ॥

तमब्रवीन्निर्जलतोयदाभो हलायुधोनन्तरजं प्रतीतः ।
प्रीतोस्मि द्रष्ट्वा हि पितृष्वसारं पृथां विपुक्तां सह कौरवाग्र्यैः ॥ २४ ॥

The kings attacked Arjuna and Bhīmasena. Then Bhīmasena uprooted a tree and roaring, seized it as a stick and stood at Arjuna's side. Having seen the strength of Bhīmasena, Arjuna became fearless. Śrī Kṛṣṇa noticed the heroism of Arjuna and Bhīma. He spoke to Baladeva: "O Saṅkarṣaṇa, the one who has won the tournament is certainly Arjuna. And the one who has uprooted that huge tree and who wants to defeat the kings with it, he is Bhīma: none on earth can perform such an act. And the one with eyes like a lotus, white complexion, and long nose who went out of the arena before that was Yudhiṣṭhira. And with them there were also the two princes, Nakula and Sahadeva. I have heard that they with Kuntī have just saved themselves from the fire in the lacquer-house." Baladeva said: "I would be very happy to see the Pāṇḍavas and Kuntī." **[15-24]**

॥ इति श्री कां० मा० राजकोपोनाम षोडशोध्यायः॥

Here ends the sixteenth chapter of the Kāmpilyamahātmya.

17

The *Brāhmaṇas* Side with Arjuna

वैशम्पायन उवाच -

अजिनानि विधुन्वन्तः करकांश्च द्विजर्षभाः ।
उचुस्ते भीर्न कर्त्तव्या वयं योत्स्यामहे परान् ॥ १ ॥

तानेवम्बादिनो विप्रानर्जुनः प्रहसन्निव ।
उवाच प्रेक्षका भूत्वा यूयं तिष्ठत पार्श्वतः ॥ २ ॥

अहमेनानजिह्माग्रैः शतशो विकिरन् शरैः ।
वारयिष्यामि सङ्क्रुद्धान् मन्त्रैराशीविषानिव ॥ ३ ॥

इति तद्धनुरादाय शुल्कावाप्तं महाबलः ।
भ्रात्रा भीमेन सहितस्तस्थौ गिरिरिवाचलः ॥ ४ ॥

ततः कर्णमुखान् दृष्ट्वा क्षत्रियान् युद्धदुर्मदान् ।
सम्पेततुरभीतौ तौ गजौ प्रतिगजाविव ॥ ५ ॥

ऊचुश्च वाचः परुषास्ते राजानो युयुत्सवः ।
आहवे हि द्विजस्यापि वधो दृष्टो युयुत्सतः ॥ ६ ॥

इत्येवमुक्त्वा राजानः सहसा दुद्रुवुर्द्विजान् ।
ततः कर्णो महातेजा जिष्णुं प्रतिययौ रणे ॥ ७ ॥

युद्धार्थी वासिताहेतोर्गजं प्रति गजो यथा ।
भीमसेनं ययौ शल्यो मद्राणामीश्वरो बली ॥ ८ ॥

दुर्योधनादयः सर्वे ब्राह्मणैः सह सङ्गताः ।
मृदुपूर्वमयत्नेन प्रत्ययुध्यंस्तदाहवे ॥ ९ ॥

ततोर्जुनः प्रत्यविध्यदापतन्तं शितैः शरैः ।
कर्णं वैकर्तनं श्रीमान् विकृष्य वलवद्धनुः ॥ १० ॥

तेषां शराणां वेगेन शितानां तिग्मतेजसाम ।
विमुह्यमानो राधेयो यत्नात् तमनुधावति ॥ ११ ॥

तावुभावप्यनिर्देश्यौ लाघवाज्जयकाङ्क्षिणौ ।
अयुध्येतां सुसंरब्धावन्योन्यविजिगीषिणौ ॥ १२ ॥

कृते प्रतिकृतं पश्य पश्य बाहुबलं च मे ।
इति शूरार्थवचनैरभाषेतां परस्परम् ॥ १३ ॥

ततोर्जुनस्य भुजयोर्वीर्यमप्रतिमं भुवि ।
ज्ञात्वा वैकर्तनः कर्ण संरब्धः समयोधयत् ॥ १४ ॥

अर्जुनेन प्रयुक्तांस्तान वाणान् वेगवतस्तदा ।
प्रतिहन्य ननादोच्चैः सैन्यानि तदपूजयन् ॥ १५ ॥

Vaiśampāyana said —

O King, the *brāhmaṇa* with their deer-skins and their *kamaṇḍalu* said to Arjuna: "Do not worry, we will fight at your side." Arjuna laughing said: "You stay near me and look at the show. I can stop their arrows as a serpent is stopped by the proper incantation." He took up the bow (the one of the *svayaṁvara*) and with Bhīma stood motionless. Then seeing Karṇa and the other warriors they started to run against them, without any fear, like elephants would run against other elephants. The kings, considering that in the *śāstra* it is written that one can fight against the fighting *brāhmaṇa*, ran against the *brāhmaṇa*. Karṇa went in front of Arjuna and Bhīma, while Duryodhana went in front of the other *brāhmaṇa*. In the beginning there was moderate fighting. But when Arjuna saw Karṇa coming, he shot many arrows at him. Karṇa was struck and panicked. He started to fight carefully. A fiery fight arose between them. Words of challenge were said. Karṇa noticing the uncommon heroism of Arjuna started to fight with anger. He succeeded in stopping the shooting of arrows of Arjuna. The other warriors showed admiration to Karṇa. **[1-15]**

कर्ण उवाच -

तुष्यामि ते विप्रवर्य भुजवीर्यस्य संयुगे ।
अविषादस्य चैवास्य शस्त्रास्त्रविजयस्यच ॥ १६ ॥

किं त्वं साक्षाद्धनुर्वेदो रामो वा विप्रसत्तमा ।
अथसाक्षाद्धरिहयः साक्षाद्वा विष्णुरच्युतः ॥ १७ ॥

आत्मप्रक्षादनार्थं वै बाहुवीर्यपुपाश्रितः ।
विप्ररूपं विधायेदं मन्ये मां प्रतियुध्यसे ॥ १८ ॥

न हि मामाहवे क्रुद्धमन्यः साक्षाच्छचोपतेः ।
पुमान् योधयितुं शक्तः पाण्डवाद्वा किरीटिनः ॥ १९ ॥

Karṇa said —

O *vipravar* (*brāhmaṇa*), I am happy to see your ability with the weapon, the strength of your arms, your attention. Are you the *dhanurveda* (the science of archery, regarded as an *Upaveda* connected with *Yajurveda* and derived from Viśvāmitra or Bhṛgu) itself or are you Paraśurāma or Indra? Or maybe I am fighting with Viṣṇu who has assumed the appearence of a *brāhmaṇa*? Only Indra or Arjuna could fight with me. **[16-19]**

वैशम्पायन उवाच -

तमेवंवादिनं तत्र फाल्गुनः प्रत्यभाषत ।
नास्मि कर्ण धनुर्वेदो नास्मि रामः प्रतापवान् ॥ २० ॥

ब्राह्मणोस्मि युधांश्रेष्ठः सर्वशस्त्रभृतांवरः ।
ब्राह्मे पौरन्दरे चास्त्रे निष्णांतो गुरुशासनात् ॥ २१ ॥

स्थितोस्म्यत्र रणे जेतुं त्वां वै वीर स्थिरो भव ।
एवमुक्तस्तु राधेयो युद्धात् कर्णो न्यवर्त्तत ॥ २२ ॥

Vaiśampāyana said —

Arjuna answered: "I am not the *dhanurveda* nor Paraśurāma. I am a *brāhmaṇa* very good in archery. By the grace of *guru*

I could obtain the complete knowledge of the *brahmāstra*[11] and of the *Indrāstra*.[12] I will defeat you. Be ready!" Hearing these words, Karṇa left the battlefield, considering the *brāhmaṇa* to be invincible. **[20-22]**

ब्राह्मं तेजस्तदाजय्यं मन्यमानो महारथः ।
अपरस्मिन् वनोद्देशे वीरौ शल्य वृकोदरौ ॥ २३ ॥

वलिनौ युद्धसम्पन्नौ विद्यया च वलेन च ।
अन्योन्यमाह्वयन्तौ तु मत्ताविव महागजौ ॥ २४ ॥

मुष्टिभिर्जानुभिश्चैव निघ्नन्तावितरेतरम् ।
प्रकर्षणाकर्षणयोरभ्याकर्षविकर्षणः ॥ २५ ॥

आचकर्षतुरन्योन्यं मुष्टिभिश्चापि जघ्नतुः ।
ततश्चटचटाशब्दः सुघोरो ह्यभवत् तयोः ॥ २६ ॥

पाषाणसम्पातनिभैः प्रहारैरभिजघ्नतुः ।
मुहूर्त्तं तौ तदाऽन्योन्यं समरे पर्यकर्षताम् ॥ २७ ॥

ततो भीमः समुत्क्षिप्य बाहुभ्यां शल्यमाहवे ।
अपातयत् कुरुश्रेष्ठो ब्राह्मणा जहसुस्तदा ॥ २८ ॥

तत्राश्चर्यं भीमसेनश्चकार पुरुषर्षभः ।
यच्छल्यं पातितं भूमौ नावधीद्बलिनं वली ॥ २९ ॥

पातिते भीमसेनेन शल्ये कर्णे च शङ्किते ।
शङ्किताः सर्वराजानः परिवव्रुर्वृकोदरम् ॥ ३० ॥

ऊचुश्च सहितास्तत्र साध्विमौ ब्राह्मणर्षभौ ।
विज्ञायेतां क्वजन्मानौ क्वनिवासौ तथैव च ॥ ३१ ॥

को हि राधासुतं कर्णं शक्तो योधयितुं रणे ।
अन्यत्र रामाद् द्रोणाद्वा पाण्डवाद्वा किरीटिनः ॥ ३२ ॥

---

11. Name of a mythical weapon which deals infallible destruction.

12. Weapon of Indra, said to have been formed out of the bones of the *ṛṣi* Dadhīca and shaped like a circular discus, or in later times regarded as having the form of two transverse bolts crossing each other thus x.

कृष्णद्वा देवकीपुत्रात् कृपाद्वापि शरद्वतः ।
को वा दुर्योधनं शक्तः प्रतियोधयितु रणे ॥ ३३ ॥

तथैव मद्राधिपतिं शल्यं बलवतां वरम् ।
बलदेवादृते वीरात् पाण्डवाद्वा वृकोदरात् ॥ ३४ ॥

वीराद् दुर्योधनाद्वान्यः शक्तः पातयितुं रणे ।
क्रियताभवहारोस्माद्युद्धाद्ब्राह्मणसम्वृतात् ॥ ३५ ॥

ब्राह्मणा हि सदा रक्ष्याः सापराधापि नित्यशः ।
अथैतान् परिलभ्येह पुनर्योत्स्याम हृष्टवत् ॥ ३६ ॥

तांस्तथावादिनः सर्वान् प्रसमीक्ष्य क्षितीश्वरान् ।
अथान्यान् पुरुषांश्चापि तूष्णीमासीद् वृकोदरः ॥ ३७ ॥

तत् कर्म भीमस्य समीक्ष्य कृष्णः कुन्तीसुतौ तौ परिशङ्कमानः ।
निवारयामास महीपतींस्तान् धर्मेण लब्धेत्यनुनीय सर्वान् ॥ ३८ ॥

In another field Śalya and Bhīma were engaged in violent hand-to-hand combat. At a certain point Bhīma lifted Śalya and threw him onto the ground. The *brāhmaṇa* laughed and were surprised when they saw that Bhīma had not killed the fallen Śalya. The kings worried much that Śalya was defeated and surrounded Bhīma. They said: "Vah! These two *brāhmaṇa* are very strong, we should ask where they come from. Except for Paraśurāma, Arjuna, Śrī Kṛṣṇa and Duryodhana no one could confront Karṇa. Likewise for Śalya: who could face him, but Balabhadrajī, Bhīma or Duryodhana. Now stop these *brāhmaṇa*s. We should always protect the *brāhmaṇa*. Even though they might have insulted us, we don't have to be in hurry to fight with them." On hearing the kings' words, Bhīmasena fell silent. O King, Śrī Kṛṣṇa had a doubt: "These two *brāhmaṇa* are Bhīma and Arjuna. But I should persuade all the kings that they have won Draupadī according to the rules of *dharma*, and that they should not fight them." **[23-38]**

एवं ते विनिवृत्तास्तु युद्धाद्युद्धविशारदाः ।
यथावासं ययुः सर्वे विस्मिता राजसत्तमाः ॥ ३९ ॥

वृत्तो ब्रह्मोत्तरो रङ्गः पाञ्चाली ब्राह्मणैर्वृता ।
इति ब्रुवन्तः प्रययुर्ये तत्रासन् समागताः ॥ ४० ॥

ब्राह्मणैस्तु प्रतिच्छन्नौ रौरवाजिनवासिभिः ।
कृच्छ्रेण जग्मतुस्तौ तु भीमसेनधनञ्जयौ ॥ ४१ ॥

विमुक्तौ जनसम्बाधाच्छत्रुभिः परिवारितौ ।
कृष्णयानुगतौ तत्र नृवीरौ तौ विरेजतुः ॥ ४२ ॥

O King, then all the people who had participated in the *svayaṁvara* returned to their abodes, astonished that the *brāhmaṇas* had not only won the *svayaṁvara*, but had also defeated all the *kṣatriya*. Bhīma and Arjuna, followed by the *brāhmaṇa*, also went to their own dwelling place. Coming out from a mass of enemies, Bhīma and Arjuna with Draupadī were as beautiful as the sun and the moon appearing at the same time from a black mass of clouds in the day of *pūrṇamāsī*, the full-moon day (this a strange simili) **[39-42]**

पौर्णमास्यां घनैर्मुक्तौचन्द्रसूर्याविवीदितौ ।
तेषां माता वहुविधं विनाशं पर्यचिन्तयत् ॥ ४३ ॥

अनागच्छत्सु पुत्रेषु भैक्षकालेऽभिगच्छति ।
धार्तराष्ट्रैर्हता न स्युर्विज्ञाय मम पुत्रकाः ॥ ४४ ॥

मायान्वितैर्वा रक्षोभिः सुघोरैर्दृढवैरिभिः विपरीतं
मतं जात व्यासस्यापि महात्मनः ॥ ४५ ॥

इत्येव चिन्तयामास सुतस्नेहवृता पृथा ।
ततः सुप्तजनप्राये दुर्दिने मेघसंप्लुते ॥ ४६ ॥

महत्यथापराह्ने तु घनैः सूर्य इवावृतः ।
ब्राह्मणैः प्राविशत् तत्र् जिष्णुर्भार्गववेश्म तत् ॥ ४७ ॥

In the meantime Kuntī was worrying that her sons had not come back yet. She thought: "They went out for *bhikṣā*, alms, but they have not come back yet. Maybe they were killed by the sons of Dhṛtarāṣṭra, or by some horrible *rākṣasa*. But this would be contrary to what Vyāsadeva declared (the author of the *Veda*)." Kuntī was very distressed because of her deep love for her sons. In those days the sky was filled with clouds and men were sleeping most of the time.[13] Then, like the sun piercing the clouds, Arjuna arrived with the *brāhmaṇas* at the house of the *kumhāra* (potter). **[43-47]**

॥ इति श्री का० मा० राजपराभवोनामसप्तदशोऽध्यायः ॥

Here ends the seventeenth chapter of the Kāmpilyamahātmya.

13. It can be inferred that it was the month of Āṣāḍha, at the end of which the rainy season starts; also from the tale of the *gandharva* Citraratha playing in the water, it is clear that it was the hot season.

18

Draupadī is Divided Among the Five Brothers

वैशम्पायन उवाच -

गत्वा तु तां भार्गवकर्मशालां पार्थौ पृथां प्राप्य महानुभावौ ।
तां याज्ञसेनीं परमप्रतीतौ भिक्षेत्यथावेदयतां नराग्र्यौ ॥ १ ॥

कुटीगता सा त्वनवेक्ष्य पुत्रौ प्रोवाच भुङ्क्तेति समेत्य सर्वे ।
पश्चाच्च कुन्ती प्रसमीक्ष्य कृष्णां कष्टं मया भाषितमित्युवाच ॥ २ ॥

साऽधर्मभीतापरिचिन्तयन्ती तां याज्ञसेनींपरमप्रतीताम् ।
पाणौ गृहीत्वोपजगाम कुन्ती युधिष्ठिरं वाक्यमुवाच चेदम् ॥ ३ ॥

इयं तु कन्या द्रुपदस्य राज्ञस्तवानुजाभ्यां मयि संनिविष्टा ।
यथाचितं पुत्र मयापि चोक्तं समेत्य भुङ्क्तेति नृप प्रमादात् ॥ ४ ॥

मया कथं नानृतमुक्तमद्य भवेत् कुरूणामृषभ ब्रवीहि ।
पञ्चालराजस्य सुतामधर्मो न चोपसर्पेत न विभ्रमेच्च ॥ ५ ॥

Vaiśampāyana said —

Bhīma and Arjuna, after arriving at the *karmaśālā*[14] of the *kumhāra*, said to Kuntī: "We got the *bhikṣā*", referring to the winning of Draupadī. Kuntī from inside the *kuṭī* (hut) answered : "Divide it among the five." But after saying it Kuntī understood that what she had said was absurd. So, greatly worried, she took the hand of Draupadī and went to Yudhiṣṭhira. She said: "Your two younger brothers spoke to me about the winning of a *bhikṣā* and I, without seeing it,

14. The place where the pottery is made.

said to divide it among you. O best of the Kuru, tell me how I can avoid to have spoken falsely and at the same time how this girl can avoid the misdeed (of having more than one husband)." **[1-5]**

वैशम्पायन उवाच -

स एवसमुक्तोमतिमान् नृवीरो मात्रा मुहूर्तं त्ववचिन्त्य राजा ।
कुन्तीं समाश्वास्य कुरुप्रवीरो धनञ्जयं वाक्यमिदं वभाषे ॥ ६ ॥

त्वया जिता फाल्गुन याज्ञसेनी त्वयैव शौभिष्यति राजपुत्री ।
प्रज्वाल्यतामग्निरमित्रसाह गृहाण पाणिं विधिवत् त्वमस्याः ॥ ७ ॥

Dharmarāja (Yudhiṣṭhira) reassured his mother and after reflecting for a while spoke to Arjuna: "O Arjuna, you have this princess, and she will give you a good name; so now light the fire and perform the wedding ceremony." **[6-7]**

अर्जुन उवाच -

मा मां नरेन्द्र त्वमधर्मभाजं कृथा न धर्मो भवता य उक्तः ।
भवान निवेश्यः प्रथमं ततोयं भीमो महाबाहुरचिन्त्यकर्मा ॥ ८ ॥

अहं ततो नकुलोऽनन्तरं मे पश्चादयं सहदेवस्तरस्वी ।
वृकोदरोऽहं च यमौ च राजन्नियं च कन्या भवतो नियोज्याः ॥ ९ ॥

एवंगते यत् करणीयमत्र धर्म्यं यशस्यं कुरुतद्विचिन्त्य ।
पाञ्चालराजस्य हितं च यत् स्यात् प्रशाधि सर्वे हि वशे स्थितास्ते ॥ १० ॥

Arjuna said —

O King, don't make me responsible for a sinful action. What you are saying is not according to the *dharma*. First you should marry and then Bhīma should marry. After that I will marry and after me Nakula and Sahadeva. So now find a solution by which the *dharma* will not be neglected and the name of King Drupada will not be spoiled. We are under your authority. **[8-10]**

वैशम्पायन उवाच -

जिष्णोर्वचनमाज्ञाय भक्तिस्नेहसमन्वितम् ।

दृष्टिं निवेशयामासुः पाञ्चाल्यां पाण्डुनन्दनाः ॥ ११ ॥

दृष्ट्वा ते तत्र पश्यन्तीं सर्वे कृष्णां यशस्विनीम् ।
सम्प्रेक्ष्यान्योन्यमासीना हृदयैस्तामधारयन् ॥ १२ ॥

तेषां तु द्रौपदीं दृष्ट्वा सर्वेषाममितौजसाम् ।
संप्रमथ्येन्द्रियग्रामं प्रादुरासीन्मनोभवः ॥ १३ ॥

काम्यं हि रूपं पाञ्चाल्या विधात्रा विहितं स्वयम् ।
वभूवाधिकमन्याभ्यः सर्वभूतमनोरमम् ॥ १४ ॥

तेषामाकारभावज्ञः कुन्तीपुत्रो युधिष्ठिरः ।
द्वैपायनवचः कृत्स्नं सस्मार मनुजर्षभः ॥ १५ ॥

स हि तानब्रवीत् पूर्वं कृष्णद्वैपायनो मुनिः ।
निर्दिष्टा भवतां पत्नी कृष्णा पार्षत्यनिन्दिता ॥ १६ ॥

अथोवाच पुनर्भ्रातृन् मिथोभेदभषान्नृपः ।
सर्वेषां द्रौपदी भार्या भविष्यति हि नः शुभा ॥ १७ ॥

Vaiśampāyana said —

O King, listening to the words of Arjuna the Pāṇḍavas looked at Draupadī, Yudhiṣṭhira and Bhīma with devotion and at Nakula and Sahadeva with affection. For a moment everyone was looking at each other, listening to what Draupadī was saying. In all of them the god of desire arose, because her beauty had been made directly by the creator, Brahmājī, and it was much more charming than any other woman's. Yudhiṣṭhira understood their intentions by their faces. He remembered the words of Vyāsajī. He had told the Pāṇḍavas that Draupadī would become the wife of all five of them. So as not to make any divergence from the aforesaid instruction, King Yudhiṣṭhira said: "Draupadī will marry us all." **[11-17]**

वैशम्पायन उवाच -

भ्रातुर्वचस्तत् प्रसमीक्ष्य सर्वे ज्येष्ठस्य पाण्डोस्तन यास्तदानीम् ।
तमेवार्थं ध्यायमाना मनोभिः सर्वे च ते तस्थुरदीनसत्त्वाः ॥ १८ ॥

वृष्णि प्रवीरस्तु कुरुप्रवीरानाऽऽशङ्कमानः सहरौहिणेयः ।
जगाम तां भार्गवकर्मशालां यत्रासते ते पुरुषप्रवीराः ॥ १९ ॥

तत्रोपविष्टं पृथुदीर्घबाहुं ददर्श कृष्णः स च रौहिणेयः ।
अजातशत्रुं परिवार्य तांश्चाप्युपोपविष्टान् ज्वलनप्रकाशान् ॥ २० ॥

ततोऽब्रवीद्वासुदेवोभिगम्य कुन्तीसुतं धर्मभृतां वरिष्ठम् ।
कृष्णोहमस्मीति निपीड्य पादौ युधिष्ठिरस्याजमीढस्य राज्ञः ॥ २१ ॥

तथैव तस्याप्यनु रौहिणेयस्तौ चापि दृष्ट्वा कुरवोऽभ्यनन्दन् ।
पितृष्वसुश्चापि यदुप्रवीरावगृह्णतां भारतमुख्य पादौ ॥ २२ ॥

अजातशत्रुश्च कुरुप्रवीरः पप्रच्छ कृष्णं कुशलं विलोक्य ।
कथं वयं वासुदेव त्वयेह गूढा वसन्तो विदिताश्च सर्वे ॥ २३ ॥

तमब्रवीद्वासुदेवः प्रहस्य गूढोप्यग्निर्ज्ञायत एव राजन् ।
तं विक्रमं पाण्डवेयानतीत्य कोन्यः कर्त्ता विद्यते मानुषेषु ॥ २४ ॥

दिष्ट्या सर्वे पावकाद्विप्रमुक्ता यूयं घोरात् पाण्डवाः शत्रु साहाः ।
दिष्ट्या पापो धृतराष्ट्रस्य पुत्रः सहामात्यो न सकामो भविष्यत् ॥ २५ ॥

भद्रं वोस्तु निहितं यद्गुहायां विवर्द्धयध्वं ज्वलना इवैधमानाः ।
मा वो विदुः पार्थिवाः केचिदेव यास्यावहे शिविरायैव तावत् ॥ २६ ॥

सोनुज्ञातः पाण्डवेनाव्ययश्रोः प्रायाच्छीघ्रं बलदेवेन सार्द्धम् ॥ २७ ॥

Vaiśampāyana said —

When Yudhisṭhira said that they all started to think how they could marry the same woman. Then Śrī Kṛṣṇa and Baladeva came to meet the Pāṇḍavas. They sat among them and after touching the feet of Kuntī they said: "We are Kṛṣṇa and Baladeva." Yudhisṭhira asked them how they could have recognised them. Śrī Kṛṣṇa laughing answered that even the hidden fire cannot be hidden. Who could have won the tournament of the *svayaṁvara* and all the rest if not the Pāṇḍavas. He said: "You escaped from a terrible fire and have prevented the sinful desire of Duryodhana. I am very happy with this. You will succeed with the task you have in mind. That is all, now I will go to my abode." After saying this, Śrī Kṛṣṇa took his leave of King Yudhisṭhira and quickly returned to his residence. **[18-27]**

॥ *इति श्री का० मा० रामकृष्णागमनोनामाष्टादशोऽध्यायः* ॥
Here ends the eighteenth chapter of the Kāmpilyamahātmya.

19

Dr̥ṣṭadyumna Secretly Watches the Pāṇḍava's Talk and Drupada's Anxiety to Know the Facts

वैशम्पायन उवाच -

धृष्टद्युम्नस्तु पाञ्चाल्यः पृष्ठतः कुरुनन्दनौ ।
अन्वगच्छत् तदा यान्तौ भार्गवस्य निवेशने ॥ १ ॥

सोऽज्ञायमानः पुरुषानवधाय समन्ततः ।
स्वयमारान्निलोनोभूद् भार्गवस्य निवेशने ॥ २ ॥

Vaiśampāyana said —

O King, the son of Drupada, Dhr̥ṣṭadyumna, had secretely followed the Pāṇḍavas. He also arrived near the house of the *kumhāra* but stayed hidden from the Pāṇḍavas. **[1-2]**

सायं च भीमस्तु रिपुप्रमाथी जिष्णुर्यमौ चापि महानुभावौ ।
भैक्ष्यं चरित्वा तु युधिष्ठिराय निवेदयाञ्चक्रुरदीनसत्त्वाः ॥ ३ ॥

ततस्तु कुन्ती द्रुपदात्मजां तामुवाच काले वचनं वदान्या ।
त्वमग्रमादाय कुरुष्व भद्रे वलिं च विप्राय च देहि भिक्षाम् ॥ ४ ॥

ये चान्नमिच्छन्ति ददस्व तेभ्यः परिश्रिता ये परितो मनुष्याः ।
ततश्च शेषं प्रविभज्य शीघ्रमर्द्धं चतुर्द्धा च ममात्मनश्च ॥ ५ ॥

अर्द्धं च भीमाय च देहि भद्रे य एष नागर्षभतुल्यरूपः ।
गौरो युवा संहननोप्पन्न एषोहि वीरो बहुभुक् सदैव ॥ ६ ॥

सा हृष्टरूपेव च राजपुत्री तस्या वचः साधु विशङ्कमाना ।
यथावदुक्तं प्रचकार साध्वी ते चापि सर्वे वुभुजुस्तदन्नम् ॥ ७ ॥

कुशैस्तु भूमौ शयनं चकार माद्रीपुत्रः सहदेवस्तरस्वी ।
यथास्वकीयान्यजिनानि सर्वे संस्तीर्य वीराः सुषुपुर्द्धण्याम् ॥ ८ ॥

अगस्त्यशास्तामभितो दिशं तु शिरांसि तेषां कुरुसत्तमानाम् ।
कुन्ती पुरस्तात् तु वभूव तेषां पादान्तरे चाथ वभूव कृष्णा ॥ ९ ॥

अशेत भूमौ सह पाण्डुपुत्रैः पादोपधानीव कृता कुशेषु ।
न तत्र दुःखं मनसापि तस्या न चावमेने कुरुपुङ्गवास्तां न् ॥ १० ॥

ते तत्र शूराः कथयाम्वभू वुः कथा विचित्राः पृतनाधिकाराः ।
अस्त्राणि दिव्यानि रथांश्च नागान् खड्गान् गदाश्चापि परश्वधांश्च ॥ ११ ॥

तेषां कथास्ताः परिकीर्त्यमानाः पञ्चालराजस्य सुतस्तदानीम् ।
शुश्राव कृष्णां च तदा निषण्णां ते चापि सर्वे ददृशुर्मनुष्याः ॥ १२ ॥

धृष्टद्युम्नो राजपुत्रस्तु सर्वं वृत्तं तेषां कथितुं चैव रात्रौ ।
सर्व राज्ञे द्रुपदायाखिलेन निवेदयिष्यंस्त्वरितो जगाम ॥ १३ ॥

पञ्चालराजस्तु विषण्णरूपस्तान् पाण्डवान प्रतिविन्दमानः ।
धृष्टद्युम्नं पर्यपृच्छन्महात्मा क्व सा गता केननीता च कृष्णा ॥ १४ ॥

कच्चिन्न शूद्रेण न हीनजेन वैश्येनवा करदेनोपपन्ना ।
कच्चित् पदं मूर्घ्नि न पङ्कदिग्धं कच्चिन्न माला पतिता श्मशाने ॥ १५ ॥

कच्चित् सवर्णप्रवरो मनुष्य उद्रिक्तवर्णोप्युत एव कच्चित् ।
कच्चिन्न वामो मम मूर्घ्नि पादः कृष्णाभिमर्शेन कृतोद्य पुत्र ॥ १६ ॥

कच्चिन्न तप्स्ये परमप्रतीतः संयज्य पार्थेन नरर्षभेण ।
वदस्व तथ्येन महानुभाव कोसौ विजेता दुहितुर्ममाद्य ॥ १७ ॥

विचित्रवीर्यस्य सुतस्य कच्चित् कुरुप्रवीरस्य धृयन्ति पुत्राः ।
कच्चित्तु पार्थेन यवीयसाद्य धनुर्गृहीतं निहतं च लक्ष्यम् ॥ १८ ॥

In the evening Bhīma, Arjuna, Nakula and Sahadeva brought the alms of the day to King Yudhiṣṭhira. Then Kuntī turned towards Draupadī and said: "O noble woman, offer the first part of this *bhikṣā* in sacrifice and also feed the *brāhmaṇa*s and the other guests. The remaining will be divided in two portions. One part you shall give to Bhīma, who always eats a lot, and the other part you will divide in six parts and give to Yudhiṣṭhira, Arjuna, Nakula, Sahadeva, me and you." Draupadī did exactly what Kuntī had ordered. Everyone got his food. Then Sahadeva spread out some *kuśa* grass on the ground and everyone rested on their own deer skin. They all lay with their heads southward with Kuntī at the side of the head and Draupadī at the side of the feet. There was not any regret in the mind of Draupadī. The Pāṇḍavas started to talk about the army and weapons. Dhṛṣṭadyumna and his attendants listened and understood all their plans. Dhṛṣṭadyumna (understanding they were not *brāhmaṇas* but *kṣatriyas*) went to tell everything to his father. These words came from the mouth of King Drupada: "Tell me, O son, who took Draupadī? Are they *śūdra*, *vaiśya*, *varṇasaṅkara* (mixed caste), *brāhmaṇa* or *kṣatriya*? Who got her? Who didn't deign to put his left foot on my head? Has she fallen in the hands of a low people? O how lucky I would be if she had become related to Arjuna, speak truely! Are the Pāṇḍu's sons here around, was Arjuna the one who hit the target?" **[3-18]**

॥ *इति श्री का० मा० द्रुपदचिन्तानामैकोनविंशोऽध्यायः* ॥

Here ends the nineteenth chapter of the Kāmpilyamahātmya.

20

Dṛṣṭadyumna Tells Facts to his Father

वैशम्पायन उवाच -

ततस्तथोक्तः परिहृष्टरूपः पित्रे शशंसाथ स राजपुत्रः ।
धृष्टद्युम्नः सीमकानां प्रवर्हौं वृत्तं यथा येन हृता च कृष्णा ॥ १ ॥

यः कार्मुकाग्रं कृतवानधिज्यं लक्ष्यं च यः पातितवान् पृथिव्याम् ॥ २ ॥

असज्जमानश्च ततस्तरस्वी वृतो द्विजाग्र्यैरभिपूज्यमानः ।
चक्राम वज्रीव दितेः सुतेषु सर्वैश्च देवैर्ऋषिभिश्च जुष्टः ॥ ३ ॥

कृष्णा प्रगृह्याजिनमन्वयात् तं नागं यथा नागवधूः प्रहृष्टा ।
अमृष्यमाणेषुनराधिपेषु क्रुद्धेषु वै तत्र समापतत्सु ॥ ४ ॥

ततोपरः पार्थिवसङ्घमध्ये प्रबृद्धमारुज्य महीप्ररोहम् ।
प्रकालयन्नेव स पार्थिवीघान् क्रुद्धोन्तकः प्राणभृतो यथैव ॥ ५ ॥

तौ पार्थिवानां मिषतां नरेन्द्र कृष्णामुपादाय गतौ नराग्र्यो ।
विभ्राजमानाविंव चन्द्रसूर्यौ बाह्या पुराद्भार्गवकर्मशालाम् ॥ ६ ॥

तत्रोपविंष्टार्चिरिवानलस्य तेषां जनित्रीति मम प्रतर्कः ।
तथाविधैरेव नरप्रवीरैरुपोपविष्टैस्त्रिभिरग्निकल्पैः ॥ ७ ॥

तस्यास्ततस्तावभिवाद्य पादावुक्ता च कृष्णा त्वभिवादयेति ।
स्थितां च तत्रैव निवेद्य कृष्णां भिक्षाप्रचाराय गता नराग्र्याः ॥ ८ ॥

तेषां तु भैक्ष्यं प्रतिगृह्य कृष्णा दत्वा वलिं ब्राह्मणसाच्च कृत्वा ।
तां चैव वृद्धां परिवेष्य तांश्च नरप्रवीरान् स्वयमप्यभुङ्क्त ॥ ९ ॥

सुप्तास्तु ते पार्थिव सर्व एव कृष्णा तु तेषां चरणीपधाने ।
आसीत् पृथिव्या शयनं च तेषां दर्भाजिनाग्रास्तरणोपपन्नम् ॥ १० ॥

ते नर्दमाना इव कालमेघाः कथा विचित्राः कथयाम्बभूवुः ।
न वैश्यशूद्रौपयिकीः कथास्ता न च द्विजानां कथयन्ति वीराः ॥ ११ ॥

निःसंशयं क्षत्रियपुङ्गवास्ते यथा हि युद्धं कथयन्ति राजन् ।
आशा हि नो व्यक्तमियं समृद्धा मुक्तान हि पार्थान् शृणुमोग्निदाहात् ॥ १२ ॥

यथाहि लक्ष्यं निहतं धनुश्च सज्यं कृतं तेन तथा प्रसह्य ।
यथाहि भाषन्ति परस्परं ते छन्ना ध्रुव ते प्रचरन्ति पार्थाः ॥ १३ ॥

Vaiśampāyana said —

Thus Dhṛṣṭadyumna happily told his father all the news: "O King, the one who pierced the target, who looked like Indra surrounded by the other gods as he was surrounded by the *brāhmaṇa* and whom Draupadī followed; and the other who got angry and scared away all the kings by using a tree as his club, they went to the house of a *kumhāra* out of town. At that house there was also an old woman, brilliant like a flame, whom I suppose to be their mother. And like the three domestic fires, *dakṣiṇa*, *gārhapatya*, *āhavanīya*, three valiant men were sitting near the old woman. The former two and Draupadī touched the woman's feet and after leaving Draupadī there with her they went to beg for alms. After that, they shared the *bhikṣā* in the right way and ate it. Then they spread out some *kuśa* grass and their deer skins and lay down. Draupadī lay at the feet of the five brothers. Then they started to speak. The conversation was not of a *brāhmaṇa* nor of a *śūdra* nor a *vaiśya*. They were speaking of warfare: I think that they are sons of a king. From the way he could pull the bow and pierce the golden fish, and the talk they had, I am almost sure that they are the Pāṇḍavas under the disguise of *brāhmaṇa*." **[1-13]**

ततः स राजा द्रुपदः प्रहृष्टः पुरोहितं प्रेषयामांस तेषाम् ।
विद्याम युष्मानितिभाषमाणो महात्मनः पाण्डुसुतास्तु कच्चित् ॥ १४ ॥

गृहीत्वाक्यो नृपतेः पुरौधा गत्वा प्रशंसामभिधाय तेषाम् ।
वाक्यं समृद्धं नृपतेर्यथावदुवाच चानुक्रमविक्रमेण ॥ १५ ॥

विज्ञातुमिच्छत्यवनीश्वरो वः पञ्चालराजो वरदो वरार्हाः ।
लक्ष्यस्य वेद्धारमिमं हि दृष्ट्वा हर्षस्य नान्तं प्रतिपद्यते सः ॥ १६ ॥

आख्यात च ज्ञातिकुलानुपूर्वीं पदं शिरस्सु द्विषतां कुरुध्वम् ।
प्रह्लादयध्वं हृदयं ममेदं पञ्चालराजस्य च सानुगस्य ॥ १७ ॥

पाण्डुर्हि राजा द्रुपदस्य राज्ञः प्रियः सखा चात्मसमो बभूवः ।
तस्यैष कामो दुहिता ममेयं स्नुषां प्रदास्यामि हि कौरवाय ॥ १८ ॥

अयं हि कामो द्रुपदस्य राज्ञो हृदिस्थितो नित्यमनिन्दताङ्गाः ।
यदर्जुनो वै पृथुदीर्घबाहुर्धर्मेण विन्देत सुतां ममैताम् ॥ १९ ॥

कृतं च तत् स्यात् सुकृतं ममेदं यशश्च पुण्यं च हितं तदेतत् ।
अथोक्तवाक्यं हि पुरोहितं स्थितं ततो विनीतं समुदीक्ष्य राजा ॥ २० ॥

समीपतो भीमसेनं शशास प्रदीयतां पाद्यमस्मै तथार्घ्यः ।
मान्यः पुरोधा द्रुपदस्य राज्ञस्तस्मै प्रयोज्यभ्यधिका हि पूजा ॥ २१ ॥

भीमस्ततस्तत् कृतवान नरेन्द्र तां चैव पूजां प्रतिगृह्य हर्षात् ।
सुखोपविष्टं हि पुरोहितं तदा युधिष्ठिरो ब्राह्मणामित्युवाच ॥ २२ ॥

पाञ्चालराजेन सुता निसृष्टा स्वधर्मदृष्टेन यथा न कामात् ।
प्रदिष्टशुल्का द्रुपदेन राज्ञा सा तेन वीरेण तथानुवृत्ता ॥ २३ ॥

न तत्र वर्णेषु कृता विवक्षा न वापि शीले न कुले न गोत्रे ।
कृतेन सज्येन हि कार्मुकेण विद्धेन लक्ष्येन हि सा विसृष्टा ॥ २४ ॥

सेयं तथानेन महात्मनेह कृष्णा जिता पार्थिवसङ्घमध्ये ।
नैवं गते सौमकिरद्य राजा सन्तापमर्हत्यसुखाय कर्तुम् ॥ २५ ॥

कामश्च योसौ द्रुपदस्य राज्ञः स चापि सम्पत्स्यति पाथिवस्य ।
सम्प्राप्यरूपां हि नरेन्द्रकन्यामिमामहं ब्राह्मण साधु मन्ये ॥ २६ ॥

न तद्धनुर्मन्दवलेन शक्यं मौर्व्या समायोजयितुं तया हि ।
न चाकृतास्त्रेण न हीनजेन लक्ष्यं तथा पातयितुं न शक्यम् ॥ २७ ॥

तस्मान्न तापं दुहितुर्निमित्तं पाञ्चालराजोर्हति कर्तुमद्य ।
न चापि तत्पातनमन्यथेह कर्तुंहि शक्यं भुवि मानवेन ॥ २८ ॥

एवंब्रुबत्येव युधिष्ठिरे तु पञ्चालराजस्य समीपतोन्यः ।
तत्राजगामाशुनरो द्वितीयो निवेदयिष्यन्निह सिद्धमन्नम् ॥ २९ ॥

King Drupada was happy to hear that those people were really the Pāṇḍavas but sent his *purohita* there to confirm this. The *purohita* went there and full of admiration took the message of his king to Yudhiṣṭhira: "O King, King Drupada wants to know you; he is very happy with the result of the tournament. For this reason tell me the name of your family and deign to put the foot on the head of your enemies and doing so make happy the heart of the king of Pañcāla and his family. King Pāṇḍu has been a very good friend of King Drupada and he wanted to marry his daughter to the Pāṇḍurāja's family. By giving to Arjuna his daughter as wife he has accomplished his duty." After listening to these words Yudhiṣṭhira said to the near Bhīmasena: "Offer King Drupada's *purohita* water to wash his hands and feet (as it is custom for respected guests)." When the *purohita* sat again, King Yudhiṣṭhira said: "We have rightly won following the rules set by King Drupada. There was not any discrimination of dynasty or family: the man who could pierce the target would obtain Draupadī as his wife. As according to this he has won Draupadī, now King Drupada should not feel remorse for what has already happened. And the desire of Drupada (to marry Draupadī to Arjuna) will also be fulfilled. We deserve the daughter of Drupada and it is right that she is with us. None without nobility and strength could use that bow. As Drupada should not have any regret." While King Yudhiṣṭhira was speaking, another messenger from Drupada arrived there to invite them for a meal. **[14-29]**

॥ इति श्री का० मा० पुरोहितयुधिष्ठिरसम्वादोनाम विंशोध्यायः॥

Here ends the twentieth chapter of the Kāmpilyamahātmya.

21

King Drupada Invites the Bridegroom's Family

दूत उवाच -

जन्यार्थमन्नं द्रुपदेन राज्ञा विवाहहेतोरुपसंस्कृतं च ।
तदाप्नुवध्वं कृतसर्वकार्याः कृष्णां च तत्रैव चिरं न कार्यम् ॥ १ ॥

इमेरथाः काञ्चनपद्मचित्राः सदश्वयुक्ता वसुधाधिपार्हाः ।
एतान् समारुह्य परैत सर्वे पञ्चालराजस्य निवेशंन तत् ॥ २ ॥

The Messenger said —

King Drupada has ordered a banquet to be prepared for the bridegroom's family. Please come and take part in it. On account of the marriage bring also Draupadī with you. Here there are some chariots ready for you, O king, now you may sit on them and come to the king's palace. **[1-2]**

वैशम्पायन उवाच -

ततः प्रयाताः कुरुपुङ्गवास्ते पुरोहितं तं परियाप्य सर्वे ।
आस्थाय यानानि महान्ति तानि कुन्ती च कृष्णा च सहैकयाने ॥ ३ ॥

श्रुत्वा तु वाक्यानि पुरोहितस्य यान्युक्तवान भारत धर्मराजः ।
जिज्ञासयेवाथ कुरूत्तमानां द्रव्याण्यनेकान्युपसंजहार ॥ ४ ॥

फलानि माल्यानि च संस्कृतानि यज्ञाङ्गपात्राण्यथ पुस्तकानि ।
गाश्चैव राजन्नथ चैव रज्जूर्वीजानि चान्यानि कृषीनिमित्तम् ॥ ५ ॥

अन्येषु शिल्पेषु च यान्यपि स्युः सर्वाणि कृत्यान्यखिलेन तत्र ।
क्रीडानिमित्तान्यपि यानि तत्र सर्वाणि तत्रोपजहार राजा ॥ ६ ॥

वर्माणि चर्माणि च भानुमन्ति खड्गा महान्तोश्वरथा विचित्राः ।
धनूंषि चाग्र्याणि शराश्च चित्राः शक्त्यृष्टयः काञ्चनभूषणाश्च ॥ ७ ॥

प्रासा भुशुण्ड्यश्च परश्वधाश्च सांग्रामिकं चैय तथैव सर्वम् ।
शय्यासनान्युत्तमवस्तुवन्ति तथैव वासो विविधं च तत्र ॥ ८ ॥

कुन्ती तु कृष्णां परिगृह्य साध्वीमन्तःपुरं द्रुपदस्याविवेश ॥ ९ ॥

तान् सिंहविक्रान्तगतीन् निरीक्ष्यमहर्षभाक्षानजिनोत्त ।
रीयान् गूढोत्तरांसान् भुजगेन्द्रभोगप्रलम्बवाहून् पुरुषप्रवीरान् ॥ १० ॥

राजा च राज्ञः सचिवाश्च सर्वे पुत्राश्च राज्ञः सुहृदस्तथैव ।
प्रेष्याश्च सर्वे निखिलेन राजन् हर्ष समापेतुरतीव तत्र ॥ ११ ॥

ते तत्र वीराः परमासनेषु सपादपीठेष्यविशङ्कमानाः ।
यथानुपूर्वं विविशुर्नराग्र्यास्तथा महार्हेषु न विस्मयन्तः ॥ १२ ॥

उच्चावचं पार्थिवभोजनीयं पात्रीषु जाम्बूनदराजतीषु ।
दासाश्च दास्यश्च सुमृष्टवेषाः सम्भोजकाश्चाप्युपजह्रुरन्नम् ॥ १३ ॥

ते तत्र भुक्त्वा पुरुषप्रवीरा यथात्मकामं सुभृशप्रतीताः ।
उत्क्रम्य सर्वाणि वसूनि राजन् साङ्ग्रामिकं ते विविशुर्नृवीराः ॥ १४ ॥

तल्लक्षयित्वा द्रुपदस्यपुत्रो राजा च सर्वैः सह मन्त्रिपुत्रैः ।
समर्थयामासुरुपेत्य हृष्टाः कुन्तीसुतान् पार्थिव राजपुत्रान् ॥ १५ ॥

Vaiśampāyana said —

After taking leave of the *purohita*, every one of the Pāṇḍavas sat on a different chariot and with Draupadī and Kuntī on their own chariot they went to Drupada's court. On the other side King Drupada, after listening to the speech of Dharmarāja, reported by his *purohita*, got ready many things to check the behaviour of the winner of the *svayaṁvara* and of his companions. Fruits, garlands, the tools for sacrifice, books, cows, ropes, many kind of seeds, tools for tilling the soil, and hand-made weapons and toys, armours, shields, swords, horses and chariots, bows, arrows, gold plated daggers, javelins, *bhuśuṇḍī*,[15] battle axes and other things

---

15. A special spear with hooks all around; maybe a fire-arm.

related to battle; and also beds, seats, and very precious clothes were gathered there.

Draupadī and Kuntī went into the queens' residence and there they were made welcome by the wives of Drupada. On the other side, moving like lions but looking like bulls, wearing their deer-skins, with square shoulders and arms as long as serpents, the Pāṇḍavas entered. The king and all his court were very happy to see them coming. They approached and first Yudhiṣṭhira, then Bhīmasena and so on, they all sat on the seats. Then the servants, the maiden and the *brāhmaṇa* qualified to prepare food started to serve different kinds of dishes worthy to be offered to kings, on gold and silver plates.

The Pāṇḍavas took as much food as they liked and then, after standing up, they saw all the things that had been collected by King Drupada. The Pāṇḍavas did not mind any of those things but stopped in front of the weapons and the handicraft related to battle, noticing that the king and all his counsellors had decided that they were surely princes. **[3-15]**

॥ *इति श्री कां० मा० पाण्डवपरीक्षणं नामैकविंशोऽध्यायः* ॥

Here ends the twenty-first chapter of the Kāmpilyamahātmya.

22

King Drupada Meets the Pāṇḍavas; Yudhiṣṭhira Explains How the Five are Draupadī's Husbands

वैशम्पायन उवाच -

तत आहूयपाञ्चाल्यो राजपुत्रं युधिष्ठिरम् ।
परिग्रहेण ब्राह्मेण परिगृह्य महाद्युतिः ॥ १ ॥

पर्यपृच्छददीनात्मा कुन्तीपुत्रं सुवर्चसम् ।
कथं जानीम भवतः क्षत्रियान् ब्राह्मणानुत ॥ २ ॥

वैश्यान् वा गुणसम्पन्नानथवा शूद्रयोनिजान् ।
मायामास्थाय विप्रांश्च चरतः सर्वतोदिशम ॥ ३ ॥

कृष्णाहेतोरिह प्राप्ता देवाः संदर्शनार्थिनः ।
ब्रवीतु नो भवान् सत्य संदेहो ह्यत्र नो महान् ॥ ४ ॥

अपि नः संशयस्यान्ते मनः संतुष्टिमावहेत ।
अपि नो भागधेयानि शुभानि स्युः परन्तप ॥ ५ ॥

इच्छया ब्रूहि तत् सत्यं सत्यं राजसु शोभते ।
इष्टापूर्त्तेन च तथा वक्तव्यमनृतं न तु ॥ ६ ॥

श्रुत्वा ह्यमरसङ्काश तव वाक्यमरिन्दम ।
ध्रुवं विवाहकरणमास्थास्यामि विधानतः ॥ ७ ॥

Vaiśampāyana said —

Then King Drupada called Yudhiṣṭhira and greeting him as a *brāhmaṇa*, he said: "How are we able to know if you are a *kṣatriya* or a *brāhmaṇa*. Or maybe a *vaiśya* or even a *śūdra*? Are you a *devatā* who has come in the disguise of a *brāhmaṇa* to see Draupadī? Tell us the truth for we are very suspicous. O Parantapa, don't you think that by clearing this suspicion we will be reassured? Speak the truth, because truth is the brilliance of the royal court. The witness of every *yajña* and every action done according to the *dharma* is said to be true, never false. O splendid hero, first introduce yourself and then we will celebrate the marriage." **[1-7]**

युधिष्ठिर उवाच -

मा राजन् विमना भूस्त्वं पाञ्चाल्य प्रीतिरस्तुते ।
ईप्सितस्ते ध्रुवः कामः सम्वृत्तोयमसंशयम् ॥ ८ ॥

वयं हि क्षत्रिया राजन् पाण्डोः पुत्रा महात्मनः ।
ज्येष्ठं मां विद्धि कौन्तैयं भीमसेनार्जुनाविमौ ॥ ९ ॥

आभ्यां तव सुतां राजन् निर्जिता राजसंसदि ।
यमौ च तत्र कुन्ती च यत्र कृष्णा व्यवस्थिता ॥ १० ॥

व्येतु ते मानसं दुःखं क्षत्रियाः स्मी नरर्षभ ।
पद्मिनीव सुतेयं ते ह्रदादन्यह्रदं गता ॥ ११ ॥

इति सत्यं महाराज सर्वमेतद्ब्रवीमि ते ।
भवान् हि गुरुरस्माकं परमं च परायणम् ॥ १२ ॥

Yudhiṣṭhira said —

O King, be happy; your desire has been fulfilled. We are *kṣatriya*, sons of King Pāṇḍu. I am the first son of Kuntī, Yudhiṣṭhira. These two are Bhīmasena and Arjuna. They have won Draupadī in front of the assembly of the kings. And these two are Nakula and Sahadeva. Kuntī is near Draupadī. Now you dispel every doubt from your mind because the exceptionally charming Draupadī has passed from your noble family to ours, like a beautiful lotus may pass from a deep lake to another. O king, what I am saying is true, you are greater than us and our protector. **[8-12]**

वैशम्पायन उवाच -

ततः स द्रुपदो राजा हर्षव्याकुल लोचनः ।

प्रतिवक्तु मुदायुक्तो नाशकत् तं युधिष्ठिरम् ॥ १३ ॥

यत्नेन तु स तं हर्षं संनिगृह्य परन्तप ।
अनुरूपं तदा वाचा प्रत्युवाच युधिष्ठिरम् ॥ १४ ॥

पप्रच्छ चैनं धर्मात्मा यथाते प्रमुद्रता पुरात् ।
स तस्मै सर्वमाचख्यावानुपूर्व्येण पाण्डवः ॥ १५ ॥

तच्छ्रुत्वा द्रुपदोराजा कुन्तीपुत्रस्य भाषितम् ।
विगर्हयामास तदा धृतराष्ट्रं नरेश्वरम ॥ १६ ॥

आश्वासयामास च तं कुन्तीपुत्रं युधिष्ठिरम् ।
प्रतिजज्ञे च राज्याय द्रुपदो वदताम्वरः ॥ १७ ॥

ततः कुन्ती च कृष्णा च भीमसेनार्जुनावपि ।
यमौ च राज्ञा संदिष्टं विविशुर्भवनं महत् ॥ १८ ॥

तत्र ते न्यवसन् राजन् यज्ञसेनेन पूजिताः ।
प्रत्याश्वस्तस्तती राजा सह पुत्रैरुवाच तम् ॥ १९ ॥

गृह्णातु विधिवत् पाणिमद्यायं कुरुनन्दनः ।
पुण्येऽहनि महाबाहुरर्जुनः कुरुतां क्षणम् ॥ २० ॥

तमब्रवीत् ततो राजा धर्मात्मा च युधिष्ठिरः ।
ममापि दारसम्बन्धः कार्यस्तावद्विशाम्पते ॥ २१ ॥

Vaiśampāyana said —

O King! The eyes of King Drupada filled with joy and he could not say a word. Then hardly containing his deep joy Drupada asked Yudhiṣṭhira to tell him what had happened since they had left Hastināpura and he narrated everything in order. Drupada after being acquainted to what had happened in Hastināpura, started to speak ill of Dhṛtarāṣṭra, and to console Yudhiṣṭhira he promised to give him the kingdom. Then he gave the order to host Kuntī, Draupadī and the Pāṇḍavas in the main palace. There they went to stay, accompanied by King Drupada. Then he asked Yudhiṣṭhira: "Today is an auspicious day for the marriage between Arjuna and Draupadī and the celebration to the gods." Dharmarāja Yudhiṣṭhira answered: "Firstly celebrate my wedding." **[13-21]**

द्रुपद उवाच -

भवान् वा विधिवत पांणि गृह्णातु दुहितुर्भम।
यस्य वा मन्यसे वीर तस्य कृष्णामुपादिश ॥ २२ ॥

King Drupada said —

You are assuming airs; the marriage will be celebrated with Arjuna. **[22]**

युधिष्ठिर उवाच -

सर्वेषां महिषी राजन् द्रोपदी नो भविष्यति।
एवं हि व्याहृतं पूर्वं मम मात्रा विशाम्पते ॥ २३ ॥

अहमप्यनिविष्टो वै भीमसेनश्च पाण्डवः।
पार्थेन विजिता चैषा रत्नभूता सुता तव ॥ २४ ॥

एष नः समयो राजन् रत्नस्य सह भोजनम्।
न च तं हातुमिच्छामः समय राजसत्तम ॥ २५ ॥

सर्वेषां धर्मतः कृष्णा महिषी नो भविष्यति।
आनुपूर्व्येण सर्वेषां गृह्णातु ज्वलने करान् ॥ २६ ॥

Yudhiṣṭhira said —

O King, Draupadī will be the queen of all us five. Our mother has already said that. I and Bhīmasena are still unmarried; Arjuna has won Draupadī, brilliant like a jewel. Among us brothers we keep the vow to share whatever precious stone we get. O king, we don't want to break this promise: for this reason Draupadī will be the wife of us five. And we five will perform the marriage with her in front of the fire. **[23-26]**

द्रुपद उवाच -

एकस्य वह्व्यो विहिता महिष्यः कुरुनन्दन।
नैकस्या वहवः पुंसः श्रूयन्ते पतयः क्वचित् ॥ २७ ॥

लोकवेदविरुद्धं हि नाधर्मं धर्मविच्छुचिः।
कर्तुमर्हसि कौन्तेय कस्मात् ते बुद्धिर् द्रशी ॥ २८ ॥

King Drupada said —

O son of the Kuru, there can be a man with many women but not a woman with many men. It is not becoming for you to commit actions against the *dharma*, the *Veda* and nature. O son of Kuntī, how can you have such an idea? **[27-28]**

युधिष्ठिर उवाच -

सूक्ष्मो धर्मो महाराज नास्य विद्मो वयं गतिम् ।
पूर्वेषामानुपुर्व्येण यातं वर्त्मानुयामहे ॥ २९ ॥

न मे वागनृतं प्राह नाधर्मे धीयते मतिः ।
एवमेव वदत्यम्बा मम चैतन्मनोगतम् ॥ ३० ॥

एष धर्मो ध्रुवो राजंश्चरैनमविचारयन् ।
मा च शङ्का तत्र ते स्यात् कथञ्चिदपि पार्थिव ॥ ३१ ॥

Yudhiṣṭhira said —

O King, we don't know the essence of *dharma*, we only follow that path that the previous generations have followed which is inspired by the dictum — "the order of the mother is the form of the protector." I don't lie, nor does my mind go in the direction of *adharma*. I am repeating what my mother said. This is truely the *dharma*, you should not have any doubt about it. **[29-31]**

द्रुपद उवाच -

त्वं च कुन्ती च कौन्तेय धृष्टद्युम्नश्च मे सुतः ।
कथयन्त्वितिदर्त्तव्यं श्वः काले करवामहे ॥ ३ ॥

King Drupada said —

Whatever conclusion you, Kuntī and Dhṛṣṭdyumna will reach, that I will do tomorrow.

॥ *इति श्री कां० मा० द्रुपदयुधिष्ठिरसम्वादो नामः द्वाविंशोऽध्यायः* ॥

Here ends the twenty-second chapter of the Kāmpilyamahātmya, the dialogue between Drupada and Yudhiṣṭhira

23

Vyāsa Arrives at King Drupada's Court

वैशम्पायन उवाच -

ते समेत्व ततः सर्वे कथयन्तिस्म भारत ।
अथ द्वैपायनो राजन्नभ्यागच्छद्यदृच्छया ॥ १ ॥

ततस्ते पाण्डवाः सर्वे पाञ्चाल्यश्च महायशाः ।
प्रत्युत्थाय महात्मानं कृष्णं सर्वेभ्यवादयन् ॥ २ ॥

प्रतिनन्द्य स ता पूजां पृष्टवा कुशलमन्ततः ।
आसने कांचने शुद्धे निषसाद महामनाः ॥ ३ ॥

अनुज्ञातास्तु ते सर्वे व्यासेनामिततेजसा ।
आसनेषु महार्हेषु निषेनुर्द्विपदांवराः ॥ ४ ॥

ततो मुहूर्त्तान्मधुरां वाणीमुच्चार्य पार्षतः ।
पप्रच्छ तं महात्मानं द्रौपद्यर्थं विशाम्पते ॥ ५ ॥

कथमेका वहूना स्याद्धर्मपत्नी न सङ्करः ।
एतन्मे भगवान् सर्वं प्रब्रवीतु यथातथम् ॥ ६ ॥

Vaiśampāyana said —

While they were talking in such a way, unexpectedly Vyāsajī arrived there. King Drupada and all the Pāṇḍavas rose to touch his feet. Vyāsajī accepted their homage and inquiring after their health he went to sit on a golden seat. Then the others with his permission sat down in very rich seats. After sometime Drupada asked Vyāsajī with sweet words what to do about the marriage: "O *muni*, according to *dharma* can there be a wife for many men, or is it a mere sin? Please tell us." **[1-6]**

व्यास उवाच -

अस्मिन् धर्मे विप्रलब्धे लोकवेदविरोधके ।
यस्य यस्य मतं यद्यच्छ्रोतुमिच्छामि तस्यतत् ॥ ७ ॥

Vyāsajī said —

It is very difficult to find a description of such a marriage in the *dharmaśāstra*, because of its being unnatural and against the *Veda*. First you express your opinion about this. **[7]**

द्रुपद उवाच -

अधर्मोयं मम मतो विरुद्धो लोकवेदयोः ।
नह्येका विद्यते पत्नी बहूनां द्विजसत्तम ॥ ८ ॥

न चाप्याचरितः पूर्वैरयं धर्मो महात्मभिः ।
न चाप्यधर्मो विद्वद्भिश्चरितव्यः कथञ्चन ॥ ९ ॥

ततोहं न करोम्येनं व्यवसायं क्रियां प्रति ।
धर्मः सदैव संदिग्धः प्रतिभाति हि मे त्वयम् ॥ १० ॥

King Drupada said —

O sage, as you say, as it is unnatural and against the *Veda* I think that this belongs to *adharma*. It has never happened that many men have had the same woman. There has never been a noble man before, who did such a thing; so also now it should not be done. I have many doubts about this and I cannot make a decision. **[8-10]**

धृष्टद्युम्न उवाच -

यवीयसः कथं भार्यां ज्येष्ठो भ्राता द्विजर्षभ ।
ब्रह्मन् समभिवर्तेत सद्वृत्तः संस्तपोधन ॥ ११ ॥

न तु धर्मस्य सूक्ष्मत्वाद्गतिं विद्मः कथञ्चन ।
अधर्मो धर्म इतिवा व्यवसायो न शक्यते ॥ १२ ॥

कर्तुमस्मद्विधैर्ब्रह्मंस्ततोयं न व्यवस्यते ।
पंचाना महिषी कृष्णा भवत्विति कथञ्चन ॥ १३ ॥

Dhṛṣṭdyumna said —

I am the little brother of the spouse. How can I say anything? I don't know the subtle way of the *dharma*, so I cannot judge if this is against the *dharma* or not. I cannot say if Draupadī can be the wife of five brothers. **[11-13]**

युधिष्ठिर उवाच -

न में वागनृतं प्राह नाधर्मे धीयते मतिः ।
वर्तते हि मनोमेऽत्र नैषोऽधर्मः कथञ्चन ॥ १४ ॥

श्रूयते हि पुरा विप्र जटिला नाम गौतमी ।
ऋषीनध्यासितवती सप्त धर्मभृताम्बरा ॥ १५ ॥

तथैव मुनिजावार्क्षी तपोभिर्भावितात्मनः ।
सङ्गताभूद्दश भ्रात्न्नेकनाम्नः प्रचेतसः ॥ १६ ॥

गुरोर्हि वचनं प्राहुर्द्धर्म्यं धर्मज्ञसत्तमाः ।
गुरूणां चैव सर्वेषां माता परमको गुरुः ॥ १७ ॥

सा चाप्युक्तवती वाचं भेक्ष्यवद् भुज्यतामिति ।
तस्मादेतदहं मन्ये परं धर्मं द्विजोत्तम् ॥ १८ ॥

Yudhiṣṭhira said —

O 'twice-born', I never speak falsely and my mind never falls into *adharma*. But now my mind itself accepts the idea of Draupadī as the wife of us five. So this is not against the *dharma*.

Moreover in the *Purāṇa* there is the description of the wife of seven *ṛṣi*, named Jaṭilā Gautamī. There is also the story of the *muni* Kaṇḍu and the *apsarā* Pramlocā who had a daughter, Vārkṣī (Māriṣā), who married the ten Pracetas.[16]

---

16. They were the 10 sons of Prācīna-barhis by a daughter of Varuṇa, progenitor of Dakṣa.

Furthermore it is considered according to the *dharma* to follow the order of the *guru*. And we know that amongst the *gurus* mother is pre-eminent. Thus my mother has said that we should share Draupadī as a *bhikṣā*. For these reasons I believe that this marriage is really according to the *dharma*. **[14-18]**

कुन्त्युवाच -

एवमेतद्यथा प्राह धर्मचारी युधिष्ठिरः ।
अन्नृतान्मे भयं तीव्रं मुच्येऽहमनृतात् कथम् ॥ १९ ॥

Kuntī said —

Yudhiṣṭhira is speaking the truth. I am afraid of falsity and I will not lose this attitude now. **[19]**

व्यास उवाच -

अनृतान्मोक्ष्यसे भद्रे धर्मश्चैष सनातनः ।
ननु वक्ष्यामि सर्वेषां पाञ्चाल शृणु मे स्वयम् ॥ २० ॥
यथाऽ यं विंहितो धर्मो यतश्चायं सनातनः ।
यथा च प्राह कौन्तेयस्तथा धर्मो न संशयः ॥ २१ ॥

Vyāsajī said —

O noble one, to avoid doing falsity is an old rule of the *dharma*. O Drupada, listen. What Yudhiṣṭhira has just said belongs to *sanātana dharma*, there is no doubt about it. Listen also to the reasons why. **[20-21]**

वैशम्पायन उवाच -

तत उत्थाय भगवान व्यासो द्वैपायनः प्रभुः ।
करे गृहीत्वा द्रुपद राजवेश्म समाविशत् ॥ २२ ॥
पाण्डवाश्चापि कुन्ती च धृष्टद्युम्नश्च पार्षतः ।
विविशुर्यत्र तत्रैव प्रतीक्षन्ते स्म तावुभो ॥ २३ ॥
ततो दैवपायनस्तस्मै नरेन्द्राय महात्मने ।
आचख्यौ तद्यथा धर्मो बहूनामेकपत्निता ॥ २४ ॥

Vaiśampāyana said —

Then Vyāsajī rose from there and taking Drupada by the hand entered the royal palace. The Pāṇḍavas, Kuntī, and also Dhṛṣṭadyumna followed them to hear what the sage was going to say. There Vyāsajī told Drupada a precedent by which Draupadī had to become the wife of the five Pāṇḍavas. **[22-24]**

॥ *इति श्री कां० मा० व्यासागमनं नाम त्रयोविंशोऽध्यायः* ॥

Here ends the twenty-third chapter of the Kāmpilyamahātmya.

24

The Story of the Five Indras, Pūrvendrā

व्यास उवाच -

पुरा वै नैमिषारण्ये देवाः सत्रमुपासते ।
तत्र वेवस्वतो राजन् शामित्रमकरोत् तदा ॥ १ ॥

ततो यमो दीक्षितस्तत्र राजन् नामारयत् कंचिदपि प्रजानाम् ।
ततः प्रजास्ता बहुला बभूवः कालाति पातान्मरणप्रहीणाः ॥ २ ॥

सोमश्च शक्रो वरुणः कुबेरः साध्या रुद्रा वसवोऽथाश्विनौ च ।
प्रतापतिर्भुवनस्य प्रणेता समाजग्मुस्तत्र देवास्तथाऽन्ये ॥ ३ ॥

ततो ब्रवन लोकगुरुं समेता भयात् तीव्रान्मानुषाणां प्रवृद्धया ।
तस्माद्भयादुद्विजन्तः सुखेप्सवः प्रयाम सर्वे शरणं भवन्तम् ॥ ४ ॥

Vyāsajī said —

O King, before the *devatā*s were in the Naimiṣāraṇya performing *yajña*. There Yamarāja slaughtered all the animals appropriate for the sacrifice. Yamarāja did not accept any other life as *dīkṣā* for the sacrifice. As Death was absent from the earth the number of creatures grew to too many. Then Candramā, Indra, Varuṇa, Kubera, all the Sādhyas, all the Rudras, all the Vasus, both of the Aśvinikumāras, and other *devatā*s went to Brahmājī. They said to him: "The number of men has grown too much and we are afraid; we are worried and we have come to get your protection." **[1-4]**

ब्रह्मोवाच -

वेवस्वतो व्यापृतः सत्रहेतोस्तेन त्विमे न म्रियन्ते मनुष्याः ।
तस्मिन्नैकाग्रे कृतसर्वकार्ये तत् एषां भवितैवान्तकालः ॥ ५ ॥

वैवस्वतस्यैव तनुर्विभक्ता वीर्येण युष्माकमुत प्रवृद्धा ।
सेषामन्तो भविता ह्यन्तकालो न तत्र वार्यं भविता नरेषु ॥ ६ ॥

Brahmājī said —

Yamarāja is engaged in killing animals for the sacrifice: this is the reason why he doesn't kill anyone anymore. When the sacrifice is completed it will be the end for mankind. Another form of Yamarāja, created by your power, will destroy mankind. **[5-6]**

व्यास उवाच -

ततस्तु ते पूर्वजदेववाक्यं श्रुत्त्वा जग्भुर्यत्र देवा यजन्ते ।
समासीनास्ते समेता महाबला भागीरथ्यां दद्दशुः पुण्डरीकम् ॥ ७ ॥

द्रष्ट्वा च तद्विस्मितास्ते वभूवुस्तेषामिन्द्रस्तत्र शूरो जगाम ।
सोऽपश्यद्योषामथ पावकप्रभां यत्र देवा गङ्गा सततं प्रसूता ॥ ८ ॥

सा तत्र योषा रुदती जलार्थिनी गङ्गां देवी व्यवगाह्य व्यतिष्ठत् ।
तस्याश्रुविन्दुः पतितो जले यस्तत् पद्ममासीदथ तत्र काञ्चनम् ॥ ९ ॥

तदद्भुतं प्रेक्ष्य वज्री तदानीमपृच्छत् तां योषितमन्तिकाद्वै ।
का त्वं भद्रे रोदिषि कस्य हेतोर्वाक्यं तथ्यं कामयेऽहंब्रवीहि ॥ १० ॥

Vyāsajī said —

After listening to Brahmājī the *devatā*s went to the place mentioned above. On the road they sat on the banks of the Gaṅgā. There they saw a lotus flower in the water. They looked at it with wonder. Then Indra tried to catch it, but when he got near to it he saw a woman luminous like the fire, the goddess of fortune, Svargaśrī. She had come there to take some water and she was standing in the middle of the river crying. Her tears were falling into the river, but when they touched the water, were becoming golden lotuses.

Seeing this wonder, Indra approached her and asked: "Who are you, O noble woman? And why are you crying? Tell me the truth." **[7-10]**

स्त्र्युवाच -

त्वं वेत्स्यसे मामिह यास्मि शक्र यदर्थं चाहं रोदिमि मन्दभाग्या ।
आगच्छ राजन् पुरतो गमिष्ये द्रक्ष्यसि तद् रोदिमि यत्कृतेऽहम् ॥ ११ ॥

The Woman said —

O Indra, come near: see who I am and why I am crying. **[11]**

व्यास उवाच -

तां गच्छन्तीमन्वगच्छत् तदानीं सोपश्यदारात् तरुणं दर्शनीयम् ।
सिद्धासनस्थं युवतीसहायं क्रीडन्तमक्षैर्गिरिराज मूर्ध्नि ॥ १२ ॥

तमब्रवीद्देवराजो ममेदं त्वं विद्धि विद्वन् भुवनं वशे स्थितम ।
ईशोहमस्मीति समन्युरब्रवीद्दृष्ट्वा तमक्षैः सुभृशं प्रमत्तम् ॥ १३ ॥

क्रुद्धं च शक्रं प्रसमीक्ष्य देवो जहास शक्रं स शनैरुदैक्षत ।
संस्तम्भितोभूदथ देवराजस्तेनेक्षितः स्थाणुरिवावतस्थे ॥ १४ ॥

यदा तु पर्याप्तमिहास्य क्रीडया तदा देवीं रुदतीं तामुवाच ।
आनीयतामेष यतोहमारान्नैनँ दर्पः पुनरप्याविशेत ॥ १५ ॥

ततः शक्रः स्पृष्ट मात्रस्तया तु स्रस्तैरङ्गैः पतितोभूद् धरण्याम् ।
तमब्रवीद्भगवानुग्रतेजा मैवं पुनः शक्र कृथाः कथञ्चित् ॥ १६ ॥

निवर्त्तयैनं च महाद्रिराजं बलं च वीर्यं च तवाप्रमेयम् ।
छिद्रस्य चैवाविशमध्यमस्य यत्रासतेत्वद्विधाः सूर्यभासः ॥ १७ ॥

स तद्विवृत्य विवरं महागिरेस्तुल्यद्युतींश्चतुरोन्यान् ददर्श ।
स तानभिप्रेक्ष्य बभूव दुःखितः कच्चिन्नाहं भविता वै यथेमे ॥ १८ ॥

ततो देवो गिरिशो बज्रपाणिं विवृत्य नेत्रे कुपितो भ्युवाच ।
दरीमेतां प्रविश त्वं शतक्रतो यन्मां बाल्यादवमंस्थाः पुरस्तात् ॥ १९ ॥

उक्तस्त्वेवं विभुना देवराजः प्रावेपतार्तो भृशमेवाभिषङ्गात् ।
स्त्रस्तैरङ्गैरनिलेनेव नुन्नमश्वत्थपत्रं गिरिराजमूर्ध्नि ॥ २० ॥

स प्राञ्जलिर्वै वृषवाहनेन प्रवेपमानः सहसैवमुक्त ।
उवाच देवं बहुरूपमुग्रमद्याशेषस्य भुवनस्य त्वमाद्यः ॥ २१ ॥

तमब्रवीदुग्रवर्चाः प्रहस्य नैवंशीलाः शेषमिहाप्नुवन्ति ।
एतेप्येवं भवितारः पुरस्तात् तस्मादेता दरीमाविश्य शेष्व ॥ २२ ॥

तत्र ह्येवं भवितारो न संशयो योनिं सर्वे मानुषीमाविशध्वम् ।
तत्र यूयं कर्म कृत्वाऽविषह्यं बहूनन्यान् निधनं प्रापयित्वा ॥ २३ ॥

आगन्तारः पुनरेवेन्द्रलोकं स्वकर्मणा पूर्वजितं महार्हम् ।
सर्वं मया भाषितमेतदेवं कर्तव्यमन्यद्विविधार्थयुक्तम् ॥ २४ ॥

Vyāsajī said —

Then Indra followed the woman to the peak of a mountain where a young form of Śivajī was sitting in *siddhāsana* and was playing with a young form of 'Pārvatī'. On seeing this Indra became angry and said to them: "I am the lord of the world and everything is subject to me (how dare you act like that in front of me?)." Śivajī laughed and slowly turned his eyes towards him. Indra stood firmly in front of him.

When Śivajī finished playing, he called the crying woman and reassured her. He asked her to bring Indra to him so that he would not be so arrogant the next time. When Indra was touched by the woman his whole body became infirm and he fell to the ground. Śivajī told Indra not to dare to behave like that anymore. "You are very valiant, — Śivajī said — now you must go inside that cave in the mountain: there you will find four Indras identical to you." Then Indra went into the cave and there he found four people identical to him. He did not enter and wanted to go somewhere else. But Śivajī became enraged and opening his eyes said to Indra: "You have disrespected me, so now you also go inside the cave." Fearing a curse, Indra started to tremble as the leaves of a *pīpal* tree on the top of a mountain would tremble in a strong wind. Indra folded his hands and admitted the supremacy of Śiva. Śiva said: "But you must stay inside the cave with the four Indras for some time. Then you five will become men. After performing very difficult tasks and fighting with many people you will come again in *svarga*." You must do what I have just said. **[12-24]**

पूर्वेन्द्रा ऊचुः -

गमिष्यामी मानुषं देवलोकाद्दुराधरो विहितो यत्र मोक्षः ।
देवानस्मानादधीरन् जनन्यां धर्मो वायुर्मघवानश्विनौ च ॥ २५ ॥

Pūrvendra (the previous Indras) said —

We shall all go from the *devaloka* to the *manuṣyaloka* from where it is hard to be released, but our birth will be possible through the god Dharma, the god Pavana (the air), Indra and the Aśvinīkumāras. **[25]**

व्यास उवाच -

एतच्छ्रुत्वा वज्रपाणिर्वचस्तु देवश्रेस्ठं पुनरेवेदमाह ।
वीर्येणाहं पुरुषं कार्यहेतोर्दद्यामेषां पञ्चमं मत्प्रसूतम् ॥ २६ ॥

तेषा कामं भगवानुग्रधन्वा प्रादादिष्टं संनिसर्गाद् यथोक्तम् ।
तां चाप्येषां योषितं लोककान्तां श्रियं भार्यां व्यदधान्मानुषेषु ॥ २७ ॥

तैरेवसार्द्धं तु ततः स देवो जगाम नारायणमादिदेवम् ।
अनन्तमव्यक्तमजं पुराणं सनातनं विश्वमनन्तरूपम् ॥ २८ ॥

स चापि तद्व्यदधात् सर्वमेव ततः सर्वे संवमूबुर्द्धरण्याम् ।
ये ते पूर्वं शक्ररूपा निवद्धास्तस्यां दर्यां पर्वतस्योत्तरस्य ॥ २९ ॥

इहैवते पाण्डवा वीर्यवन्तः शक्रस्यांशः पाण्डवः सव्यसाची ।
एवमेते पाण्डवाः संवभूबुर्ये ते राजन् पूर्वमिन्द्रा वभूवुः ॥ ३० ॥

अस्त्रैर्दिव्यैर्मानुषान् योधयित्वा संगन्तारः पुनरेवेन्द्रलोकम् ।
लक्ष्मीश्चैषा पूर्वमेवीपदिष्टा भार्या यैषां द्रौपदी दिव्यरूपा ॥ ३१ ॥

कथं हि स्त्री कर्मणा ते महीतलात् समुत्तिष्ठेदन्यतो दैवयोगात् ।
यस्या रूपं सोमसूर्यप्रकाशं गन्धश्चास्या क्रोशमात्रात् प्रवाति ॥ ३२ ॥

इदं चान्यत् प्रीतिपूर्वं नरेन्द्र ददामि ते वरमत्यद्भुतं च ।
दिव्यं चक्षुः पश्य कुन्तीसुतांस्त्वं पुण्यैर्दिव्यैः पूर्वदेहै रुपेतान् ॥ ३३ ॥

Vyāsajī said (addressing Drupada) —

Indra heard the speech of the four in the cave and said to Mahādeva: "These four will become men and by my seed a man will be born." Śiva granted Indra this boon. Then Śiva ordered that Svargaśrī (the crying woman) should be their wife, and all together they went to Nārāyaṇa, the primeval god. There he confirmed the same things said by Śiva.

O King, then the four in the cave became the four Pāṇḍavas and from a part of the lord of heaven, Indra, Arjuna was produced. In this way the five Indras became the five Pāṇḍavas. They would defeat the men with the *divyāstra* and then reach heaven again. And Svargaśrī is their wife, Draupadī, from before. O King, how can a normal woman appear from the soil without divine intervention? No one has the shape shining like the sun and the moon, whose scent carries for one *kosa*. O king, I give you another marvellous gift. Now see through the *divya-dṛṣṭi* (the divine faculty of vision) these Pāṇḍavas as they were the five Indras. **[26-33]**

वैशम्पायन उवाच -

ततो व्यासः परमोदारकर्मा शुचिर्विप्रस्तपसा तस्य राज्ञः ।
चक्षुर्दिव्यं प्रददौ तांश्च सर्वान् राजाऽपश्यत् पूर्वदेहैर्यथावत् ॥ ३४ ॥

ततो दिव्यान् हेमकिरीटमालिनः शक्रप्रख्यान् पावकादित्यवर्णान् ।
वद्धापीडांश्चचारुरूपांश्च यूतो व्यूढोरस्कांस्तालमात्रान् ददर्श ॥ ३५ ॥

दिव्यैर्वस्त्रैररजोभिः सुगन्धैर्माल्यैश्चोग्र्यैःशोभमाना नतीव ।
साक्षात् त्र्यक्षान् वा वसूंश्चापि रुद्रानादित्यान् वा सर्वगुणोपपन्नान् ॥ ३६ ॥

तान् पूर्वेन्द्रानभिवीक्ष्याभिरूपान् शक्रात्मजं चेन्द्ररूपं निरीक्ष्य ।
प्रीती राजा द्रुपदो विस्मितश्च दिव्यां मायां तामवेक्ष्याप्रमेयाम् ॥ ३७ ॥

तां चैवाग्रयां स्त्रियमतिरूपयुक्तां दिव्यां साक्षात् सीमवन्हि प्रकाशाम् ।
योग्यां तेषां रूपतेजोयशोभिः पत्नीं मत्वा हृष्टवान पार्थिवेन्द्रः ॥ ३८ ॥

स तद् दृष्ट्वा महदाश्चर्यरूपं जग्राह पादौ सत्यवत्याः सुतस्य ।
नैतच्चित्रं परमर्षेत्वयीति प्रसन्नचेताः स उवाच चैनम् ॥ ३९ ॥

Vaiśampāyana said —

Then Vyāsajī gave to Drupada the *divya-dṛṣṭi* so that he could see the five brothers in the form of five Indras. In that form they were wearing golden crowns and garlands; they had the splendour of Agni and Sūrya, with wide chests; they looked very young and very tall. Wearing *divya-vastra* (divine clothes) and adorned with garlands of fragrant flowers, they appeared like a tangible Mahādeva or the Vasus, the Rudras or the Ādityas. Seeing the four Indras and as the fifth Indra himself, King Drupada became very happy and full of wonder. And considering Draupadī, now in the form of Svargalakṣmī as the right wife for them, he became very content. In front of such a prodigy he fell at the feet of Vyāsajī and said: "O *maharṣi*, among the *muni*s nothing is a surprise for you." **[34-39]**

॥ *इति श्री कां० मा० पञ्चेन्द्रोपाख्यानं नाम चतुर्विंशोऽध्यायः* ॥

Here ends the twenty-fourth chapter of the Kāmpilyamahātmya.

25

The Precedent of How Draupadī Came to Get Five Husbands

व्यास उवाच -

आसीत् तपोवने काचिद्दृषेः कन्या महात्मनः ।
विलग्नमध्या सुश्रोणी सुभ्रूः सर्व गुणान्विता ॥ १ ॥

कर्मभिः स्वकृतैः सा तु दुर्भगा समपद्यत ।
नाध्यगच्छत् पतिं सा तु कन्या रूपवती सती ॥ २ ॥

तपस्तप्तुमथारेभे पत्यर्थमसुखा ततः ।
तोषयामास तपसा सा किलोग्रेण शङ्करम् ॥ ३ ॥

तस्याः स भगवांस्तुष्टस्तामुवाच यशस्विनीम् ।
वरं वरय भद्रं ते वरदोस्मीति शङ्करः ॥ ४ ॥

सैवमुक्ताऽब्रवीत् कन्या देवं वरदमीश्वरम् ।
पतिं सर्वगुणोपेतमिच्छामीति पुनःपुनः ॥ ५ ॥

तामथ प्रत्युवाचेदमीशानो वदतांवरः ।
पञ्च ते पतयो भद्रे भविष्यन्ति न संशयः ॥ ६ ॥

विश्वभुग् भूतधामा च शिविरिन्द्रः प्रतापवान् ।
शान्तिश्चतुर्थस्तेषां वै तेजस्वी पञ्चमः स्मृतः ॥ ७ ॥

एवमुक्ता ततः कन्या देवं वरदमऽब्रवीत् ।
एकमिच्छाम्यहं देवत्त्वत्प्रसादात् पति प्रभो ॥ ८ ॥

पुनरेवाब्रवीद् देव इदं वचनमुत्तमम् ।
पञ्चकृत्वस्त्वयोक्तोहं पतिं देहीति वै यतः ॥ ९ ॥

तत् तथा भविता भद्रे वचस्तद् भद्रमस्तु ते ।
देहमन्यं गतायाश्च सर्वमेतद् भविष्यति ॥ १० ॥

Vyāsajī said —

Once upon a time, in a forest a *ṛṣi* had a daughter. She was beautiful and endowed with good qualities. Unfortunately she could not find a husband. So she undertook very hard asceticism in order to get a husband. Śiva was pleased by her attitude and so he asked her: "O noble woman, ask for a boon!" Then she repeated five times the wish to have a husband complete with all the virtues. Then Śiva said: "You will have five husbands respectively named Viśvabhuka, Bhūtadhāmā, Śivi, Śānti and Tejasvī. She answered that she wanted just one husband and how could she manage with five. Śiva said that she had said five times *patidehi*, give me a husband, so it would certainly happen. **[1-10]**

व्यास उवाच -

सैषा देवी रुचिरा देवाजुष्टा पञ्चानामेका स्वकृतेनेह कर्मणा ।
सृष्टा स्वयं देवपत्नी स्वयम्भुवा श्रुत्वा राजन् द्रुपदेष्टं कुरुष्व ॥ ११ ॥

Vyāsajī said —

O king, that Devī, Svargalākṣmī, is this Draupadī. She was produced by Brahmājī to be in another life the wife of the five Indras and in this life the wife of the Pāṇḍavas. Now decide to do what you will. **[11]**

॥ इति श्री का० मा० मुनिकन्योपाख्यानं नाम पञ्चविंशोऽध्यायः ॥
Here ends the twenty-fifth chapter of the Kāmpilyamahātmya.

26

Draupadī Marries the Five Pāṇḍavas

द्रुपद उवाच -

अश्रुत्वैवं वचनं ते महर्षे मया पूर्वंयतितं संविधातुम्।
न वै शक्यं विहितस्यापयानं तदेवेदमुपषन्नं विधानम्॥ १॥

दिष्टस्य ग्रन्थिरनिवर्त्तनीयः स्वकर्मणा विहितं नेह किञ्चित्।
कृतं निमित्तं हि वरैकहेतोस्तदेवेदभुपयन्नं विधानम्॥ २॥

यथैव कृष्णोक्तवती पुरस्तान्नैकान् पतीन् मे भगवान् ददातु।
स चाप्येव वरमित्यब्रवीत् तां देवो हि वेत्ता परमं यदत्र॥ ३॥

यथा चैवं विहितः शङ्करेण धर्मोऽधर्मो वा नात्र ममापराधः।
गृह्णन्त्विमे विधिवत् पाणिमस्या यथोपजोषं विहितैषां हि पत्नी॥ ४॥

Drupada said —

O sage, even without hearing your speech I had already realised that the disposition produced by the *deva* cannot be withdrawn. The nuptial knots written in the book of Time cannot be untied. My personal decision could not change anything. I was looking for one husband for my daughter and I got five. Only Śiva knows the secret beyond the five-fold request previously made by the daughter of the sage to get a husband and the equivalent boon granted by Śiva. I cannot find any fault with what Śiva does, may it be *dharma* or *adharma*. I will give the five Pāṇḍavas my daughter in marriage. **[1-4]**

वैशम्पायन उवाच -

ततोऽब्रवीत् स मुनिर्द्धर्मराजमद्यैव पुण्याहमुत पाण्डवेय।

अद्य पौष्ययोगमुपैति चन्द्रमाः पाणिं कृष्णायास्त्वं गृहाणाद्य पूर्वम् ॥ ५ ॥

ततो राजा यज्ञसेनःसपुत्रो जन्यार्थमुक्तं बहु तत्तदग्र्यम् ।
समानयामास सुतां च कृष्णामाप्लाव्य रत्नैर्बहुभिर्विभूष्य ॥ ६ ॥

ततस्तु सर्वे सुहृदो नृपस्य समाजग्मुः सहिता मन्त्रिणश्च ।
द्रष्टुं विवाहं परम प्रतीता द्विजाश्च पौराश्च यथा प्रधानाः ॥ ७ ॥

ततोस्य वेश्माग्र्यजनोपशोभितं विस्तीर्णपद्मोत्पलभूषिताजिरम् ।
बलौघरत्नौघविचित्रमावभौ नभो यथा निर्मलतारकावृतम् ॥ ८ ॥

ततस्तु ते कौरवराजपुत्रा विभूषिताः कुण्डलिनो युवानः ।
महार्हवस्त्रा वरचन्दनोक्षिताः कृताभिषेकाः कृतमङ्गलक्रियाः ॥ ९ ॥

पुरोहितेनाग्निसमानवर्चसा सहैव धौम्येन यथाविधि प्रभो ।
क्रमेण सर्वे विविशुस्ततः सदा महर्षभा गोष्ठमिवाभिनन्दिनः ॥ १० ॥

ततः समाधाय स वेदपारगो जुहाव मन्त्रैर्ज्वलितं हुताशनम् ।
युधिष्ठिरं चाप्युपनीय मन्त्रवन्नियोजयामास सहैव कृष्णया ॥ ११ ॥

प्रदक्षिणं तौ प्रगृहीतपाणी परिणाय्ययामास स वेदपारगः ।
ततोभ्यनुज्ञायतमाजिशोभितं पुरोहितो राजगृहाद्विनिर्ययौ ॥ १२ ॥

क्रमेण चानेन नराधिपात्मजा वरस्त्रियास्ते जगृहुस्तदा करम् ।
अहन्यहन्युत्तमरूपधारिणो महारथाः कौरववंशवर्द्धनाः ॥ १३ ॥

इदं च तत्राद्भुतरूपमुत्तमं जगाद देवर्षिरतीतमानुषम् ।
महानुभावा किल सा सुमध्यमा वभूव कन्यैव गतेगतेऽहनि ॥ १४ ॥

कृते विवाहे द्रुपदो धनं ददौ महारथेभ्यो बहुरूपमुत्तमम् ।
शतं रथानां वरहेममालिनां चतुर्युजां हेमखलीनमालिनाम् ॥ १५ ॥

शतं गजानामपि हेममालिनां शतं गिरीणामिव हेमशृङ्गिणाम् ।
तथैव दासीशतमग्र्ययौवनं महार्हवेषाभरणाम्बरस्रजम् ॥ १६ ॥

पृथक् पृथग दिव्यदृशां पुनददौ तदा धनं सौमकिरग्निसाक्षिकम् ।
तथैव वस्त्राणि विभूषणानि प्रभावयुक्तानि महानुभावः ॥ १७ ॥

कृते विवाहे च ततस्तु पाण्डवाः प्रभूतरत्नामुपलभ्य तां श्रियम् ।
विजह्रु रिन्द्रप्रतिमा महाबलाः पुरे तु पाञ्चालनृपस्य तस्य ह ॥ १८ ॥

Vaiśampāyana said —

Then Vyāsajī said to Yudhiṣṭhira: "Today is an auspicious

day. The moon is in the *nakṣatra* of the constellation of Puṣya, marry Draupadī today."[17]

Then Drupada gave as dowry to the five husbands all the things that had been assembled there. Draupadī was bathed and adorned with beautiful clothes and jewels.

The *mitra mantrī* (the counsellor) of King Drupada and the inhabitants of the town gathered there to see the wedding. On that occasion the royal palace filled with important men, decorated with flowers, gold and precious stones, illuminated by thousands of stars and seemed embellished by the sky itself. The young Pāṇḍavas, after taking a bath, applied sandalwood paste and put on earrings and rich clothes. Then accompanied by their *purohita* Dhaumya they entered the *maṇḍapa* where the wedding was to be celebrated with the same gait of five bulls entering a cattle pen. There the sage Dhaumya reciting the proper *mantra*s performed a *havana*. Then he tied the clothes of Draupadī to that of Yudhiṣṭhira and the two, hand in hand, made the ritual *pradakṣiṇā*. After that Dhaumya took leave of them and went home. In the same way everyday each one of the Pāṇḍavas was married to her. O King, Nārada was present there to see the wonder of a young girl getting married everyday. King Drupada gave to each of them gold necklaces as a dowry, hundreds of chariots drawn by quadrille of horses with golden reins, hundreds of big elephants with golden garments and the same number of young servants finely dressed. Then the right offerings were made to the witnessing sacrificial fire. After receiving this great wealth, the Pāṇḍavas started to live happily in Kāmpilya. **[5-18]**

॥ इति श्री का० मा० द्रौपदीविवाहोनाम षड्विंशोऽध्यायः॥

Here ends the twenty-sixth chapter of the Kāmpilyamahātmya.

17. Even though in this *nakṣatra* it is prohibited to celebrate any marriage, by the order of such an important man as Vyāsa it was acceptable.

27

Kuntī Blesses Draupadī After the Wedding

वैशम्पायन उवाच -

पाण्डवैः सह संयोगं गतस्य द्रुपदस्य ह ।
न वभूव भयं किञ्चिद् देवेभ्योपि कथंचन ॥ १ ॥

कुन्तीमासाद्य ता नार्यो द्रुपदस्य महात्मनः ।
नाम सङ्कीर्त्तयन्त्योऽस्या जग्मुः पादौ स्वभूर्द्धभिः ॥ २ ॥

कृष्णा च क्षौमसम्वीता कृतकौतुकभङ्गला ।
कृताभिवादना श्वश्वास्तस्थौ प्रह्वा कृताञ्जलिः ॥ ३ ॥

रूपलक्षणसम्पन्नां शीलाचारसमन्विताम् ।
द्रोपदीमवदत् प्रेम्णा पृथाऽऽ शीर्वचनं स्नुषाम् ॥ ४ ॥

यथेन्द्राणी हरिहये स्वाहा चैव विभावसौ ।
रोहिणी च यथा सोमे दमयन्ती यथा नले ॥ ५ ॥

यथा वैश्रवणे भद्रा वसिष्ठेऽरुन्धती यथा ।
यथा नारायणे लक्ष्मीस्तथा त्व भव भर्तृषु ॥ ६ ॥

जीवसूर्वीरसूर्भद्रे बहुसौख्यसमन्विता ।
सुभगा भोगसम्पन्ना यज्ञपत्नी पतिव्रता ॥ ७ ॥

अतिथीनागतान् साधून वृद्धान् वालांस्तथा गुरून ।
पूजयन्त्या यथान्यायं शश्वद्गच्छन्तु ते समाः ॥ ८ ॥

कुरूजाङ्गलमुख्येषु राष्ट्रेषुनगरेषु च ।
अनु त्वमभिषिच्यस्व नृपतिं धर्मवत्सला ॥ ९ ॥

पतिभिर्निर्जितामुर्वी विक्रमेण महा बलैः ।
कुरू ब्राह्मणसात् सर्वामश्वमेधे महाक्रतौ ॥ १० ॥

पृथिव्यां यानि रत्नानि गुणवन्ति गुणान्विते ।
तान्याप्नुहि त्वं कल्याणि सुखिनी शरदां शतम ॥ ११ ॥
तथा च त्वाऽभिनन्दामि वध्वऽद्य क्षौमसम्वृताम् ।
तथा भूयोऽभिनन्दामि जातपुत्रां गुणान्विताम् ॥ १२ ॥

Vaiśampāyana said —

As he was closely related to the Pāṇḍavas, King Drupada became fearless of every kind of being, including *devatās*.

His queens introduced themselves; each repeating their name they went to Kuntī and bowed their heads to her feet. And also Draupadī, well-dressed with the proper wedding clothes, *kṣauma* (linen), with many ornaments, touched the feet of her mother-in-law and stood with her hands folded in front of her. Then Kuntījī endowed with beauty, virtue and straight-forward behaviour gave her blessings to her daughter-in-law: "O noble woman, may you be a faithful wife to your husbands as Indrāṇī was to Indra, Svāhā to Agni, Rohiṇī to Candramā, Damayantī to Nala, Bhadrā to Kubera, Arunadhatī to Vasiṣṭha, and Lakṣmī to Nārāyaṇa. May your sons be blessed with a long life and be valiant. May you be happy, lucky and become the sacrifical fire; may your husbands perform their *yajña.* May you spend many years serving the guests, the *sādhus*, the old and the young, the *guru.* Now that you are the queen of the *mahārāja* of the country of the Kurus, you should go there with your husbands to perform an *abhiṣeka.* Pay the *brāhmaṇas* to perform the *aśvamedha*, to celebrate their victory over all the earth. O Kalyāṇī, you have all the precious stones and wealth of this earth, may you live for one hundred years. As I see you now wearing the *kṣauma*, so I hope to see you with a son in your lap." **[1-12]**

वैशम्पायन उवाच -

ततस्तु कृतदारेभ्यः पाण्डुभ्यः प्राहिणोद्धरिः ।
वैदूर्यमाणिचित्राणि दिव्यान्याभरणानि च ॥ १३ ॥

वासांसि च महार्हाणि नानादेश्यानि माधवः ।
कम्वलाजिनरत्नानि स्पर्शवन्ति शुभानि च ॥ १४ ॥

शयनासनयानानि विविधानि महान्ति च ॥ ।
वैदूर्यवज्रचित्राणि शतशो भाजनानि च ॥ १५ ॥

रूपयौवनदाक्षिण्यैरुपेताश्च स्वलंकृताः ।
प्रेष्याः सम्प्रददौ कृष्णो नानादेश्या मनोहराः ॥ १६ ॥

गजान् विनीतान् भद्रांश्च सदश्वांश्च स्वलंकृतान् ।
रथांश्च दान्तान् सौवर्णान् शुभ्रैः पट्टैरलंकृतान् ॥ १७ ॥

कोटिशश्च सुवर्णं च तेषामकृतकं तथा ।
बीथीकृतममेयात्मा प्राहिणोन्मधुसूदनः ॥ १८ ॥

तत् सर्वं प्रतिजग्राह धर्मराजो युधिष्ठिरः ।
मुदा परमया युक्तो गोविन्दप्रियकाम्यया ॥ १९ ॥

Vaiśampāyana said —

During the wedding many jewels arrived, fine clothes and leather from different countries; big palanquins and different kinds of seats and beds; vehicles, bowls studded with jewels, many young beautiful servants, trained *bhadrajāti* elephants, wonderful horses, and chariots adorned with ivory. Hundred of thousands of coins and a lot of gold were offered by Śrī Kṛṣṇa. Dharmarāja accepted all that with love. **[13-19]**

ततस्ते पाण्डवाः सर्वे नारदेन प्रवोधिताः ।
समयं चक्रिरे राजन् परस्परवशंगताः ॥ २० ॥

याज्ञसेन्या सहासीनमन्योऽन्यं योऽवलोकयेत् ।
स तु द्वादश वर्षाणि ब्रह्मचारी बने बसेत् ॥ २१ ॥

मासं मासमिचं सर्वानस्मानेकैकशस्तथा ।
उपासीत प्रसूतेश्च विवेकार्थं पृथक् पृथक् ॥ २२ ॥

Then according to the teaching of Nārada, the Pāṇḍavas made a joint vow: when Draupadī is with one of them the other four will not approach, and if one approaches he will spend twelve years in the forest under a vow of chastity.

Draupadī will stay one month in turn with each one of the Pāṇḍavas, so that it will be possible to determine whose son will be. **[20-22]**

॥ *इति श्री का० मा० द्रौपदीविवाहोपसंहारो नाम सप्तविंशोऽध्यायः* ॥

Here ends the twenty-seventh chapter of the Kāmpilyamahātmya.

28

The Story of Kāleśvara Mahādeva

वैशम्पायन उवाच -

वृत्ते स्वयम्वरे राजन् निवृत्तेषु च राजसु ।
विवाहे विहिते चापि पाञ्चाल्याः पाण्डुनन्दनैः ॥ १ ॥

वसत्सु चैव काम्पिल्ये पाण्डवेषु महात्मसु ।
सस्मार द्रौपदी देवं शङ्करं लोकशङ्करम् ॥ २ ॥

ध्यायत्या हृदयात् तस्याः शिवलिंग मनोरमम् ।
प्रादुर्वभूव तद् द्रष्ट्वा साऽभवद्धर्षविह्वला ॥ ३ ॥

विचारयामास तदा स्वपितुर्भवने स्थिता ।
करिष्ये स्थापनं चास्य विधिदृष्टेन कर्मणा ॥ ४ ॥

निश्चित्यैवं स्वमनसाऽनुज्ञाप्य पितरं तथा ।
समारेभेऽथ तद्राजन् विधातुं पतिसम्मता ॥ ५ ॥

तत आहूय विप्रेन्द्रान् वेद*veda*ङ्गपारगान ।
पितुः पुरोहितं चापि धौम्यं च स्वपुरोहितम् ॥ ६ ॥

भृत्वा प्रतिष्ठासम्भारान् सर्वान् प्राथमकल्पिकान् ।
तल्लिङ्गं स्थापयामास वेदोक्तविधिना नृप ॥ ७ ॥

जन्हुजादक्षिणे तीरे काम्पिल्यादुत्तरे तथा ।
स्थापयित्वाऽथ तन्नाम चक्रे कालेश्वरं स्फुटम् ॥ ८ ॥

ततः सा द्रौपदीरूपा गिरिजा राजसत्तम ।
पुरोक्तं शम्भुना स्मृत्वा तुष्टा तुष्टाव तं नता ॥ ९ ॥

Vaiśampāyana said —

O King, on the occasion of the *svayaṁvara* the other kings came back. The Pāṇḍavas stayed for sometime at the wedding. It was then that Draupadī remembered Śiva and from her heart a *śivaliṅgam* appeared. Because of that Draupadī was very happy. She decided to install it. So with the assent of her father and of her husbands she called the *brāhmaṇa* competent in the reciting of the *Veda*s. Then she also invited the *purohita* of her father and her *purohita*, Dhaumya. The *devapratiṣṭhā*, the rite of immission of life into any statue, was performed. Using the best things fit for the sacrifice and according to the Vedic lore, the *liṅgam* was installed on the south bank of the Gaṅgā and at the northern side of Kampilapura. It became known by the name of Kāleśvara. After that the form of Pārvatī, Draupadī, started to praise Śivajī. **[1-9]**

शिव कालेश सुराधिप चन्द्रललाम। रागबिरोधविवर्जित भर्जितकाम॥
कृतकाम्पिल्लपुरान्तिकबास महेश। निर्जरनिर्झरिणीधर हर गिरिजेश॥
क्षीरसमुद्रसुतापतिपूजितपाद्। नित्य निरीह निरञ्जन बीतविवाद्॥
भालबिलोचन संसृतिमोचन देव। अन्धक सूदन शर्व सुपर्वऽपतेब॥
पर्बतनाथसुताकृतबामशरीर। निजजनबृजिनपयोवहनिवहसमीर॥
योगिजनामलमानसपङ्कजमित्र। वासवगर्बविमईक चित्रचरित्र॥
रावणवाणसमर्चितपादसरोज। प्रमथगणाथिपते भव भर्ग विभोऽज॥
दक्षप्रजापतियज्ञविनाशक रुद्र। कुरु कल्याणं करुणासुधासमुद्र॥
द्रुपदसुताऽपररूपा सैव शिवा हि। भवदनुशासननिष्ठा कृपया पाहि॥
सुचिरं भवद्विरहतः स्बिन्ना साऽथ। तदऽरं निजलोकं मां प्रापय नाथ॥

दोहा - सङ्कीत्यैवं द्रौपदी पतिता यच्चरणे हि।
दत्तकवेरपि चित्तगं देव तदेव बिंधेहि॥

The *Śivastuti* made by Draupadī; *chanda baravai*, 12-17-19.

"O Śiva, Lord of the *deva* and of the Time, the beautiful moon is on your head. You, Destroyer of Kāmadeva, are beyond love and hatred. O Maheśa, you have kindly made your residence near Kāmpilya. Hara, Lord of Girijā, who keeps on his head the river Gaṅgā. Your feet are always worshipped by the husband of the daughter of the milk ocean (Nārāyaṇa and Lakṣmī). You are everlasting, uncontaminated, desireless and above all disputes. On your forehead you have the third eye. O Lord, you are the destroyer of the worldly sins. You are the killer of Andhaka. O Sarva, you are the lord of all the festivities. You have made the left part of your body with the daughter of the Himālayas. You are like a wind that drives away the clouds of sins of your devotees. The Sun who blooms the lotus of the pure mind of the *yogīs*. Destroyer of the pride of Indra. Your behaviour is wonderful. Your lotus feet are worshipped by Rāvaṇa and Bāṇāsura. You are the lord of the *gaṇas* like Pramatha and others. Pure being, lustre, all-pervading, unborn, Rudra the destroyer of the sacrifice of Dakṣa, ocean of nectar of kindness, do good to me. The daughter of King Drupada is Pārvatī herself. She has strong faith in your discipline. Please protect her because she feels sad being separated from You for so long. So, O Lord, make me attain your *loka*.

(The poet Durgadatta also prays that Śiva, after hearing the prayer of Draupadī, who fell upon the feet of the Lord, will grant the same (Śivaloka) as Draupadī asks.)

ततः प्रसन्नः प्रत्यक्षं तामाह भगवान् भवः ।
एकोहं पञ्चधा प्रादुर्भूतोस्मि त्वत्कृते ऽनघे ॥ १० ॥

या मूर्तयः पुराणे मे पृथगाख्याः पृथग्गुणाः ।
ता एव पञ्च पाञ्चालि त्वदर्थं प्रकटीकृताः ॥ ११ ॥

ऊर्ध्वरोमा सूर्यतेजस्तुल्या चन्द्रमसः समा ।
कुबेरसद्वशी तुर्या ब्रह्मरूपा च पंचमी ॥ १२ ॥

तमेगुणाथ त्रिगुणा सात्विकी राजसी तथा ।
निर्गुणा पंचमी तत्र तां तु पशयन्ति योगिनः ॥ १३ ॥

भीमो धर्मः सहसुरो नकुलोऽथ धनञ्जयः ।
ताभ्यो यथाक्रमं जाता इत्युक्त्वाऽन्तर्हितो हरः ॥ १४ ॥

Then Śiva appeared there and spoke to Draupadī saying: "O Draupadī, just for you I have manifested myself in this five-fold shape. In my *Purāṇa*[18] there is the description of the qualities and the names of every one of my five forms. Those *mūrti* themselves are present here (in the forms of the Pāṇḍavas). Among them, from the *tāmasika mūrti* Ūrddharoma Bhīmasena has sprung. From the form of Sūrya, endowed with all three qualities, Yudhiṣṭhira. From the form of Candramā, mainly *sāttvika*, Sahadeva. Nakula appeared from the *rājasika mūrti* of Kubera. From my essence beyond qualities, *brahmarūpa nirguṇa*, Arjuna came into existence. In him you should see no more than a *yogī*."[19] So saying Śiva disappeared. **[10-14]**

---

18. *Śiva Purāṇa*.

19. In Bhīmasena the *tamoguṇa* was prevailing, because of this he was often irascible. In Yudhiṣṭhira there was the *satoguṇa* prevailing while he was following the orders of *dharma*; he was caught by *rajoguṇa* when he fought against Droṇa and when he was lying; then he was under the influence of *tamoguṇa* when he played dice without thinking of the consequences. So he had all the three qualities because he was produced by the form of the Sun, made of the triple *Veda*. In the *Bhaviṣya Purāṇa* it is said that: *trayīmāyayā triguṇātmadhāriṇe*. And also in the *Bhagavad-Gītā* it is stated that *traiguṇyaviṣayā vedāḥ* as also in *Śrimadbhāgavatam*.

    Sahadeva, who knows astrology and who is skilled in breeding cows, was mainly *sāttvika*. He inherited this quality by the moon.

    In Nakula the *rajoguṇa* was predominant because of his being produced by the *rājasikamūrtī* of Kubera, the king of the *yakṣas* who are adored by *rājasika* beings. The *Gītā* states that: 'The *sāttvika* beings adore the *devas*, the *rājasika* beings adore the *yakṣas*.'

    Arjuna was representative of the *nirguṇa*, as ordered by Kṛṣṇa. In fact in the *Gītā* Arjuna is called *nistraiguṇyo bhavā'rjuna*. And also Arjuna accepted to perform the order of Kṛṣṇa: *kariṣye vacanaṁ tava*.

कालश्वरशिवस्थानाद्राजन्नेकधनुर्मिते ।
पौरन्दर्यां सुप्रसिद्धं सिद्धपीठमितिस्मृतम् ॥ १५ ॥

यः स्नात्वा जान्हवीतोयेऽभ्यर्च्य कालेश्वरं हरम् ।
सिद्धपीठे तपः कुर्यात स याति परमां गतिम् ॥ १६ ॥

यः सावित्रीमनुदिनं त्रीणि वर्षाण्यतन्द्रितः ॥ ।
जपेत् तत्रायुतमितां सिद्धासौ जायते नरः ॥ १७ ॥

यः पुरश्चरणं कुर्यात् सावित्र्याः सिद्धपीठके ।
ब्रह्मचारी यताहारी सोपि सिद्धेश्वरो भवेत ॥ १८ ॥

त्र्यम्बकेति ऋचं सम्यक् सिद्धपीठे जपेन्नरः ।
षडक्षरं मनुं वापि सोपि सिद्धिमवाप्नुयात् ॥ १९ ॥

यः श्रावणे सोमवारे कालेशं क्षीरधारया ।
स्नापयेन्मनुजः सोपि शिवलोके महीयते ॥ २० ॥

घृतप्रदीपं यो नित्यं दद्यात् कालेश्वरालये ।
भास्वरास्तस्य जायन्ते सर्वे लोका न संशयः ॥ २१ ॥

शिवरात्रिव्रती तत्र कुर्याज्जागरणं तुयः ।
स्तुवन् देवं नाममन्त्रैः प्रणवाद्यैर्नमोन्तकैः ॥ २२ ॥

धूपैर्दीपैश्च नैवेद्यैः पुङ्गीताम्बूलकचन्दनैः ।
पञ्चामृतैः शुभैः पुष्पैर्बिल्वपत्रैर्मनोहरैः ॥ २३ ॥

वस्त्रमाल्यादिभिः पूजां कुर्वंस्तद्गतमानसः ।
नरो न निरयं याति शिवलोकं प्रयाति सः ॥ २४ ॥

शिवसूक्तं व्रती यस्तु पठेन्नित्यं तदन्तिके ।
सोपि शम्भुगणो भूत्वा मोदते मनुजाधिप ॥ २५ ॥

यद्दक्षयापि यः कश्चिन्निवसेत् तत्र मानवः ।
सङ्कीर्णो हीनवर्णो वा सोपि पापैः प्रमुच्यते ॥ २६ ॥

O King, four hands eastward from Kāleśvara there is a *siddhapīṭha*. The devotee who after bathing in the Gaṅgā and making *pūjā* in the Kāleśvara temple makes *tapas* in this place obtains an auspicious life. The man who will daily recite 10000 times the *gāyatrī mantra* for a period of three years, will obtain the *siddhi*. The one who under the vow of *brahmacarya* will perform the *puraścaraṇa* of the *gāyatrī* will also obtain *siddhi.* The man who will recite there the *tryambakam* or the six-syllable *mantra* will never have obstacles in his life. In the month of *śrāvaṇa*, on Monday, the one who will wash with milk the Kāleśvara *liṅgam* will obtain the *Śivaloka*. One who will light a *dīpaka* there will never go in darkness while in the post-mortem. Staying awake during the night called *Śivarātri*, singing *bhajana* and *kīrtana*, offering *dhūpa*, *dīpaka*, fruits, *tāmbūla*, sandalwood, flowers, *belpatra*, clothes, garlands: who will perform the *pūjā* of the Kāleśvara, he will never go to any hell, but on the contrary he will reach the *Śivaloka*. The one who fasts there and recites the Śiva-*stuti* will become a *gaṇa* of Śiva. And the *śūdra* or the one of mixed caste, who arrives there by chance, will be freed from every sin. **[15-26]**

॥ इति श्री का० भा० कालेश्वरशिवस्थापनं नामाष्टाविंशोऽध्यायः ॥

Here ends the twenty-eighth chapter of the Kāmpilyamahātmya.

29

The Kāleśvara Temple

वैशम्पायन उवाच -

अत्रैवोदाहरन्तीममितिहासं पुरातनम्।
श्रृणुष्वैकमना राजन कथयामि तवाग्रतः ॥ १ ॥

केचित् पंचमहापापा अवन्त्यामभवन् नृप ।
मिथ्या वाचो द्यूतरता धर्ताः स्तेनाः सुरापिनः ॥ २ ॥

तेषां निवसतां तत्र बहुकालः समत्यगात्।
ततो मृत्युवशं प्राप्ता याम्यैर्नीता यमालये ॥ ३ ॥

तत्र ते प्रेतपतिना पातिता नरकेऽशुचौ ।
शरदामयुतं घोरा बुभुजुर्याम्ययातनाः ॥ ४ ॥

ततः पंचपि संजाताः पंचावारं च गर्दभाः ।
सप्तवारं सारमेयाश्चतुर्वारं वलीमुखाः ॥ ५ ॥

ततः पंचापि ते प्राप्ता योनिं चाण्डालसंज्ञिताम ।
तत्रापि दुःखनिवहं बहन्तो निधनंगताः ॥ ६ ॥

पुनरेकोऽभवत् तक्षा द्वितीयः पश्यतीहरः ।
तृतीयो मालिकस्तुर्यो व्याधः कैवर्त्तकोपरः ॥ ७ ॥

एवं पञ्चापि ते पापा एकग्रामे प्रजज्ञिरे ।
तेषां राजन् महाप्रीतिरन्योन्यं समजायत ॥ ८ ॥

एकचित्तास्ततः सर्वे दुराचारा दुराशयाः ।
परदाररताश्चौरा हिंसका धनवर्जिताः ॥ ९ ॥

देशाद्देशं भ्रमन्तस्ते कदाचिद्दैवयोगतः ।
प्राप्ताः पञ्चालविषये यत्र कालेश्वरो हरः ॥ १० ॥

तत्रावसन् बहुतिथं भिक्षावृत्तिपरायणाः ।
वसतां तत्र विप्राणां सेवां चक्रुर्विमत्सराः ॥ ११ ॥

दयार्द्रहृदया विप्रास्तेभ्यः स्वोच्छिष्ठभोजनम् ।
ददुर्भुक्तानि वस्त्राणि दीनेभ्यो दीनवत्सलाः ॥ १२ ॥

एवं निवसतां तेषां बहुकाले गते नृप ।
पूर्वजन्मचरित्राणां प्रज्ञानं समजायत ॥ १३ ॥

अथ कश्चिद्द्विजश्रेष्ठोधर्मदत्तःइतिश्रुतः ।
तान् पर्यपृच्छत् सकलान् के यूयं पापकारिणः ॥ १४ ॥

Vaiśampāyana said —

O King, I will tell you a story of this place. Listen to it.

In the town of Ujjain there were five great sinners. These five rogues used to lie, gamble, steal and drink. When they died many years later, they went to *Yamaloka*. There they had to suffer the pains of hell for 10000 years. Then they were born five times as donkeys, seven times as dogs and four times as monkeys. After those births they were born as *cāṇḍāla*, and also that time they had to experience much suffering. Then they passed through the births of carpenter, goldsmith, gardener, *bhīla* and boatman. They always stayed together, living in the same village, but every time they were committing sins. By a lucky chance, wandering from country to country, they arrived at Pañcāla and stopped at the Kāleśvara temple. There they performed the adoration of Śiva and served the *brāhmaṇa*s, living on alms. The *brāhmaṇa*s started to give to the five brothers the rest of their own food and their already-worn clothes. After living like that for sometime, they remembered their previous lives, *jāti smaraṇa*. One day a *brāhmaṇa* called Dharmadatta asked them: "Who are you? " **[1-14]**

पापिन ऊचुः -

वयं पुराऽवन्तिपुर्यां जाताः पापकृतो द्विजाः ।
ततो वर्षायुतं भुक्त्वा घोरा नरकयातनाः ॥ १५ ॥

ततश्च गार्दभीं योनिं कौक्कुरीं मार्कटीं तथा ।
पञ्चसप्तचतुर्वारं भुक्त्वा चाण्डालतां गताः ॥ १६ ॥

इदानीं व्याधकैवर्तकलादत्वष्टमालिकाः ।
संजाताः कर्मशेषेण भ्रमन्तोऽत्र समागताः ॥ १७ ॥

अस्मास्वेको गुरुस्त्रीगो वन्हिदो गरदोऽपरः ।
उच्छिष्टदायी विप्रेभ्यः पञ्चमो हरमूर्त्तिहृत् ॥ १८ ॥

ब्रह्मन् क्षेत्रप्रभावाच्च महतां दर्शनात् तथा ।
गतजन्मस्मृतिर्जाता त्राह्यस्मान्शरणागतान् ॥ १९ ॥

The Sinners said —

We were *brāhmaṇa*s in Ujjain, but we behaved badly. So we had to spend 10000 years in hell. Later we had to be born five times as donkeys, seven times as dogs, four times as monkeys, and after that we became wretched *cāṇḍāla*. Then because of other kārmic residues we had to undergo the births of carpenter, goldsmith, *bhīla*, boatman and gardener. Wandering around we arrived here. We are violators of the *guru*'s wife, pyromaniacs; we poison and disrespect the *brāhmaṇa*s; we are also stealers of the *mūrti* of Śiva. O *vipra*, by the influence of this Kālī *kṣetra* and by the sight of the sages we have remembered our previous lives. We take refuge in you, please protect us. **[15-19]**

धर्मदत्त उवाच -

मा भैष्ट पापिनः प्रातः शिवरात्रिर्भविष्यति ।
यूयं तत्र व्रतं कृत्वा पूजयध्वं वृषध्वजम् ॥ २० ॥

रात्रौ जागरणं चैव कार्यं कालेश्वरालये ।
एवं कृते तु भवतां भविष्यति शुभा गतिः ॥ २१ ॥

Dharmadatta said —

O Sinners, don't fear. Tomorrow it will be *Śivarātri* and you will fast and make *pūjā* to Śiva at the Kāleśvara temple; by staying awake all night in that temple your path will be auspicious. **[20-21]**

वैशम्पायन उवाच -

एवमुक्तास्ततस्तेन धर्मदत्तद्विजेन ते ।
शिवरात्रिव्रतं चक्रुः कालेश्वरशिवालये ॥ २२ ॥

ततस्तेषां नृपश्रेष्ठ सर्वेषामेव तत्क्षणम् ।
भस्मसादघसङ्घोभूत् तृणराशिरिवानले ॥ २३ ॥

स्वधर्मे मतिरुत्पन्ना श्रियमापुरचंचलाम् ।
पशूनथाप्यरोगित्वं पुत्रपौत्रादिसन्ततिम् ॥ २४ ॥

धर्मदत्तस्ततस्तेभ्यो मन्त्रं पंचाक्षरं ददौ ।
तज्जप्यनिरताः सर्वे व्यतीयुः सकलां जनिम् ॥ २५ ॥

मृत्युकाले तु सम्प्राप्ते शिवभक्तिपरायणाः ।
संसारबन्धनान्मुक्ता गतवन्तोऽभयं शिवम् ॥ २६ ॥

Vaiśampāyana said —

O King, listening to the words of the *brāhmaṇa*, they all spent the whole night of *Śivarātri* at the temple of Kāleśvara, observing the fast, and in that time they were cleansed from all their sins. They also got more consciousness of their *dharma*, a large fortune, animals, sons and nephews and freedom from illness. Then Dharmadatta taught them the five-syllable *mantra*, and they spent the rest of their lives repeating it. And after death they were able to reach and reside in the *Śivaloka*. **[22-26]**

जनमेजय उवाच -

महर्षिवर सर्वज्ञ सर्वज्ञानमहोदधे ।
पंचाक्षरस्य माहात्म्यं श्रोतुमिच्छामि तत्त्वतः ॥ २७ ॥

Janamejaya said —

O *maharṣi*, we would like to hear the eulogy of the five-syllable *mantra*. Please tell us. **[27]**

वैशम्पायन उवाच -

पंचाक्षरस्य माहात्म्यं वर्षकोटिशतैरपि ।
अशक्यं विस्तराद् वक्तुं ततः संक्षेपतः शृणु ॥ २८ ॥

नमस्कारादिसंयुक्तं शिवायेत्यक्षरत्रयम् ।
जिह्वाग्रे वर्त्तते यस्य सफलं तस्य जीवितम् ॥ २९ ॥

अन्त्यजो वाऽधमो वापि मूर्खो वा पण्डितोपि वा ।
पंचाक्षरजपे निष्ठो मुच्यते पापसंचयात् ॥ ३० ॥

सदाचारविहीनस्य पतितस्यान्त्यजस्य च ।
पंचाक्षरात् परं नास्ति परित्राणं कलौ युगे ॥ ३१ ॥

इत्युक्तं परमेशेन देव्या पृष्टेन शूलिना ।
हिताय सर्वलोकस्य कलिजानां विशेषतः ॥ ३२ ॥

पंचाक्षरः पंचवक्त्रःपांचाली पंच पाण्डवाः ।
पांचालराजः पंचैते पंचत्वेपि स्मृताः शुभाः ॥ ३३ ॥

राजन्नेवं समाख्यातस्तव कालेश्वरोद्भवः ।
तन्महत्त्वं च संप्रोक्तं किं भूयः श्रोतुमिच्छसि ॥ ३४ ॥

Vaiśampāyana said —

O King, the complete eulogy of the five-syllable *mantra* cannot be said even in a thousand years. Listen just to some of it. The man who keeps always on his tongue the *mantra namaḥ śivāya* will have a successful life. The most wretched idiot of the lowest caste or the wisest *brāhmaṇa*, whoever recites this *mantra*, is absolved from every sin. By reciting the *pañcākṣara mantram* even the most wayward person can find redemption. It was told by Śaṅkarjī to Pārvatī. It is auspicious also to remember it at the time of death. O King, I have told you the origin of the Kāleśvara temple and its *māhātmya*. Now tell me what you would like to hear.[20] **[28-34]**

॥ इति श्री का० मा० कालेश्वरकथोपसंहारोनामैकोनत्रिंशोऽध्यायः ॥

Here ends the twenty-ninth chapter of the Kāmpilyamahātmya.

---

20. In *Mbh*, Draupadī is considered to be Svargaśrī, Lakṣmī, and the five *indriya*, the faculties, are the five Pāṇḍavas. In the manuscript in possession of the author it is written that Pārvatī was Draupadī and the five forms of Śiva the five Pāṇḍavas. But in other *Purāṇa*s and in the seventh *parva* of the *Pṛthvīrājarāso* it is written that Indrāṇī was cursed by Kāmadhenu to become Draupadī. These inconsistencies are due to differences of times, and do not question the validity of the myth.

यः काम्पिल्यपुराधिनाथसुतया संस्थापितो द्वापरे द्वारे यस्य सुरापगोत्तरवहा + सन्तापहा पापहा ॥ भृत्यानामपहृत्य कृत्यनिवहं संपादयत्याशु शं तं वन्दे कलिकालजालशमनं कालेश्वरं शङ्करम् ॥ १ ॥

भी शम्भोऽहं भवाम्भोनिधिविविधमरुल्लोलकल्लोलपातैरा ऽऽनीतीऽतीवभीतो नीजविधिबशतस्त्वत्पदाम्भोजमूलम् ॥ तद् दृष्टिं हर्षबृष्टिं कुरु मयि कृपया भो यया खिन्नचित्तो दुर्गादत्तो भवत्तोऽवरममरवरं प्रार्थयेऽन्यं शरण्यम् ॥ २ ॥

Prayer of Durgadatta —

I, Durgadatta, bow down before Śaṅkara who is the Lord of Time and pacifier of the effects of time in kaliyuga. He was consecrated by the daughter of the king of Kāmpilya during the dvāpara age.[21] *The divine river Gaṅgā flows northward in front of Kāmpilya's gate. The Lord removes the effect of karma from his devotees and gives peace immediately.* [1]

O Lord, I have been brought before you from the ocean of the world, being tossed and thrown by the waves created by different types of air, mārūta. I am extremely afraid. By my own fate I have come near your lotus-feet. Therefore look at me and shower happiness over me in kindness so that the afflicted Durgadatta, being lower in grade, may become noble by your immortal boon and be able to surrender to You because he has taken shelter in You. This is the prayer. [2]

---

21. *Uttaravāhinī*, flowing northward Gaṅgā and *pūrvavāhinī*, flowing eastward Sarasvatī are considered meritorious. — *PadmaP.*

30

The Story of Śikhaṇḍī[22]

जनमेजय उवाच -

शिखण्डिनः समुत्पत्तिं श्रोतुमिच्छामि साम्प्रतम् ।
यः पुरा वनिता भूत्वा पश्चात् पुरुषतां गतः ॥ १ ॥

Janamejaya said —

I would like to hear about the origin of Śikhaṇḍī, who became a man after having been a woman. **[1]**

वैशम्पायन उवाच -

एवमेव पुरा राजन् गाङ्गेयो रणमूर्द्धनि ।
सुयोधनेनानुयुक्तः स यदाह शृणुष्व तत् ॥ २ ॥

Vaiśampāyana said —

The same question was put by Duryodhana to Bhīṣma in the beginning of the war of Bhārata. Listen to this. **[2]**

दुर्योधन उवाच -

कथं शिखंडी गाङ्गेय कन्या भूत्वा पुरा तदा ।
पुरुषोभूद्यु धिश्रेष्ठ तन्मे ब्रहि पितामह ॥ ३ ॥

22. The story of Śikhaṇḍī is found in *Mbh.*, I, 1, 182; I, 63, 130; I, 63-67; V, 192, and VI, 13-15.

Duryodhana said —

O Pitāmaha, please tell me how Śikhaṇḍī after being born as a girl was then born as a boy. **[3]**

भीष्म उवाच -

भार्या तु तस्य राजेन्द्र द्रुपदस्य महीपतेः ।
महिषीं दयिता ह्यासीदपुत्रस्य विशाम्पते ॥ ४ ॥

एतस्मिन्नेव काले तु यज्ञसेनो महीपतिः ।
अपत्यार्त्थं महाराज तोषयामास शङ्करम ॥ ५ ॥

अस्मद्वधार्थं निश्चित्य तपो घोरं समाश्रितः ।
ऋते कन्यां महादेव पुत्रो मे स्यादिति ब्रुवन् ॥ ६ ॥

भगवन् पुत्रमिच्छामि भीष्मं प्रतिचिकीर्षया ।
इत्युक्त आह देवस्तं स्त्रीपुमांस्ते भविष्यति ॥ ७ ॥

निवर्त्तस्व महीपाल नैतज्जात्वन्यथा भवेत् ।
स च गत्वा स्वनगरं भार्यामिदमुवाच ह ॥ ८ ॥

कृतो यत्नो महादेवस्तपसाऽऽराधितो मया ।
कन्या भूत्वा पुमान भावी प्रत्युक्तोस्मीति शम्भुना ॥ ९ ॥

पुनः पुनर्याच्यमानो दिष्टमित्यब्रवीच्छिवः ।
तदन्यथा न भविता भवितव्यं हि तत् तथा ॥ १० ॥

ततः सा नियता भूत्वा ऋतुकाले मनस्विनी ।
पत्नी पाञ्चालराजस्य द्रुपद प्रविवेश ह ॥ ११ ॥

लेभे गर्भं यथाकालं विधिद्रुष्टेन कर्मणा ।
पार्षतस्य महीपाल यथा मां नारदोब्रवीत् ॥ १२ ॥

ततो दधार सा देवी गर्भं राजीवलोचना ।
तां स राजा प्रियां भार्यां द्रुपदः कुरुनन्दन ॥ १३ ॥

पुत्रस्नेहान्महावाहुः सुखं पर्यचरत् तदा ।
सर्वानभि प्रायकृतान भार्यालभत कौरव ॥ १४ ॥

Bhīṣma said —

O King, the queen of Drupada had no sons. Then in order to kill me (Bhīṣma) they started to undertake very strict austerity to please Śiva. King Drupada said: "O Bhagavān, I want a son who will be able to kill Bhīṣma!" Then Śiva said to him: "You will first have a daughter and then a son. Accept this as inevitable." After reaching his home he told his wife everything that had occurred. He said: "Even though I insisted a lot, Lord Śiva said that first a girl will be born and then a boy." In the right time and after an ablution, King Drupada and his queen performed a rite in the same way of the *puṁsavan saṁskāra*[23] and became pregnant. O King, I have heard this story from Nārada. King Drupada desirous of a son was fulfilling every whim of his beloved wife.[24] **[4-14]**

अपुत्रस्य सतो राज्ञो यज्ञसेनस्यभूपते ।
यथाकालं तु सा देवी महिषी द्रुपदस्य ह ॥ १५ ॥

कन्यां प्रवररूपां हि प्राजायत नराधिप ।
अपुत्रस्य तु राज्ञः सा द्रुपदस्य मनस्विनी ॥ १६ ॥

ख्यापयामास राजेन्द्र पुत्रो ह्येष ममेति वै ।
ततः स राजा द्रुपदः प्रच्छन्नाया नराधिप ॥ १७ ॥

पुत्रवत् पुत्रकार्याणि सर्वाणि समकारयत् ।
रक्षणं चैव मन्त्रस्य महिषी द्रुपदस्य सा ॥ १८ ॥

चकार सर्वयत्नेन ब्रुवाणा पुत्र इत्युत ।
न च तां वेद नगरे कश्चिदन्यत्र पार्षतात् ॥ १९ ॥

श्रद्दधानो हि तद्वाक्यं देवस्याच्युततेजसः ।
छादयामास तां कन्यां पुमानिति च सोऽब्रवीत् ॥ २० ॥

जातकर्माणि सर्वाणि कारयामास पार्थिवः ।
पुम्वद्विधानयुक्तानि शिखण्डीति च तं विदुः ॥ २१ ॥

अहमेकस्तु चारेण वचनान्नारदस्य च ।
ज्ञातवान् देववाक्येन अम्बायास्तपसा तथा ॥ २२ ॥

---

23. The ceremony which is performed during the third month of conception.

24. If a pregnant woman is not satisfied in her desires the son is spoiled.

At the right time King Drupada had a daughter but her parents hid her sex and performed all the rites as if she was a boy. And trusting the words of Śiva they gave her a masculine name: Śikhaṇḍī. No one knew the real identity of Śikhaṇḍī. I learnt from a messenger, or Nārada, that Śiva had once said to Ambā: "Next you will be born as a girl who will kill Bhīṣma; after that you will be born as a boy." And Ambā, the daughter of the King of Kāśī, said: "I will destroy Bhīṣma."[25] **[15-22]**

॥ इति श्री का० मा० शिखण्ड्युत्पत्तिवर्णनं नाम त्रिंशोऽध्यायः ॥

Here ends the thirtieth chapter of the Kāmpilyamahātmya.

25. This tale is described in the Udyoga-Parva, *adhyāya* 187.

31

Śikhaṇḍī Marries the Daughter of the King Hiraṇvarmā

भीष्म उवाच -

ततो लेख्यादिषु तथा शिल्पेषु द्रुपदात्मजः ।
इष्वस्त्रे चैव राजेन्द्र द्रोणशिष्यो वभूव ह ॥ १ ॥

तस्य माता महाराज राजानं वरवर्णिनी ।
चोदयामास भार्यार्थं कन्यायाः पुत्रवत् तदा ॥ २ ॥

ततस्तां पार्षतो दृष्ट्वा कन्यां सम्प्राप्तयौवनाम् ।
स्त्रियं मत्वा महाचिन्तां प्रपेदे सह भार्यया ॥ ३ ॥

Bhīṣma said —

Then Śikhaṇḍī became disciple of Droṇācārya. There he learnt how to read and write and the art of using weapons. One day the queen approached the king to speak about Śikhaṇḍī's marriage. Seeing her/him so young, the king and the queen got worried. **[1-3]**

राजोवाच -

कन्या ममेयं सम्प्राप्ता यौवनं शोकवर्द्धिनी ।
मया प्रच्छादिता चेयं वचनात् तस्य धूर्जटेः ॥ ४ ॥

The King said —

Trusting the words of Śiva I have kept her hidden until now, but this girl is going to give me some problems. **[4]**

राज्ञ्युवाच -

न तन्मिथ्या महाराज भविष्यति कथञ्चन ।

त्रैलोक्यकर्त्ता कस्माद्धि वृथा वक्तु मिहार्हति ॥ ५ ॥

यदि ते रोचते राजन वक्ष्यामि शृणु मे वचः ।
श्रुत्वेदानीं प्रपद्येथाः स्वां मतिं पृषतात्मज ॥ ६ ॥

क्रियतामस्य यत्नेन विधिवद् दारसंग्रहः ।
भविता तद् वचस्तथ्यमिति मे धीयते मतिः ॥ ७ ॥

एवं तौ निश्चयं कृत्वा तस्मिन् कार्येऽथ दम्पती ।
वरयांचक्रतुः कन्यां दशार्णाधिपतेः सुताम ॥ ८ ॥

हिरण्यवर्मेतिनृपो योऽसौ दाशार्णकः स्मृतः ।
स च प्रादान्महीपाल कन्यां तस्मै शिखण्डिने ॥ ९ ॥

स च राजा दशार्णेषु महानासीत् सुदुर्जयः ।
हिरण्यवर्मा दुर्धर्षो महासेनो महाबलः ॥ १० ॥

कृते विवाहे तु तदा सा कन्या राजसत्तम ।
यौवनं समनुप्राप्ता सा च कन्या शिखण्डिनी ॥ ११ ॥

कृतदारः शिखण्डी च काम्पिल्यं पुनरागमत् ।
हिरण्यवर्मणो राज्ञः सुतामादाय पार्थिव ॥ १२ ॥

The Queen said —

O my king, the words of the Lord of the three worlds must come true. If you can understand me, please reflect also on my words. I think that this girl will certainly become a man; so we should contact some kings who have daughters to marry. The two asked the king of Daśārṇa, Hiraṇyavarmā, to marry his daughter to Śikhaṇḍī, and he accepted their proposal. King Hiraṇyavarmā was well known in that country. After the wedding Śikhaṇḍī stayed there sometime, but then, still being very young, he came to Kampila with her/his bride. **[5-12]**

दशार्णाधिपतेः कन्या ज्ञात्वा तां तु शिखण्डिनीम् ।
धात्रीणां च सखीनां च व्रीडयाना न्यवेदयत् ॥ १३ ॥

ततस्ता राजशार्दूल धात्र्यो दाशार्णिकास्तदा ।
जग्मुरार्तिं परां प्रेष्याः प्रेषयामासुरेव च ॥ १४ ॥

ततो दशार्णाधिपतेः प्रेष्याः सर्वा न्यवेदयन् ।
विप्रलम्भं यथावृत्तं स च चक्रोध पार्थिवः ॥ १५ ॥

शिखण्ड्यपि महाराज पुम्वद्राजकुले तदा ।
विजहार मुदा युक्तः स्त्रीत्वं नैवातिरोचयन् ॥ १६ ॥

ततः कतिपयाहस्य तच्छ्रुत्वा भरतर्षभ ।
हिरण्यवर्मा राजेन्द्र रोषादार्तिं जगाम ह ॥ १७ ॥

ततो दाशार्णको राजा तीव्रकोपसमन्वितः ।
दूतं प्रस्थापयामास द्रुपदस्य निवेशनम् ॥ १८ ॥

ततो द्रुपदमासाद्य दूतः काञ्चनवर्मणः ।
एकः सर्वं समुत्सार्य सहो वचनमब्रवीत् ॥ १९ ॥

दशार्णराजो राजंस्त्वामिदं वचनमब्रवीत् ।
पराभवात् प्रकुपितो विप्रलब्धस्त्वयाऽनघ ॥ २० ॥

अवमन्यसे मां नृपते नूनं दुर्मन्त्रितं तव ।
यन्मे कन्यां स्वकन्यार्थे मोहाद्याचितवानसि ॥ २१ ॥

तस्याद्य विप्रलम्भस्य फलं प्राप्नुहि दुर्मते ।
एष त्वां सजनामात्यमुच्छेत्स्यामि स्थिरो भव ॥ २२ ॥

But the daughter of King Hiraṇyavarmā discovered that Śikhaṇḍī was a woman and felt embarrassed because of it. She told everything to her companions, who had come with her there from her father's place. As she was very distressed she sent some servants to Hiraṇyavarmā. They told the king about Drupada's ruse (pretending that his daughter was a man). When Hiraṇyavarmā heard this he became very angry. On the other side Śikhaṇḍī, still in the disguise of a man, also did not feel at ease. After some days Hiraṇyavarmā received the same news again. He became very unhappy and enraged and decided to send a messenger to Kampila. In secret, the messenger said to Drupada: "O King, Hiraṇyavarmā has sent me to tell you that he is very disappointed by your deception, and that he is going to destroy you with the help of his ministers." **[13-22]**

॥ इति श्री कां० मा० शिखंडिनीविवाहो नामैकत्रिंशोऽध्यायः ॥

Here ends the thirty-first chapter of the Kāmpilyamahātmya.

32

The Anger of the King Hiraṇvarmā, Ascertaining the Real Sex of Śikhaṇḍī

भीष्म उवाच -

एवमुक्तस्य दूतेन द्रुपदस्य तदाऽनघ ।
चोरस्येव गृहीतस्य न प्रावर्त्तत भारती ॥ १ ॥

स यत्नमकरोत् तीव्रं सम्वन्धिन्यनुमानने ।
दूतैर्मधुरसंभाषैर्न तदस्तीति सन्दिशन् ॥ २ ॥

स राजा भूय एवाथ ज्ञात्वा तत्त्वमथागमत् ।
कन्येति पांचालसुता त्वरमाणोभिनिर्ययौ ॥ ३ ॥

ततः स प्रेषयामास मित्राणाममितौजसाम् ।
दुहितुर्विप्रलम्भं तं धात्रीणां वचनात् तदा ॥ ४ ॥

ततः समुदयं कृत्वा बलाना राजसत्तमः ।
अभियाने मति चक्रे द्रुपदं प्रति भारत ॥ ५ ॥

ततः स मन्त्रयामास पांचाल्यं पार्थिवं प्रति ।
तत्रेवं निश्चितं तेषामभूद्राज्ञां महात्मनाम् ॥ ६ ॥

तथ्यं भवति चेदेतद्राजन् कन्या शिखण्डिनी ।
वध्वा पांचालराजानमानयिष्यामहे गृहम् ॥ ७ ॥

अन्यं राजानमाधाय पांचालेषु नरेश्वरम् ।
घातयिष्याम नृपतिं पांचाल्यं सशिखण्डिनम् ॥ ८ ॥

तत् तदाऽनृतमाज्ञाय पुनर्दूतान् नराधिपः ।
प्रास्थापयत् पार्षताय निहन्मीति स्थिरो भव ॥ ९ ॥

Bhīṣma said —

"Listening to the words of the messenger King Drupada could not reply, he was like a thief caught redhanded. Trying to convince his daughter's father in law that it was not true, he started to speak mellifluous words to the messenger. But King Hiraṇyavarmā ascertained the real sex of Śikhaṇḍī and organised an assembly with other allied kings to speak about Drupada's deception. The assembly agreed that if Śikhaṇḍī was really a girl then King Drupada should have been caught and killed with his daughter, and another King should be put on the throne of Kampila. Upon hearing again the lies of Drupada King Hiraṇyavarmā became furious. He decided to send him a declaration of war. [1-9]

स हि प्रकृत्या वै भीरुः किल्विषी च नराधिपः ।
भयं तीव्रमनुप्राप्तो द्रुपदो धरणीपतिः ॥ १० ॥

विसृज्य दूतान् दाशार्णान् द्रुपदः शोकमूर्छितः ।
समेत्य भार्यां रहसि वाक्यमेतदुवाच ह ॥ ११ ॥

अभियास्यति मां कोपात् सम्बन्धी सुमहाबलः ।
हिरण्यवर्मा नृपतिः कर्षमाणो वरूथिनीम् ॥ १२ ॥

शिखण्डी किल पुत्रस्ते कन्येति परिशङ्कितः ।
वंचितोस्मीतिमन्वानो मां किलोच्छेत्तुमिच्छति ॥ १३ ॥

किमत्र तथ्यं सुश्रोणि मिथ्या किं ब्रूहि शोभने ।
श्रुत्वा त्वत्तः शुभं वाक्यं संविधास्याम्यहं तथा ॥ १४ ॥

अहं च संशयं प्राप्तो वाला चेयं शिखंडिनी ।
त्वं च राज्ञि महत् कृच्छ्रं संप्राप्ता वरवर्णिनि ॥ १५ ॥

मया दाशार्णको राजा वञ्चितः स महीपतिः ।
किमिदानीं करिष्यामि मूढः कन्यामिमां प्रति ॥ १६ ॥

सा त्व सर्वविमोक्षाय तत्त्वमाख्याहि पृच्छतः ।
तथा विदध्यां सुश्रोणि कृत्यमाशु शुचिस्मिते ॥ १७ ॥

शिखण्डिनि च मा भैस्त्वं विधास्ये तत्र तत्त्वतः ।
कृपयाऽहं वरारोहे वञ्जितः पुत्रधर्मतः ॥ १८ ॥

King Drupada was very scared by the belligerent intentions of the King of Daśārṇa. He dismissed the messengers and in seclusion with an upset mind he said to his wife: "O Queen, my daughter's father in law is attacking us with a big army. He has the suspicion that your son Śikhaṇḍī is a girl. You have cheated me and for that I will kill you. It is time for you to tell the truth and I will make my decision. I, you and this girl are in a big trouble. I cheated the King of Daśārṇa, and now what should I do? O Queen, because of this girl I have had to lie, so now tell me what should I do? O Śikhaṇḍī, do not fear. I am thinking of a remedy for you. Pretending you are a boy is deceiving me also." [10-18]

॥ इति श्री कां० मा० द्रुपदचिन्तानाम द्वात्रिंशोऽध्यायः॥

Here ends the thirty-second chapter of the Kāmpilyamahātmya.

33

Śikhaṇḍī's Depression; Intervent of the Yakśa Sthūṇākarṇa

भीष्म उवाच -

जानता हि नरेन्द्रेण ख्यापनार्थं परस्य वै ।
प्रकाशं चोदिता देवी वाक्यमेतदुवाच ह ॥ १ ॥

अपुत्रया मया राजन् सपत्नीनां भयादियम् ।
कन्या शिखण्डिनी जाता पुमानिति निवेदिता ॥ २ ॥

त्वया चैव नरश्रेष्ठ तन्मे प्रीत्यानुमोदितम् ।
पुत्रकर्म कृतं चैव कन्यायाः पार्थिवर्षभ ॥ ३ ॥

मया च प्रत्यभिहितं देववाक्यार्थदर्शनात् ।
कन्या भूत्वा पुमान् भावीत्येवं चैतदुपेक्षितम् ॥ ४ ॥

Bhīṣma said —

Even though King Drupada knew the real sex of Śikhaṇḍī, to save his reputation in front of the other co-wives, he asked the queen about the matter. The queen answered: "O king, fearing the dishonour of not having a son and the criticism of the co-wives, I have concealed this girl in the disguise of a boy. Furthermore you also know all this and so you agreed to perform the *saṁskāra* as if she were a boy. I trusted the words of Śiva (that she would have become a male after being a female) and I have kept the secret." **[1-4]**

एतच्छुत्वा द्रुपदो यज्ञसेनः सर्वं तत्त्वं मन्त्रविद्भ्यो निवेद्य ।
मन्त्रं राजा मन्त्रयामास राजन् यथा युक्तं रक्षणे वै प्रजानाम् ॥ ५ ॥

सम्बन्धकं चैव समर्थ्यं तस्मिन् दाशार्णके नृपतौ मानवेन्द्र ।
स्वयं कृत्वा विप्रलम्भं यथावन्मन्त्रैकाग्र्यो निश्चयं वै जगाम ॥ ६ ॥

स्वभावगुप्तं नगरमापत्काले तु भारत ।
गोपयामास राजेन्द्र सर्वतः समलंकृतम् ॥ ७ ॥

आर्तिं च परमां राजा जगामसह भार्यया ।
दशार्णपतिना सार्द्धं विरोधे भरतर्षभ ॥ ८ ॥

कथं सम्बन्धिना सार्द्धं न मे स्याद्विग्रहो महान् ।
इति संचित्य मनसा देवतामर्चयत् तदा ॥ ९ ॥

तं तु द्रष्ट्वा तदा राजन् देवी देवपरं तदा ।
अर्चां प्रयुञ्जानमथो भार्या वचनम ब्रवीत् ॥ १० ॥

देवानां प्रतिपत्तिश्च सत्यं साधु मता सताम् ।
किमु दुःखार्णवं प्राप्य तस्मादर्चयतां गुरून् ॥ ११ ॥

दैवतानि च सर्वाणि पूज्यन्तां भूरिदक्षिणम् ।
अग्नयश्चापि हूयन्तां दाशार्ण प्रतिषेधने ॥ १२ ॥

अयुद्धेन निवृत्तिं च मनसा चिन्तय प्रभो ।
देवतानां प्रसादेन सर्वमेतद्भविष्यति ॥ १३ ॥

मन्त्रिभिर्मन्त्रितं सार्द्धं त्वया पृथुललोचन ।
पुरस्यास्याऽविनाशाय यच्च राजंस्तथा कुरु ॥ १४ ॥

दैवं हि मानुषोपेतं भृशं सिद्ध्यति पार्थिव ।
परस्परविरोधाद्धि सिद्धिरस्ति न चैतयोः ॥ १५ ॥

तस्माद्विधाय नगरे विधानं सचिवैः सह ।
अर्चयस्व यथाकामं दैवयानि विशाम्भते ॥ १६ ॥

After listening to the queen's speech King Drupada consulted his ministers and started to defend himself suitably in front of the public. He sent word to tell Hiraṇyavarmā that he had not lied and that what he had heard was not true. Then he strengthened the trenches of the town and placed cannons all around to fortify the city. The king and the queen were very scared to be the enemy of King Hiraṇyavarmā. So King

Drupada decided to make a *pūjā* to his *iṣṭa-devatā* in order to reconcile with his daughter's father-in-law, Hiraṇyavarmā. Then the queen said: "The offerings to the gods are always auspicious, and I would do whatever is appropriate in times of distress. Let us perform a rich *pūjā* to the gods and also a big *havana* asking that King Hiraṇyavarmā go back to his house without fighting us. By the grace of the gods this will be granted. On the other side you should apply the protection measures that were decided by you along with your ministers. By carrying out both the two plans, of the gods and of the men, the matter is sure to succeed. So defend the city and perform the right worship to the gods." **[5-16]**

एवं सम्भाषमाणौ तौ दृष्ट्वा शोकपरायणौ ।
शिखण्डिनी तदा कन्या व्रीडितेव तपस्विनी ॥ १७ ॥

ततः सा चिन्तयामास मत्कृते दुःखितावुभौ ।
इमाविति ततश्चक्रे मतिं प्राणविनाशने ॥ १८ ॥

एवं सा निश्चयं कृत्वा भृशं शोकपरायणा ।
निर्जगाम गृहाद्राजन् गहनं निर्जनं वनम् ॥ १९ ॥

यक्षेणर्द्धिमता राजन स्थूणाकर्णेन पालितम् ।
तद्भयादेव च जनो विसर्जयति तद्वनम् ॥ २० ॥

तत्र च स्थूणभवनं सुधामृत्तिकलेपनम् ।
लाजोल्लापिकधूमाढ्यमुच्चप्राकारतोरणम् ॥ २१ ॥

शिखण्डिनी तत् प्रविश्य दुपदस्यात्मजा नृप ।
अनश्नाना बहुतिथं शरीरमुदशोषयत् ॥ २२ ॥

दर्शयामास तां स्थूणो यक्षो मार्दवसंयुतः ।
किमर्थोऽयं तवारम्भः करिष्ये ब्रूहि मा चिरम् ॥ २३ ॥

अशक्यमिति सा यक्षं पुनः पुनरुवाच ह ।
करिष्यामीति वै क्षिप्रं प्रत्युवाचाथ गुह्यकः ॥ २४ ॥

धनेश्वरस्यानुचरो वरदोऽस्मि नृपात्मजे ।
अदेयमपि दास्यामि ब्रूहि यत् ते विवक्षितम् ॥ २५ ॥

ततः शिखण्डिनी सर्वमखिलेन न्यवेदयत्।
तस्मै यक्षप्रधानाय स्थूणाकर्णाय भारत ॥ २६ ॥

अपुत्रो मे पिता यक्ष नचिरान्नाशमेष्यति ।
अभियास्यति सक्रोधो दशार्णाधिपतिर्हि तम ॥ २७ ॥

महाबलो महोत्साहः स हेमकवचो नृपः ।
तस्माद्रक्षस्व मां यक्ष मातरं पितरं च मे ॥ २८ ॥

प्रतिज्ञातं हि भवता दुःख प्रशमनं मम ।
भवेयं पुरुषो यक्ष त्वत्प्रसादादनिन्दितः ॥ २९ ॥

यावदेव स राजा वै नोपयाति पुरं मम ।
तावदेव महायक्ष प्रसादं कुरु गुह्यक ॥ ३० ॥

Hearing the speech between the king and the queen, Śikhaṇḍī felt ashamed and unhappy. He started to think: "My father and my mother are grief-stricken because of me. Why not commit suicide?" Having decided to do so he went into a wild jungle where the *yakṣa,* Sthūṇākarṇa resided. Through fear of him nobody used to go there, as his whitewashed house was there. It was filled with perfumed plants of *khas*, surrounded with high walls and had a huge door. O King, there Śikhaṇḍī stayed fasting for many days; his body became emaciated by the austerities. Only then did the *yakṣa* Sthūṇākarṇa decide to show himself to Śikhaṇḍī. With respect the *yakṣa* asked: "Why or for who are you observing such a hard *tapasyā*? Tell me what is your purpose, I will accomplish your desire." Many times Śikhaṇḍī answered that the *yakṣa* could not help him. But Sthūṇākarṇa insisted: "Whatever you are striving for I will do it now. I am servant of Kubera and so I can bestow boons. Even if your desire is a vile one I will satisfy you." So Śikhaṇḍī told the *yakṣa* the entire story of his father's desire for a male son and how the king of Daśārṇa, Hiraṇyavarmā had been deceived by concealing her true sex (the sex of Śikhaṇḍī) and making her marry his daughter. Śikhaṇḍī also said that King Hiraṇyavarmā was attacking her father: "Please save me and my parents from the mighty Hiraṇyavarmā. You have just promised to remove all my burdens. O *yakṣa*, please help me become a man, before he arrives at the court of my father." **[17-30]**

॥ *इतिश्री कां० मा० शिखण्डिनीस्थूणाकर्णसमागमो नाम त्रयस्त्रिंशोऽध्यायः* ॥
Here ends the thirty-third chapter of the Kāmpilyamahātmya.

34

Sthūṇākarṇa Gives His Masculinity to Śikhaṇḍī

भीष्म उवाच -

श्रुत्वा शिखण्डिनीवाक्यं स यक्षो भरतर्षभ ।
प्रोवाच मनसा चिन्त्य दैवेनोपनिपीडितः ॥ १ ॥

भवितव्यं तथा तद्धि मम दुःखाय कौरव ।
भद्रे कामं करिष्यामि समयं तु निबोध मे ॥ २ ॥

किञ्चित्कालान्तरे दास्ये पुंलिङ्गंस्वमिदं तव ।
आगन्तव्यं त्वया काले सत्यं चैव वदस्व मे ॥ ३ ॥

प्रभुः सङ्कल्पसिद्धोस्मि कामचारी विहङ्गमः ।
मत्प्रसादात् पुरं चैव त्राहि बन्धूंश्च केवलम् ॥४ ॥

स्त्रीलिङ्ग धारयिष्यामि तवेदं पार्थिवात्मजे ।
सत्यं मे प्रतिजानीहि करिष्यामि प्रियं तव ॥ ५ ॥

Bhīṣma said —

O King, Duryodhana, at the request of Śikhaṇḍī, the *yakṣa*, caught by ill-fortune, said: "What you are asking is not easy, but I will accomplish your desire. Listen to my promise — I will lend you my masculinity for a while but after that you must promise to come back here. I am fully-competent, with strong determination; I can move at will and fly in the sky. By my grace you will be able to protect your town and your parents. O princess, I will take your femininity, but you must swear you will come back to me." **[1-5]**

शिखण्डिन्युवाच -

प्रतिदास्यामि भगवन् पुंलिङ्गं तव सुव्रत ।
किञ्चित्कालान्तरं स्त्रीत्वं धारयस्व निशाचर ॥ ६ ॥

प्रतियाते तु दाशार्णे पार्थिवे हेमवर्मणि ।
कन्यैवाऽहं भविष्यामि पुरुषस्त्वं भविष्यसि ॥ ७ ॥

Śikhaṇḍī said —

O *yakṣa*, I will take your masculinity for a while after which I will come back and take again my femininity. When the King of Daśārṇa returns to his kingdom, I will be a woman and you will be a man again. **[6-7]**

भीष्म उवाच -

इत्यक्त्वा समयं तत्र चक्राते ताबुभौ नृप ।
अन्योन्यस्याऽभिसन्देहे तौ सङ्क्रामयतां तदा ॥ ८ ॥

स्त्रीलिङ्गं धारयामास स्थूणायक्षोथ भारत ।
यक्षरूपं च तद् दीप्तं शिखण्डी प्रत्यपद्यत ॥ ९ ॥

ततः शिखण्डी पाञ्चाल्यः पुंस्त्वमादाय पार्थिव ।
विवेश नगरं हृष्टः पितरं च समासदत् ॥ १० ॥

यथावृत्तं ततः सर्वमाचख्यौ द्रुपदस्य तत् ।
द्रुपदस्तस्य तच्छ्रुत्वा हर्षमाहारयत् परम् ॥ ११ ॥

सभार्यस्तच्च सस्मार महेश्वरवचस्तदा ।
ततः सम्प्रेषयामास दशार्णाधिपतेर्न्नृपः ॥ १२ ॥

पुरुषोयं मम सुतः श्रद्धत्तां मे भवानिति ।
अथ दाशार्णको राजा सहसाभ्यागमत् तदा ॥ १३ ॥

पञ्चालराजं द्रुपदं दुःखशोकसमन्वितः ।
ततः काम्पिल्लमासाद्य दशार्णाधिपतिर्नृप ॥ १४ ॥

प्रेषयामास सत्कृत्य दूतं ब्रह्मविदां वरम् ।
ब्रूहि मद्वचनाद् दूत पाञ्चाल्यं तं नृपाधमम् ॥ १५ ॥

यन्मे कन्यां स्वकन्यार्थे वृतवानसि दुर्मते ।
फलं तस्यावलेपस्य द्रक्ष्यस्यद्य न संशयः ॥ १६ ॥

एवमुक्तश्च तेनासौ ब्राह्मणो राजसत्तम ।
दूतः प्रयातो नगरं दशार्णनृपचोदितः ॥ १७ ॥

तत आसादयामास पुरोधा द्रुपदं पुरे ।
तस्मै पाञ्चालको राजा गामर्घ्यं च सुसत्कृतम् ॥ १८ ॥

प्रापयामास राजेन्द्र स ह तेन शिखण्डिना ।
तां पूजां नाभ्यनन्दत् स वाक्यं चेदमुवाच ह ॥ १९ ॥

यदुक्तं तेन वीरेण राज्ञा काञ्चनवर्मणा ।
यत् तेऽहमधमाचार दुहित्रास्म्यभिवञ्चितः ॥ २० ॥

तस्य पापस्य करणात् फलं प्राप्नुहि दुर्मते ।
देहि युद्धं नरपते ममाद्य रणमूर्द्धनि ॥ २१ ॥

Bhīṣma said —

Having made this promise, they exchanged their bodies. Sthūṇākarṇa became a woman and Śikhaṇḍī became a man. Then Śikhaṇḍī happily went to his father and told him what had happened. The king and the queen were overjoyed to hear what had happened. They remembered the words of Śiva. Then they sent a messenger to King Hiraṇyavarmā to confirm that Drupada's son was really a man. The enraged Hiraṇyavarmā got even more angry to hear the insistence of Drupada after deceiving him, and he decided to attack him quickly. When he arrived at Kāmpilya he sent his *purohita* as a messenger to Drupada. He said: "Tell that low man that he will soon reap the harvest of having married his daughter with mine!" O King, the *brāhmaṇa* went into the town of Kāmpilya to report the warning of Hiraṇyavarmā. King Drupada received him gladly and made Śikhaṇḍī offer him a libation, but the *purohita* did not accept anything and with harsh words delivered the words of his king, Hiraṇyavarmā: "O wretch, you have deliberately lied to me about your daughter. Now take the responsibility for that. Come in the field and fight with me. I will destroy you, your family and your people!" **[8-21]**

उद्धरिष्यामि ते सद्यः सामात्यसुतबान्धवम् ।
तदुपालम्भसंयुक्तं श्रावितः किल पार्थिवः ॥ २२ ॥

दशार्णपतिनोक्तेन मन्त्रिमध्ये पुरोधसा ।
अब्रवीद्भरतश्रेष्ठ द्रुपदः प्रणयानतः ॥ २३ ॥

यदाह मां भवान ब्रह्मन् सम्बन्धिवचनाद्वचः ।
अस्योत्तरं प्रतिवचो मम दूतो वदिष्यति ॥ २४ ॥

ततः संप्रेषयामास द्रुपदोपि महात्मने ।
हिरण्यवर्मणे दूतं ब्राह्मणं वेदपारगम् ॥ २५ ॥

समागम्य स राजानं दशार्णाधिपतिं तदा ।
तद्वाक्यमाददे राजन् यदुक्तं द्रुपदेन ह ॥ २६ ॥

आगमः क्रियतां व्यक्तः कुमाराऽयं सुतो मम ।
मिथ्यैतदुक्तं केनापि तदश्रद्धेयमित्युत ॥ २७ ॥

ततः स राजा द्रुपदस्य श्रुत्वा विमर्शयुक्तो युवतीर्वरिष्ठाः ।
सम्प्रेषयामास सुचारुरूपाः शिखण्डिनं स्त्री पुमान् वेति वेत्तुम् ॥ २८ ॥

ताः प्रेषितास्तत्त्वभावं विदित्वा प्रीत्या राज्ञे तच्छशंसुर्हि सर्वम् ।
शिखंडिनं पुरुषं कौरवेन्द्र दशार्णराजाय महानुभावम् ॥ २९ ॥

ततः कृत्वा तु राजा स आगमं प्रीतिमानथ ।
सम्बन्धिना समागम्य हृष्टो वासमुवास ह ॥ ३० ॥

शिखण्डिने च मुदितः प्रादाद्वित्तं जनेश्वरः ।
हस्तिनोऽश्वांश्च गाश्चैव दास्यश्च बहुलास्तथा ॥ ३१ ॥

पूजितश्च प्रतिययौ निर्भर्त्स्य तनयां किल ।
प्रतियाते तु दाशार्णे हृष्टरूपः शिखण्ड्यभूत् ॥ ३२ ॥

After listening to the angry words of King Hiraṇyavarmā through the mouth of the *purohita*, King Drupada with politeness said: "O *brāhmaṇa*, I will send a messenger to give an answer to my daughter's father-in-law." So Drupada also sent a *brāhmaṇa* to Hiraṇyavarmā: "Check yourself the masculinity of my son. No one has ever spoken falsely to you, do not think you have been cheated." When Hiraṇyavarmā received this information he left the previous idea of fighting and hired some young prostitutes to investigate if Śikhaṇḍī was a man or a woman. They went to Śikhaṇḍī and they ascertained his masculinity. So they returned to the king of Daśārṇa and confirmed what King Drupada had insisted on. Then the two kings met merrily and spent sometime together. Hiraṇyavarmā gave to Śikhaṇḍī many elephants, horses, cows and servants. After rebuking his daughter he left Kāmpilya with the blessing of Drupada. After he left, Śikhaṇḍī started to live happily in Kāmpilya. **[22-32]**

कस्यचित् त्वथ कालस्य कुबेरो नरवाहनः ।
लोकयात्रां प्रकुर्वाणः स्थूणस्यऽऽगान्निवेशनम् ॥ ३३ ॥

स तद्गृहस्योपरि वर्त्तमान आलोकयामास धनाधिगोप्ता ।
स्थूणस्य यक्षस्य विवेश वेश्म स्वलङ्कृतैर्माल्यगुणैर्विचित्रैः ॥ ३४ ॥

लाज्यैश्च गन्धैश्च तथा वितानैरभ्यार्चितं धूपनधूपितं च ।
ध्वजैः पताकाभिरलङ्कृतं च भक्ष्यान्नपेयामिषदन्तहोमम् ॥ ३५ ॥

तत् स्थानं तस्य दृष्ट्वा तु सर्वतः समलङ्कृतम् ।
मणिरत्नसुवर्णानां मालाभिः परिपूरितम् ॥ ३६ ॥

नानाकुसुमगन्धाढ्यं सिक्तसंमष्टशोभितम् ।
अथाब्रवीद्यक्षपतिस्तान् यक्षानऽनुगांस्तदा ॥ ३७ ॥

स्वलङ्कृतमिदं वेश्म स्थूणस्यामितविक्रमाः ।
नोपसर्पति मां चैव कस्मादद्य स मन्दधीः ॥ ३८ ॥

यस्माज्जानन् स मन्दात्मा मामसौ नोपसर्पति ।
तस्मात् तस्मै महादण्डो धार्यः स्यादिति मे मतिः ३९ ॥

Once Kubera while making a tour through the worlds arrived at the house of the *yakṣa* Sthūṇākarṇa. He got to the house of Sthūṇākarṇa and entered it. The house was adorned with very rare garlands. Inside there were perfumes of *khas* and sandalwood, the fragrance of the incenses, many banners and flags, a lot of food, pure water, meat, and other dishes. Everywhere it was decorated with precious stones and golden wreaths. Many different kind of flowers had been planted in that sparkling house. Kubera saw all this. Then he asked

Sthūṇākarṇa's servants where he was and why he did not come to welcome him, even though he knew already that he had arrived. Kubera got very angry because of this. **[33-39]**

यक्षा ऊचु -

द्रुपदस्य सुता राजन् राजो जाता शिखण्डिनी ।
तस्या निमित्ते कस्मिंश्चित प्रादात् पुरुषलक्षणम् ॥ ४० ॥

अग्रहील्लक्षणं स्त्रीणां स्त्रीभूता तिष्ठते गृहे ।
नोपसर्पति तेनासौ सव्रीडः स्त्रीसरूपवान् ॥ ४१ ॥

The Yakṣas said —

For some reason Sthūṇākarṇa has yielded his masculinity to the daughter of Drupada, and assumed her femininity. Ashamed of this he is sitting inside, not daring to come in front of you. **[40-41]**

आनीयतां स्थूण इति ततो यक्षाधिपोऽब्रवीत् ।
कर्त्ताऽस्मि निग्रहं तस्येत्युवाच स पुनः पुनः ॥ ४२ ॥

सोऽभ्यागच्छत यक्षेन्द्रमाहूतः पृथिवीपते ।
स्त्रीसरूपो महाराज तसथौ व्रीडासमन्वितः ॥ ४३ ॥

तं शशापाथ संक्रुद्धो धनदः कुरुनन्दन ।
एवमेव भवत्वस्य स्त्रीत्वं पापस्य गुह्यकाः ॥ ४४ ॥

अप्रवृत्तं सुदुर्बुद्धे यस्मादेतत त्वया कृतम ।
तस्मादद्य प्रभृत्येव स्त्री त्वं सा पुरुषस्तथा ॥ ४५ ॥

ततः प्रसादयामासुर्यक्षा वैश्रवणं किल ।
स्थूणस्यार्थे कुरुष्वान्तं शापस्येति पुनः पुनः ॥ ४६ ॥

ततो महात्मा यक्षेन्द्रः प्रत्युवाचानुगामिनः ।
सर्वान् यक्षगणांस्तात शापस्यान्तचिकीर्षया ॥ ४७ ॥

शिखण्डिनि हते यक्षाः स्वं रूपं प्रतिपत्स्यते ।
स्थूणोयक्षो निरुद्वेगो भवत्विति महामनाः ॥ ४८ ॥

इत्युक्त्का भगवान् देवो यक्षराजः सुपूजितः ।
प्रययौ सहितःसर्वैर्निमेषान्तरचारिभिः ॥ ४९ ॥

स्थूणस्तु शापं संप्राप्य तत्रैव न्यवसत् तदा ।
समये चागमत् तूर्णं शिखण्डी तं क्षपाचरम् ॥ ५० ॥

सोभिगम्याब्रवीद्वाक्यं प्राप्तोस्मि भगवन्निति ।
तमब्रवीत् ततं स्थूणः प्रीतोस्मीति पुनः पुनः ॥ ५१ ॥

आर्जवेनागतं दृष्ट्वा राजपुत्रं शिखण्डिनम् ।
सर्वमेव यथावृत्तमाचचक्षे शिखण्डिने ॥ ५२ ॥

Then Kubera said that Sthūṇākarṇa be brought there by force to be punished. The blushing female, Sthūṇākarṇa was brought into Kubera's presence. He cast a curse on him: "You have committed such a sin that you shall remain a woman forever and Śikhaṇḍī will remain a man." The *yakṣa*s begged Kubera a lot to cancel the curse, but he said that only upon the death of Śikhaṇḍī would Sthūṇākarṇa get back his masculinity. After saying this Kubera went away along with his followers, and Sthūṇākarṇa stayed there. At the right time Śikhaṇḍī returned there and noting his sincerity, Sthūṇākarṇa explained as to what had happened. **[42-52]**

यक्ष उवाच -

शप्तो वैश्रवणेनाहं त्वत्कृते पार्थिवात्मज ।
गच्छेदानीं यथाकामं चर लोकान् यथासुखम् ॥ ५३ ॥

दिष्टमेतत् पुरा मन्ये न शक्यमतिवर्तितुम् ।
गमनं तव चेतो हि पौलस्त्यस्य च दर्शनम् ॥ ५४ ॥

Sthūṇākarṇa said —

O son of king, because of you Kubera has cursed me; now you go where you want. The damage cannot be repaired, neither by your staying here nor by the coming of Kubera. **[53-54]**

भीष्म उवाच -

एवमुक्तः शिखण्डी च स्थूणायक्षेण भारत ।
प्रत्याजगाम नगरं हर्षेण महता वृतः ॥ ५५ ॥

पूजयामास विविधैर्गन्धमाल्यैर्महाधनैः ।
द्वितातीन् देवताश्चैव चैत्यानथ चतुष्पथान् ॥ ५६ ॥

द्रुपदः सह पुत्रेण सिद्धार्थेन शिखण्डिना ।
मुदं च परमां लेभे पाञ्चाल्यः सह बान्धवैः ॥ ५७ ॥

शिष्यार्थं प्रददौ चाथ द्रोणाय कुरुपुङ्गव ।
शिखण्डिनं महाराज पुत्रं स्त्रीपूर्विणं तथा ॥ ५८ ॥

प्रतिपेदे चतुष्पादं धनुर्वेदं नृपात्मजः ।
शिखण्डी सह युष्माभिर्धृष्टद्युम्नश्च पार्षतः ॥ ५९ ॥

मम त्वेतच्चरास्तात यथावत प्रत्यवेदयन् ।
जडान्धवधिराकारा ये मुक्ता द्रुपदे मया ॥ ६० ॥

एवमेष महाराज स्त्रीपुमान् द्रुपदात्मजः ।
स संभूतः कुरुश्रेष्ठ शिखण्डी रथसत्तमः ॥ ६१ ॥

Bhīṣma said —

Śikhaṇḍī was very happy to hear that and went home, and there were performed offerings to *brāhmaṇas*, *devatās*, temples and altars. King Drupada and his friends were glad to see that Śikhaṇḍī was still a man. He was made to follow Droṇācārya as his teacher. From him he learnt the *dhanurveda* along with Dhṛṣṭadyumna, you (Duryodhana) and your brothers. O King, all this story was told to me by the spies whom I had sent to Drupada's court in the disguise of madmen, mutes and blind men. This is the story of Śikhaṇḍī who after being born as a woman became a man.[26] **[55-61]**

॥ *इति श्री कां० मा० शिखण्डिपुंस्त्वप्राप्तिर्नाम चतुस्त्रिंशोऽध्यायः* ॥
Here ends the thirty-fourth chapter of the Kāmpilyamahātmya.

26. The story of Śikhaṇḍī is described in *Mbh.* Bhīṣma-Parva, chapter 9, stanza 41.

35

Description of the Dynasty of King Drupada; on the Name of Kāmpilya and of Pañcāla

जनमेजय उवाच -

कथं काम्पिल्लसञ्ज्ञेति जाता तन्नगरस्य हि ।
कुतः स कथ्यते ब्रह्मन् देशः पाञ्चालसंज्ञकः ॥ १ ॥

द्रुपदस्य च राजर्षेः कस्मिन् वंशो समुद्भवः ।
सर्वमेतत् समाचक्ष्व ममाद्य मुनिपुङ्गव ॥ २ ॥

Janamejaya said —

O *brāhmaṇa*, why is that town called Kāmpilya? Why is that region called Pañcāla? And which *vaṁśa* did King Drupada belong to? Please tell me. [1-2]

वैशम्पायन उवाच -

अजमीढस्य नीलिन्यां नीलः शान्तिस्तु नीलजः ।
शान्तेः सुशान्तिस्तत्पुत्रः पुरुजोऽर्कस्ततोऽभवत् ॥ ३ ॥

भर्म्याश्वस्तत्सुतस्तस्य पञ्चासन् मुदुलोऽग्रजः ।
तस्मात् तु ब्रह्म निर्वृत्तं गोत्रं मुद्गलसंज्ञितम् ॥ ४ ॥

सृञ्जयश्चैव राजासीदथो बृहदिषुर्नृप ।
यवीनरश्च काम्पिल्लः काम्पिल्लं येन निर्मितम् ॥ ५ ॥

भर्म्याश्वः प्राह पुत्रा मे पंचानां रक्षणाय हि ।
विषयाणामलमिमे इति पंचालसंज्ञिताः ॥ ६ ॥

इत्थं काम्पिल्लपंचालसंज्ञाहेतुः स्मृतस्तव ।
द्रुपदस्याथ राजर्षेरन्ववायं निबोध मे ॥ ७ ॥

Vaiśampāyana said —

King Ajamīḍha's queen, Nīlinī, had a son called Nīla. He begot Śānti, who begot Suśānti, who begot Puruja, who begot Arka. His son Bhṛmyāśva had five sons: Mudgala, Sṛñjaya, Bṛhadiṣu, Yavīnara and Kāmpilla. Among them Mudgala was born first, from whom the Mudgala *gotra*, lineage, sprang.[27] Sṛñjaya was a king and he founded Kāmpilya. After him came Bṛhadiṣu, Yavīnara and Kāmpilla, after whom the city took its name. King Bhṛmyāśva declared his five sons capable of protecting the country. For this reason this region is named Pañcāla (*pañca* = five). O King, I have told you from where the names of Kāmpilya and Pañcāla derive. Now listen to the genealogy of Drupada. **[3-7]**

आसीत पंचजनः पुत्रः सृञ्जयस्य महात्मनः ।
पुत्रः पंचजनस्यापि सोमदत्तो महीपतिः ॥ ८ ॥

सोमदत्तस्य दायादः सहदेवो महायशाः ।
सहदेवसुतश्चापि सोमको नाम पार्थिवः ॥ ९ ॥

सोमकस्य शतं पुत्रा वभू वुरमरोपमाः ।
तेषां जन्तुरभूज्ज्येष्ठो यवीयान् पृषतः स्मृतः ॥ १० ॥

पृषतस्य सुतो राजन् द्रुपदो नृपसत्तमः ।
तस्यापि तनया आसन सत्यजित् सत्यविक्रमः ॥ ११ ॥

पार्थस्य चक्ररक्षौ च युधामन्यूत्तमौजसौ ।
धृष्टद्युम्नश्च सेनानीः शिखण्डी स्त्रीपुमान् नृप ॥ १२ ॥

ऋक्षदेवः क्षत्रदेवः शस्त्रगुप्तस्तथैव च ।
शिखण्डितनयास्ते तु भारते निधनं गताः ॥ १३ ॥

---

27. The *gotra* of Mudgala is still present in the region. The king Mudgala, because of his meritorious behaviour, was changed into a *brāhmaṇa*, and his descendants also were held as *brāhmaṇa* kings.

क्षत्रञ्जयः क्षत्रधर्मा धृष्टद्युम्नसुतावुभौ ।
भारते निधनं प्राप्तौ धृष्टकेतुस्तु वंशकृत् ॥ १४ ॥

एष रे कथितो राजन् द्रुपदस्य मयाऽन्वयः ।
यत्राऽऽसीत् साहदेविस्तु सोमको ददतां वरः ॥ १५ ॥

सर्व एते महाराज स्मृताः पाञ्चालसंज्ञकाः ।
कथ्यन्ते सृंजयाश्चापि तथैव नृप सोमकाः ॥ १६ ॥

Sṛñjaya's son was Pañcajana, his son was Somadatta, from Somadatta Sahadeva was born, then Somaka who had 100 sons. The first of them all was Jantu and the youngest was Pṛṣata. Pṛṣata was the father of Drupada. He had five sons: Satyajīta, Yudhamanyu, Uttamauja, Dhṛṣṭadyumna and Śikhaṇḍī. Among them the second and the third defended Arjuna, whilst the fourth was his general. Śikhaṇḍī's sons were Ṛkṣdeva, Kṣetradeva, Śastragupta. Dhṛṣṭadyumna's sons, Kṣatrañjaya and Kṣatradharma, were killed in the Bhārata war. The genealogy went on through another son of Dhṛṣṭadyumna: Dhṛṣṭaketu. O King, I have told you the genealogy of King Drupada. In this the foremost was Somaka. They have all been called Pāñcāla, Sṛñjaya and Somaka.[28] **[8-16]**

सूत उवाच -

एतच्छ्रुत्वा तु कौरव्यः स वैशम्पायनोदितम् ।
पप्रच्छानन्तरं भूयः सोमकं प्रति शौनक ॥ १७ ॥

Sūta said —

After this speech of Śaunaka *ṛṣi*, the king of the Kuru asked him again about King Somaka. **[17]**

॥ *इति श्री का० मा० द्रुपदवंशवर्णनंनाम पंचत्रिशोऽध्यायः* ॥
Here ends the thirty-fifth chapter of the Kāmpilyamāhātmya.

---

28. Also today in this region there are many *kṣatriya* belonging to the Somavaṁśa who are called Somakavaṁśī.

36

The Story of King Somaka

जनमेजय उवाच -

कथंवीर्यः स राजाऽभूत् सोमकोददतांवरः ।
कर्माण्यस्य प्रभावं च श्रोतुमिच्छामि तत्त्वतः ॥ १ ॥

Janamejaya said —

Who was King Somaka, what he did and what was his influence? I want to hear about him. **[1]**

वैशम्पायन उवाच -

पारीक्षिताऽऽसोन्नृपतिः सोमको नाम धार्मिकः ।
तस्य भार्याशतं राजन् सदृशीनामभूत् तदा ॥ २ ॥

स वै यत्नेन महता तासु पुत्रं महीपतिः ।
कश्चिन्नासादयामास कालेन महता ह्यपि ॥ ३ ॥

कदाचित् तस्य वृद्धस्य घटमानस्य यत्नतः ।
जन्तुर्नाम सुतस्तस्मिन् स्त्रीशते समजायत ॥ ४ ॥

तं जातं मातरः सर्वाः परिवार्य समासते ।
सततं पृष्ठतः कृत्वा कामभोगान् विशाम्पते ॥ ५ ॥

ततः पिपीलिका जन्तुः कदाचिददशत् स्फिचि ।
स दष्टो व्यनदन्नादं तेन दुःखेन बालकः ॥ ६ ॥

ततस्ता मातरः सर्वाः प्राक्रोशन् भृशदुःखिताः ।
प्रवार्य जन्तुं सहसा स शब्दस्तुमुलोऽभवत् ॥ ७ ॥

तमार्तनादं सहसा शुश्राव स महीपतिः ।
अमात्यपर्षदो मध्ये उपविष्टः सहर्त्विजा ॥ ८ ॥

ततः प्रस्थापयामास किमेतदिति पार्थिवः ।
तस्मै क्षत्ता यथावृत्तमाचचक्षे सुतं प्रति ॥ ९ ॥

त्वरमाणः स चोत्थाय सोमकः सह मन्त्रिभिः ।
प्रविश्यान्तः पुरं पुत्रमाश्वासयदरिंदमः ॥ १० ॥

सान्त्वयित्वा तु तं पुत्रं निःक्रम्यान्तःपुरान्नृपः ।
ऋत्विजासहितो राजन्सहामात्य उपाविशत् ॥ ११ ॥

Vaiśampāyana said —

O son of Parīkṣit, King Somaka was a follower of *dharma* and he had one hundred faithful wives. Even after a lot of time he could not get any children from these queens. He was already old when he had a son from one of them called Jantu. All the other queens who were not busy with their own duties used to sit with the boy. Once an ant bit him and he started crying, and all the mothers around him also started to cry. An awful mourning sound arose. The king, his counsellors and *brāhmaṇa*s seated in the assembly heard the crying. An attendant was sent into the queens' apartment to enquire as what had happened. When he came back he explained to the king what had happened. Somaka with his ministers also went to see the child. Then he came back in the assembly to make a decision. **[2-11]**

सोमक उवाच -

धिगस्त्विहैकपुत्रत्वमपुत्रत्वं वरं भवेत् ।
नित्यातुरत्वाद् भूतानां शोक एवैकपुत्रता ॥ १२ ॥

इदं भार्याशतं ब्रह्मन् परीक्ष्य सदृशं प्रभो ।
पुत्रार्थिना मया वोढं न तासां विद्यते प्रजा ॥ १३ ॥

एकः कथञ्चिदुत्पन्नः पुत्रो जन्तुरयं मम ।
यतमानस्य सर्वासु किं नु दुःखमतः परम ॥ १४ ॥

वयश्च समतीतं मे सभार्यस्य द्विजोत्तम ।
आसां प्राणाः समायत्ता मम चात्रैकपुत्रके ॥ १५ ॥
स्यात् तु कर्म तथा युक्तं येन पुत्रशतं भवेत् ।
महता लघुना वापि कर्मणा दुष्करेण वा ॥ १६ ॥

Somaka said (to his *ṛtvija*, the performer of the sacrifice): "O *brāhmaṇa*, it is a curse to have only one son; it is better not to have any children than to have only one. To be the only son is a cause of suffering for children. I have carefully chosen these hundred queens, but still I cannot get any more sons from them. After much effort I had Jantu who is going to suffer from being the only son because I and the queens are ageing and we concentrate all our attention on him. Even if it would be very hard, please tell me some remedy by which I can have one hundred sons: I will do whatever is necessary." **[12-16]**

ऋत्विगुवाच -

अस्ति वै तादृशं कर्म येन पुत्रशतं भवेत् ।
यदि शक्नोषि तत् कर्तुमथ वक्ष्यामि सोमक ॥ १७ ॥

The Ṛtvija said —

There is a way to have one hundred sons if you can manage it. I will explain. **[17]**

सोमक उवाच -

कार्यं वा यदि वाऽकार्यं येन पुत्रशतं भवेत् ।
कृतमेवेति तद् विद्धि भगवान् प्रब्रवीतु मे ॥ १८ ॥

Somaka said —

O *brāhmaṇa*, you should understand that in order to get one hundred sons I am ready to do anything, suitable or unsuitable. Please tell me. **[18]**

ऋत्विगुवाच -

यजस्व जन्तुना राजंस्त्वं मया वितते क्रतौ ।
ततः पुत्रशतं श्रीमद् भविष्यत्यचिरेण ते ॥ १९ ॥

वपाया हूयमानाया धूमवाघ्राय मातरः ।
ततस्ताः सुमहावीर्यान् जनयिष्यन्ति ते सुतान् ॥ २० ॥

तस्यामेव तु ते जन्तुर्भविता पुनरात्मजः ।
उत्तरे चास्य सौवर्णं लक्ष्म पार्श्वे भविष्यति ॥ २१ ॥

The Ṛtvija said —

O King, if you sacrifice Jantu and offer him in the fire, *havana*, you will certainly get one hundred sons. Your queens will have to inhale the smoke rising from his burning flesh, from that they will give you formidable sons. And Jantu will also be born again from his mother. He will have a golden mark on his left side where the ant bit him. **[19-21]**

॥ इति श्री का० मा० जन्तूपाख्यानं नाम षट्त्रिंशोध्यायः॥

Here ends the thirty-sixth chapter of the Kāmpilyamahātmya.

37

Somaka Gets 100 Sons From His as Many Wives

सोमक उवाच -

ब्रह्मन् यद् यद् यथा कार्यं तत् कुरुष्व तथा तथा ।
पुत्रका मतया सर्वं करिष्यामि वचस्तव ॥ १ ॥

Somaka said —

Please do whatever is necessary; my desire to have sons is so strong. **[1]**

वैशम्पायन उवाच -

ततः स याजयामास सोमकं तेन जन्तुना ।
मातरस्तु वलात् पुत्रमऽपाकर्षुः कृपान्विताः ॥ २ ॥

हा हताः स्मेति वाशन्त्यस्तीव्रशोकसमन्विताः ।
रुदन्त्यः करुण वापि गृहीत्वा दक्षिणे करे ॥ ३ ॥

सव्ये पाणौ गृहीत्वा तु याजकोपि स्म कर्षति ।
कुररीणामिवार्तानां समाकृष्य तु तं सुतम् ॥ ४ ॥

विशस्य चैनं विधिवद् वपामस्य जुहाव सः ।
वपाया ह्रूयमानाया धूममाघ्राय मातरः ॥ ५ ॥

आर्त्ता निपेतुः सहसा पृथिव्यां कुरुनन्दन ।
सर्वाश्च गर्भानऽलभंस्ततस्ताः परमाङ्गनाः ॥ ६ ॥

ततो दशसु मासेषु सोमकस्य विशाम्पते ।
जज्ञे पुत्रशतं पूर्णं तासु सर्वासु भारत ॥ ७ ॥

जन्तुर्ज्येष्ठः समभवज्जनित्र्यामेव पार्थिव ।
स तासामिष्ठ एवासीन्न तथा ते निजाः सुताः ॥ ८ ॥

तच्च लक्षणमस्यासीत् सौवर्णं पार्श्वं उत्तरे ।
तस्मिन् पुत्रशते चाग्र्यूः स वभूव गुणैरपि ॥ ९ ॥

Vaiśampāyana said —

Then the Ṛtvija offered the son of Somaka in the *havana*. His mothers were holding him from the right side while the Ṛtvija was pulling him from the left side. Then he managed to seize him from the mothers who were crying like birds. He was cut in the ritual way and his body was offered on the fire. The smoke was inhaled by the queens who fell senseless on the ground. They all became pregnant. And after ten (lunar) months each of them had a son. The first of all was Jantu who was born from the same mother. He was very precious to all the queens, even more than their own sons. On his left side there was the golden mark and he was endowed with better qualities than all his brothers. **[2-9]**

ततः स लोकमगमत् सोमकस्य गुरुः परम् ।
अथ काले व्यतीते तु सोमकोप्यगमत् परम ॥ १० ॥

अथ तं नरके घोरे पच्यमानं ददर्श सः ।
तमपृच्छत् किमर्थं त्वं नरके पच्यसे द्विज ॥ ११ ॥

तमब्रवीद् गुरुः सोथ पच्यमानोऽग्निना भृशम् ।
त्वं मया याजितो राजस्तस्येदं कर्मणः फलम् ॥ १२ ॥

एतच्छ्रुत्वा स राजर्षिर्द्धर्मराजानमब्रवीत् ।
अहमत्र प्रवेक्ष्यामि मुच्यतां मम याजकः ॥ १३ ॥

मत्कृते हि महाभागः पच्यते नरकाग्निना ।

Then the *guru* of Somaka, the Ṛtvija, left his body, and after sometime Somaka also did the same. When he saw that the Ṛtvija had reached hell, he asked: "Why are you here?" Then the Ṛtvija said: "I am cooking in the fire because of the *yajña* I performed for you." When the king heard that he asked

46

On the Dynasty of Ugrāyuddha, the Destroyer of the Nīpas[59]

युधिष्ठिर उवाच -

उग्रायुधः कस्य सुतः कस्मिन् वंशे स जज्ञिवान्।
किमर्थं चापि भवता निहतस्तद् ब्रवीहि मे ॥ १ ॥

Yudhiṣṭhira said —

Whose son was Ugrāyuddha? To which genealogy did he belong and why did you kill him? **[1]**

भीष्म उवाच -

द्विमीढस्य तु दायादो विद्वान् राजा यवीनरः।
धृतिमांस्तस्य पुत्रस्तु तस्य सत्यधृतिः स्मृतः ॥ २ ॥

जज्ञे सत्यधृतेः पुत्रो द्रुढनेमिः प्रतापवान्।
द्रुढनेमिसुतश्चापि सुधर्मानाम पार्थिवः ॥ ३ ॥

आसीत् सुधर्मणः पुत्रः सार्वभौमः प्रजेश्वरः।
सार्वभौम इति ख्यातः पृथिव्यामेकराड विभुः ॥ ४ ॥

तस्यान्ववाये महति महान् पौरवनन्दनः।
महतश्चापि पुत्रस्तु राजा रुक्मरथः स्मृतः ॥ ५ ॥

पुत्रो रुक्मरथस्यापि सुपार्श्वो नाम पार्थिवः।
सुपार्श्वतनयश्चापि सुमतिर्नाम धार्मिकः ॥ ६ ॥

---

59. *Harivam.*, 20.

and his ancestors reached *svarga*. Every man who performs the *piṇḍadāna* with faith there will attain the best state.

O King, (1) Amāvasyā, (2) Monday, (3) Śardvīpa, (4) Mahālaya (the black fortnight of the month of Āśvin), these four alone are very sacred. If by chance these four coincide, who is the poet able to describe the greatness of such a combination? **[23-34]**

जनमेजय उवाच -

ब्रह्मन् निमन्त्रितानां तु ब्राह्मणानां निरागसाम् ।
लम्बोदरोतिसरलो गरलं दत्तवान् कथम् ॥ ३५ ॥

Janamejaya said —

O *brāhmaṇa*, why would the virtuous Lambodara have served poisoned food to the innocent *brāhmaṇas*? **[35]**

वैशम्पायन उवाच -

लम्बोदरस्य नृपते नैतत् कर्म सुदारुणम् ।
दुःशीला तस्य भार्याऽऽसीन्नामतो गुणतोपि च ॥ ३६ ॥

सा चिरं चिन्तयामास निजभर्तृविनाशनम् ।
लब्ध्वैतदन्तरं क्षीरं तया सगरलं कृतम ॥ ३७ ॥

निजदारापराधेन पूर्वजैः साकमूरुजः ।
लम्बोदरो निरालम्बः सोढवान् सुचिरं तमः ॥ ३८ ॥

Vaiśampāyana said —

That bad action was not committed by Lambodara but by his wife, who was by name and quality Duḥśīla (wicked disposition). She had been planning for sometime to kill her husband to be independent. When the opportunity arose she mixed some poison with the milk. O King, because of his wife's offence, Lambodara and all his ancestors had to suffer for a long period. **[36-38]**

॥ *इति श्री का० मा० लम्बोदरोपाख्यानं नाम चत्वारिंशोऽध्यायः* ॥

Here ends the fortieth chapter of the Kāmpilyamahātmya.

41

The Importance of Performing *Śrāddha* at Sardvīpa *Tīrtha*

सूत उवाच -

लम्बोदरगतिं श्रुत्वा विस्मितः कुरुभूपतिः ।
स वैशम्पायनं भूयो जगाद भृगुनन्दन ॥ १ ॥

Sūta said —

On hearing the story of Lambodara, King Janamejaya was awe-struck and again he asked Vaiśampāyana. **[1]**

जनमेजय उवाच -

मुने त्वया समुदिता शरद्वीपे वणिग्गतिः ।
पितृणां पिण्डदानेन तत्र नः संशयो महान् ॥ २ ॥

किमर्थमाश्वयुङ्मासकृष्णपक्षः पितृप्रियः ।
अमावास्या तथा सोमः कथमेतौ पितृप्रियौ ॥ ३ ॥

पंचालविषये यत् तद् दक्षिणे जाह्नवीतटे ।
शरद्वीपाह्वयं तीर्थं तत् कथं पितृवल्लभम् ॥ ४ ॥

यत्र लम्बोदरः स्नात्वा श्राद्धं कृत्वाऽथ तर्पणम् ।
अपापः पूर्वजैः साकं नाकलोकमवाप ह ॥ ५ ॥

Janamejaya said —

O *muni*, you said that Lambodara got the beatitude after death by offering the *piṇḍadāna* on *somavatī amāvasyā* at the Śardvīpa *tīrtha*. I have some doubts about that. Why is the black fortnight of the month of Kvāra dear to the ancestors, and why are the nights of new moon and Monday also dear to the ancestors? Why is the Śardvīpa *tīrtha* at the southern banks of the Gaṅgā in the land of Pañcāla also dear to the *pitṛ*, where Lambodara after bathing, performing *śrāddha*, and offering libation attained heaven along with his ancestors? **[1-5]**

वैशम्पायन उवाच -

सम्यगुक्तं महाराज धर्मयुक्तं वचस्तव ।
अनन्यगतिको भूत्वा शृणु सर्वं यथाक्रमम् ॥ ६ ॥

आषाढीमवधिं कृत्वा पञ्चमं पक्षमाश्रिताः ।
काङ्क्षन्ति पितरः क्लिष्टा अन्नमप्यऽन्वहं जलम् ॥ ७ ॥

तृप्ताः सम्वत्सरं यावत् तत्र पिण्डप्रदानतः ।
एतस्मात् कारणाद् राजन् पितृप्रेष्टो महालयः ॥ ८ ॥

अमावास्यां पितृश्राद्धमुक्तं वेदपुराणायोः ।
पितरः स्वामिनश्चास्यास्ततः सा पितृतुष्टिदा ॥ ९ ॥

अग्नौ प्रास्ताहुतिर्यद्वदादित्यमुपतिष्ठति ।
तद्वत् श्राद्धे दत्तमन्नं सोमस्याप्यायनं भवेत् ॥ १० ॥

यत् सोमायेतिमन्त्रेण श्राद्धेन्नं सम्प्रदीयते ।
स्वर्गस्थानां पितृणां तत् सुधारूपं प्रजायते ॥ ११ ॥

मानुषे त्वोषधीरूपं तदेव जनमेजय ।
अतः सुधाकरश्चायमोषधीशश्च कथ्यते ॥ १२ ॥

ओषधीषु च सर्वासु श्राद्धे मेध्यं परं तिलाः ।
सोमस्तद्दैवतं चातः सोमवारः पितृःप्रियः ॥ १३ ॥

सोमो हि भगवान् देवः पितृणां तर्पणं यतः ।
सोमपाः पितरश्चातः० ॥ १४ ॥

कौशिकस्य मुनेः सप्त सुताः केनापि हेतुना शुभे ।
तीर्थे शरद्वीपे चक्रवाकत्वमागताः ॥ १५ ॥

मुनिवन्मौनिनस्तत्र चक्रुस्ते परमं तपः ।
ततो जन्मान्तरे सिद्धा लेभिरे परमां गतिम् ॥ १६ ॥

तेषां तपःप्रभावाच्च शिवस्य वचनात् तथा ।
शरद्वीपाह्वयं तीर्थं पितॄणां प्रीतिवर्द्धनम् ॥ १७ ॥

लम्बोदरस्तथाऽन्येऽत्र मनुजा मनुजाधिप ।
श्राद्धं विधाय विधिवद् विशुद्धास्त्रिदिवं गताः ॥ १८ ॥

श्राद्धैः प्रीणाति हि पितॄन् सर्वकामफलैस्तु यः ।
तत्परः प्रयतः श्राद्धी प्रेत्य चेह च मोदते ॥ १९ ॥

पितरो धर्मकामस्य प्रजाकामस्य च प्रजाम् ।
पुष्टिकामस्य पुष्टिं च प्रयच्छन्ति क्षितोश्वर ॥ २० ॥

श्राद्धात् परतरं नान्यच्छ्रेयस्करमुदाहृतम् ।
धरण्यां धरणीपाल ततः श्राद्धं समाचरेत् ॥ २१ ॥

न सन्ति पितरश्चेति कृत्वा मनसि यो नरः ।
श्राद्धं न कुरुते तस्य पिबन्ति पितरो ह्यस्टक् ॥ २२ ॥

Vaiśampāyana said —

O King, the four questions you ask are very good. Now listen to the answers in due order. (1) From the full moon of the month of Āṣāḍha for five fortnights (up to the black fortnight of Āśvin) ancestors want food and water everyday. The offering of the *piṇḍadāna* in those days satisfies them for the entire year. For this reason the dark fortnight of the month of Āśvin (*kanāgat*) is dear to the *pitṛ*. (2) The Veda and the Purāṇas affirm the importance of the *piṇḍadāna* made on *amāvasyā*, new moon day, (whilst the *pūrṇimā* day is for the gods); moreover the lords of *amāvasyā* are the *pitṛ*: so the *amāvasyā* day is favourite to the ancestors. (3) As the *āhuti* offered into the fire reaches the Sun, so the food offered in the *śrāddha* rite goes to the Moon. The food offered to the *pitṛ* in the *śrāddha* with the right *mantra* (*oṁ somāya pitṛmate svadhā namaḥ*) becomes ambrosia for the *pitṛ*s who are in the *svarga*, and *oṣadhi* (wheat, barley, etc.) for the *pitṛ*s who are on the earth; for this reason the moon is called Sudhākara (receptacle of nectar) and Oṣadhīśa (lord of herbs).[46] Among the (annual) herbs, sesame is considered the most sacred and its lord is Candramā;[47] so the Śruti declares that Monday is dear to the *pitṛ*s, and Candramā likes the offerings of sesame.[48] The moon, Candramā, is a mighty god by whom the ancestors can drink the ambrosia. So another name for the *pitṛ*s is Somapā (drinkers of *soma*) and thus Somavāra is their favourite day. (4) For some reason the seven sons of Viśvāmitra became ruddy geese; at the Śardvīpa *tīrtha* they performed *tapas* like the sages. In another birth they became *siddha* and attained *mukti*. By the effect of their *tapas* and the aforesaid declaraton of Śivajī[49] the Śardvīpa *tīrtha* is very dear to the *pitṛ*s, where Lambodara and many other men obtained the best fruit from the *śrāddha* rite. O King, the man who satisfies the *pitṛ*s with the rite of *śrāddha* will get the highest happiness here and hereafter. And he will give *dharma* to the ancestors who long for *dharma*, progeny to the ones who want progeny, and wealth to the ones who want wealth. O king, in this world there is no rite more effective and beneficial then the *śrāddha*: so it is very important that every man performs it. Those people who don't perform the *śrāddha* rite without considering their ancestors, they will have to suffer the anger of the *pitṛ*s and after illness and pains their blood will dry up. **[6-22]**

॥ इति श्री का० मा० महालयादिमहत्त्ववर्णनं नामैकचत्वारिंशोऽध्यायः॥

Here ends the forty-first chapter of the Kāmpilyamāhātmya.

---

46. *tathā ca śrutiḥ soma oṣadhīnāmadhipatiḥ iti*

47. Manu: *trīṇi śrāddhe pavitrāṇī dauhitraḥ kutapastilāḥ iti*. There are two types of plants: *vanaspati* and *oṣadhi*. The former are those that grow spontaneously and last along the years, whilst the latter are those plants that are cultivated and their bearing fruit coincides with their cutting.

48. *tilosi somadevatyāḥ iti.*

49. *idaṁ tīrthaṁ mahāpuṇyamityādi.*

42

Discussion About *Śrāddha* and *Piṇḍadāna* Between Yudhiṣṭhira and Bhīṣma

जनमेजय उवाच -

कथं विहितमस्माभिः श्राद्धं प्रीणाति वै पितॄन्।
एतद् वेदितुमिच्छामः श्राद्धस्य फलमुत्तमम्॥ १॥

Janamejaya said —

O *muni*, how are the ancestors satisfied by the *śrāddha* performed by men? Please tell me about it. **[1]**

वैशम्पायन उवाच -

शरतल्पगतं भीष्ममेवमेव पुरा नृप।
अपृच्छद्धर्मराजोपियन्मां त्वं परिपृच्छसि॥ २॥

Vaiśampāyana said —

O King, the same question was put by King Yudhiṣṭhira to Bhīṣmajī, while the latter was lying on the battleground, impaled on a bed of arrows. **[2]**

युधिष्ठिर उवाच -

वर्त्तन्ते पितरः स्वर्गे केषांचिन्नरके पुनः।
प्राणिनां नियतं वापि कर्मजं फलमुच्यते॥ ३॥

श्राद्धानि चैव कुर्वन्ति फलकामाः सदा नराः।
अभिसन्धाय पितरं पितुश्च पितरं तथा॥ ४॥

पितुः पितामहं चैव त्रिषु पिण्डेषु नित्यशः ।
तानि श्राद्धानि दत्तानि कथं गच्छन्ति वै पितॄन् ॥ ५ ॥

कथं च शक्तास्ते दातुं नरकस्थाः फलं पुनः ।
के बा ते पितरोऽन्ये स्म कान् यजामो वयं पुनः ॥ ६ ॥

देवा अपि पितॄन् स्वर्गे यजन्तीति च नः श्रुतम् ।
एतदिच्छाम्यहं श्रोतुं विस्तरेण महाद्युते ॥ ७ ॥

स भवान् कथयत्वेतां कथाममितबुद्धिमान् ।
यथा दत्तं पितॄणां हि तारणायेह जायते ॥ ८ ॥

Yudhiṣṭhira said —

The ancestors of some are in *svarga* whilst the ancestors of others are in *naraka* (hell), and all creatures will receive the fruit of their own *karma*. Man performs *śrāddha* in the hope of getting sons, riches, and other benefits. They give the *piṇḍa* to the father, grandfather and great-grandfather: how does that offering reach the ancestors? How can the ancestors who are in hell give the fruit of the *piṇḍadāna*? In this case is the donor of the fruit another *pitṛ*? And if the donor is another one should we offer to our own ancestors or straight to the donor? And we have also heard that the gods who are at present in heaven also adore the *pitṛ*s: who are those *pitṛ*s? Please tell me that in detail, so that I can understand how my offering of food and water rescues my ancestors. **[3-8]**

भीष्म उवाच -

अत्र ते कीर्तयिष्यामि यथाश्रुतमरिन्दम ।
पित्रा मम पुरा गीतं लोकान्तरगतेन वै ॥ ९ ॥

श्राद्धकाले मम पितुर्मया पिण्डः समुद्यतः ।
तं पिता मम हस्तेन भित्त्वा भूमिमयाचत ॥ १० ॥

हस्ताभरणपूर्णेन केयूराभरणेन च ।
रक्ताङ्गुलितलेनाथ यथा दृष्टः पुरा मया ॥ ११ ॥

नैष कल्पे विधिर्दृष्ट इति संचिन्त्य चाप्यहम् ।
कुशेष्वेव ततः पिण्डं दत्तवानविचारयन् ॥ १२ ॥

ततः पिता मे सुप्रीतो वाचा मधुरया तदा ।
उवाच भरतश्रेष्ठ प्रीयमाणो मयाऽनघ ॥ १३ ॥

त्वया दायादवानस्मि कृतार्थोऽमुत्र चेह च ।
सत्पुत्रेण त्वया पुत्र धर्मज्ञेन विपश्चिता ॥ १४ ॥

मया तु तव जिज्ञासा प्रयुक्तैषा दृढव्रत ।
व्यवस्थानं तु धर्मेषु कर्तुं लोकस्य चानघ ॥ १५ ॥

यथा चतुर्थं धर्मस्य रक्षिता लभते फलम् ।
पापस्यापि तथा मूढः फलं प्राप्नोत्यरक्षिता ॥ १६ ॥

प्रमाणं यद्धि कुरुते धर्माचारेषु पार्थिवः ।
प्रजास्तदनुवर्त्तन्ते प्रमाणाचरितं सदा ॥ १७ ॥

त्वया च भरतश्रेष्ठ वेदधर्माश्च शाश्वताः ।
कृताः प्रमाणं प्रीतिश्च मम निर्वर्तिताऽतुला ॥ १८ ॥

तस्मात् तवाहं सुप्रीतः प्रीत्या च वरमुत्तमम् ।
ददामि तं प्रतीच्छ त्वं त्रिषु लोकेषु दुर्लभम् ॥ १९ ॥

न ते प्रभविता मृत्युर्यावज्जीवितुमिच्छसि ।
त्वत्तोऽभ्यनुज्ञां संप्राप्य मृत्युः प्रभविता तव ॥ २० ॥

किं वा ते प्रार्थितं भूयो ददामि वरमुत्तमम् ।
तद् ब्रूहि भरतश्रेष्ठ यत् ते मनसि वर्त्तते ॥ २१ ॥

Bhīṣma said —

O King, now listen to what I have heard from my father, Śāntanu, when I went to the other world. When I was offering the *piṇḍadāna* I wanted to put the *piṇḍa* directly into his hand but he took his hand away and said: "Put it on the ground." His hand was like I could see it when he was alive, with the rings and other ornaments, and his fingers and palm were red. I thought that the *śāstra*s do not say that the *piṇḍadāna* must be offered straight into the hand and so I put the *piṇḍa* on some *kuśa* grass. Then my father became glad and said: "O son, with you I have been happy in both the worlds, you know *dharma* and are also intelligent. I have proved your faith to the *dharma* and your honour. The defender of *dharma* gets one quarter of the *dharma*, and the destroyer of the honour of *dharma* gets one quarter of the sin. As the king gives evidence of the *dharma* by deeds so his subjects will do as well. O son, you have accepted the *sanātana dharma* declared by the Veda and for this I am very happy with you. I give you a boon renowned in the three worlds; take it. You will live as long as you want, and death will come by your command. If you have any another requests, tell me." **[9-21]**

इत्युक्तवन्तं तमहमभिवाद्य कृतांजलिः ।
अब्रुवं कृतकृत्योहं प्रसन्ने त्वयि सत्तम ॥ २२ ॥
यदि त्वनुग्रहं भूयस्त्वत्तोऽर्हामि महाद्यु ते ।
प्रष्टुमिच्छामि वै किञ्चिद् व्याहृतं भवता स्वयम् ॥ २३ ॥
स मामुवाच धर्मात्मा ब्रूहि भीष्म यदिच्छसि ।
छेत्तास्मि संशयं सर्वं यन्मां पृच्छसि भारत ॥ २४ ॥
ततोऽपृच्छमहं तातं तत्रान्तर्हितमेव हि ।
गतं सुकृतिनां लोकं कौतुहलसमान्वितः ॥ २५ ॥
श्रूयन्ते पितरो देवा देवानामपि देवताः ।
देवाश्च पितरोन्ये वा कान यजामो वयं पुनः ॥ २६ ॥
कथं च दत्तमस्माभिः श्राद्धं प्रीणाति वै पितॄन् ।
लोकान्तरगतांस्तात किं नु श्राद्धस्य वा फलम् ॥ २७ ॥
कान् यजन्ति स्म वै लोकाः सदेवनरदानवाः ।
सयक्षोरगगन्धर्वाः सकिन्नरमहोरगाः ॥ २८ ॥
अत्र मे संशयस्तीव्रः कौतूहलसमन्वितः ।
तद् ब्रूहि मम धर्मज्ञ सर्वज्ञो ह्यसि मे मतः ॥ २९ ॥

After hearing this, I bowed to him and with folded hands I said: "I am beholden to make you happy. But if you have more mercy for me I would ask you some more questions." He listened to my request and said: "Ask me." So I continued: "I have heard that *pitṛ*s are also gods. And that Indra and the other gods adore the *pitṛ*s; and the *pitṛ* also adore Indra and the others. And others (like my father, etc.) are also called *pitṛ*s. So who among these three should I adore? And how does the food that I have offered reach my ancestors who have gone to the other worlds? And what is the fruit that one obtains by performing *śrāddha*? *Devatā*, *daitya*, *manuṣya*, *yakṣa*, *sarpa*, *gandharva*, *kinnara*, who do these beings worship? The *pitṛ*s, are little more than the gods, so how can the gods adore them? And if they are greater than the gods, how can we, men with few merits, adore them? I have many doubts on this matter. So please answer me, you who are omniscent." **[22-29]**

शान्तनुरुवाच -

संक्षेपेणैव ते वक्ष्ये यन्मां पृच्छसि भारत ।
पितरश्च यथोद्भूताः फलं श्राद्धस्य चाऽनघ ॥ ३० ॥

पितॄणां कारणां श्राद्धे शृणु सर्वं समाहितः ।
आदिदेवसुतास्तात पितरो दिवि देवताः ॥ ३१ ॥

तान् यजन्ति स्म वै लोकाः सदेवासुरमानवाः ।
सयक्षोरगगन्धर्वाः सकिंनरमहोरगाः ॥ ३२ ॥

आप्यायिताश्च ते श्राद्धैः पुनराप्याययन्ति च ।
जगत् सदेवगन्धर्वमिति ब्रह्मानुशासनम् ॥ ३३ ॥

तान् यजस्व महाभाग श्राद्धैरग्र्यैरतन्द्रितः ।
ते ते श्रेयो विधास्यन्ति सर्वकामफलप्रदाः ॥ ३४ ॥

त्वया चाराध्यमानास्ते नामगोत्रादिकीर्त्तनैः ।
अस्मानाप्याययिष्यन्ति स्वर्गस्थानपि भारत ॥ ३५ ॥

मार्कण्डेयस्तु ते शेषमेतत् सर्वं प्रवक्ष्यति ।
एष वै पितृभक्तश्च विदितात्मा च भारत ॥ ३६ ॥

उपस्थितश्च श्राद्धेऽद्य ममैवानुग्रहाय वै ।
एन पृच्छ महाभागमित्युक्त्वान्तरधीयत ॥ ३७ ॥

Śāntanu said —

O Bhīṣma, I will answer in brief what you are asking: the

origin of the *pitṛ*s and the fruit of the *śrāddha*. Listen to the reason for adoring the *pitṛs* in the *śrāddha* rite. The *pitṛ*s who are in the sky are the sons of Brahmājī. They are praised by the gods and the others. And when they are satisfied by the gods, thanks to their yogic strength they satisfy the whole world. That is to say, that the offerings of the *yajamāna* on earth are accepted by the *pitṛ* in the sky and then distributed to the *pitṛ* on the earth: in this way the desires of the *yajamāna* are also fulfilled. If the father, grandfather, and others of the *yajamāna* attain *mokṣa*, then the *yajamāna* will have his *dharma*, *dhana* and *kāma* accomplished. O Bharata, if you perform their *pūjā* (of the *pitṛs*) they will grant you all happiness. You should adore them after uttering the name of our *gotra*. Thus they will satisfy us (your father, and others). The rest of the questions will be answered by Mārkaṇḍeya, a *ṛṣi* who is a devotee of *pitṛs* and knower of *ātman*. Please be kind with me and ask Mārkaṇḍeya, who is sitting today in the *śrāddha*. After saying this Śāntanu disappeared. **[30-37]**

॥ *इतिश्री का० मा० पितृकल्पे भीष्मशान्तनुसम्वादोनाम द्विचत्वारिंशोऽध्यायः* ॥
Here ends the forty-second chapter of the Kāmpilyamahātmya.

43

The Talk Between Mārkaṇḍeya and Sanatkumāra on *Pitarā* and *Devatā*[50]

भीष्म उवाच -

ततोहं तस्य वचनान्मार्कण्डेयं समाहितः ।
प्रश्नं तमेवान्वपृच्छं यन्मे पृष्टः पुरा पिता ॥ १ ॥

स मामुवाच धर्मात्मा मार्कण्डेयो महातपाः ।
भीष्म वक्ष्यामि कात्स्न्येंन शृणुष्व प्रयतोऽनघ ॥ २ ॥

अहं पितृप्रसादेन दीर्घायुष्ट्वमवाप्तवान् ।
पितृभक्त्यैव लब्धं च प्राग् लोके परमं यशः ॥ ३ ॥

सोऽहं युगस्य पर्यन्ते बहुवर्षसहस्रिके ।
अधिरुह्य गिरिं मेरुं तपोऽतप्यं सुदुश्चरम् ॥ ४ ॥

ततः कदाचित् पश्यामि दिव्यं प्रज्वाल्य तेजसा ।
विमानं महदायान्तमुत्तरेण गिरेस्ततः ॥ ५ ॥

तस्मिन् विमाने पर्यङ्के ज्वलितादित्यसंनिभम् ।
अपश्यं तत्र चैवाहं शयानं दीप्ततेजसम् ॥ ६ ॥

अङ्गुष्ठमात्रं पुरुषमग्नावग्निमिवाहितम् ।
सोहं तस्मै नमस्कृत्य प्रणम्य शिरसा विभुम् ॥ ७ ॥

संनिविष्टं विमानस्थं पाद्यार्घ्याभ्यामपूजयम् ।
अपृच्छं चैव धर्मज्ञं विद्याम त्वां कथं विभो ॥ ८ ॥

तपोवीर्यात् समुत्पन्नं नारायणगुणात्मकम् ।
दैवतं ह्यसि देवानामिति मे धीयते मतिः ॥ ९ ॥

50. *Harivam.*, 17, 18.

स मामुवाच धर्मात्मा स्मयमान इवानघ ।
न ते तपः सुचरितं येन मामवबुध्यसे ॥ १० ॥

क्षणेनैव प्रमाणं स बिभ्रदन्यदनुत्तमम् ।
रूपेण न मया कश्चिद् दृष्टपूर्वः पुमान् क्वचित् ॥ ११ ॥

Bhīṣma said —

Then according to the order of my father, I put the same questions to Mārkaṇḍeya *ṛṣi*. He said to me: "Listen Bhīṣma! By the grace of the *pitṛs* I have lived for a very long time and also acquired glory. I passed many years performing *tapas* on Mount Sumeru. Once I saw a very brilliant and big *vimāna,* approaching from the north. On that a very radiant man as tall as a thumb was lying on a bedstead. I bowed with reverence to him. And after ritually washing his feet, I asked him — Who are you? Are you Nārāyaṇa, who has assumed a body as a consequence of my asceticism, or are you a *deva*, or just the fruit of my imagination?" Then smiling he said — "Your *tapas* is not over yet, so you cannot know me." After saying this he immediately assumed a colossal body that I had never seen before. **[1-11]**

सनत्कुमार उवाच -

विद्धि मां ब्रह्मणः पुत्रं मानसं पूर्वजं विभोः ।
तपोवीर्यात् समुत्पन्नं नारायणगुणात्मकम् ॥ १२ ॥

सनत्कुमार इति यः श्रुतो देवेषु वै पुरा ।
सोऽस्मि भार्गव भद्रं ते कं कामं करवाणि ते ॥ १३ ॥

ये त्वन्ये ब्रह्मणः पुत्रा यवीयांसस्तु ते मम ।
भ्रातरः सप्त दुर्द्धर्षास्तेषां वंशाः प्रतिष्ठिताः ॥ १४ ॥

क्रतुर्वसिष्ठः पुलहः पुलस्त्योऽत्रिस्तथाङ्गिराः ।
मरीचिश्च तथा धीमान् देवगन्धर्वसेविताः ॥ १५ ॥

वयं तु यतिधर्माणः संयोज्यात्मानमात्मनि ।
प्रजाधर्मं च कामं च व्यपहाय महाद्युते ॥ १६ ॥

यथोत्पन्नस्तथैवाहं कुमार इति विद्धि माम्।
तस्मात सनत्कुमारेति नामैतन्मे प्रतिष्ठितम्॥ १७॥

मद्भक्त्या ते तपश्चीर्णं मम दर्शन काङ्क्षया।
एष दृष्टोस्मि भवता क कामं करवाणि ते ॥ १८॥

Sanatakumāra said —

I was born from the heat of the *tapas* of Brahmājī. I am his mind-born elder son, and I am made of pure *sattva-guṇa*. I am Sanatakumāra and I come to you, ask me whatever you want. I have seven brothers of royal dynasty. They are (1) Kratu, (2) Vasiṣṭha, (3) Pulaha, (4) Pulastya, (5) Atri, (6) Aṅgirā, (7) Marīci. They have progeny but I am *yati* (ascetic), and I am always connected with *Īśvara*, and celibate since the beginning. For this reason I am called Sanatakumāra[51] (lit. 'always a youth'). You have made *tapas* so that you deserve to meet me. Tell me what can I do for you. **[12-18]**

मार्कण्डेय उवाच -

अनुज्ञातो भगवता प्रीयमाणेन भारत।
ततोऽहमेनमेवार्थं तमपृच्छं सनातनम्॥ १९॥

पृष्टः पितृणां सर्गं च फलं श्राद्धस्य चानघ।
चिच्छेद संशयं भीष्म स तु देवेश्वरो मम॥ २०॥

स मामुवाच धर्मात्मा कथान्ते बहुवार्षिके।
रमे त्वयाऽहं विप्रर्षे शृणु सर्वं यथातथम्॥ २१॥

देवानसृजतब्रह्मा मां यक्ष्यन्तीति भार्गव।
तमुत्सृज्य तथात्मानमयजंस्ते फलार्थिनः॥ २२॥

ते शप्ता ब्रह्मणा मूढा नष्टसंज्ञा दिवौकसः।
न स्म किंचिद् विजानन्ति ततो लोकोप्यमुह्यत॥ २३॥

शप्तास्ते प्रणता भूयः प्रायाचन्त पितामहम्।
अनुग्रहाय लोकानां ततस्तानऽब्रवीदिदम्॥ २४॥

---

51. Lit. 'always a youth'.

प्रायश्चित्तं चरध्वं वै व्यभिचारो हि वः कृतः ।
पुत्राश्च परिपृच्छध्वं ततो ज्ञानमवाप्स्यथ ॥ २५ ॥
प्रायश्चित्तक्रियार्थं ते पुत्रान् पप्रच्छुरार्तवत् ।
तेभ्यस्ते प्रयतात्मानः शशंसुस्तनयास्तदा ॥ २६ ॥
प्रायश्चित्तानि धर्मज्ञा वाङ्मनःकर्मजानि वै ।
शंशन्ति कुशला नित्यं चक्षुर्भ्यामपि नित्यशः ॥ २७ ॥
प्रायश्चित्तार्थतत्त्वज्ञा लब्धसंज्ञा दिवौकसः ।
गम्यतां पुत्रकाश्चेति पुत्रैरुक्ताश्च ते तदा ॥ २८ ॥
अभिशप्तास्तु ते देवाः पुत्रवाक्येन निन्दिताः ।
पितामहमुपागच्छन् संशयच्छेदनाय हि ॥ २९ ॥

Mārkaṇḍeya said —

O Bhīsma, then I asked him these questions: the origin of the *pitṛ*s and the fruit of the *śrāddha*. Many years later he answered me: "Listen, Brahmājī first created the gods with the hope that they would worship him. But they abandoned him and started to look after only themselves in the form of the senses, *indriya*s." Thus Brahmājī cursed them: "You will lose knowledge." So they all became idiots. In that way also man, following the course of the gods, became stupid. Then the gods took refuge in Brahmājī, asking his pardon. So he said to them: "You have committed an offence by neglecting the order of seniority (older). To expiate this sin you will have to be instructed by your sons (man)." So they asked their sons and their sons taught them. Good speech, concentration of mind, the way of saluting by bowing the body: they explained the ways to atone for this misdeed. By this expiation and by getting some knowledge, their sons told the gods: "Sons, now go." So the gods went to Brahmājī for clarification: "How could our sons call us 'sons'?" **[19-29]**

ततस्तानब्रवीद् देवो यूयं वै ब्रह्मवादिनः ।
तस्माद् यदुक्तं युष्माकं तत् तथा न तदन्यथा ॥ ३० ॥

यूयं शरीरकर्तारस्तेषां देवा भविष्यथ ।
ते तु ज्ञानप्रदातारः पितरो वो न संशयः ॥ ३१ ॥

अन्योन्यं पितरो यूयं ते चैवेति न संशयः ।
देवाश्च पितरश्चैव तदु वुध्यध्वं दिवौकसः ॥ ३२ ॥

ततस्ते पुनरागम्य पुत्रानूचुर्दिवौकसः ।
ब्रह्मणा छिन्नसन्देहाः प्रीतिमन्तः परस्परम् ॥ ३३ ॥

यूयं वै पितरोऽस्माकं यैर्वयं प्रतिबोधिताः ।
धर्मज्ञाः कश्च वः कामः को वरो वः प्रदीयताम् ॥ ३४ ॥

उक्ताश्च यस्माद् युष्माभिः पुत्रका इति वै वयम् ।
तस्माद् भवन्तः पितरो भविष्यन्ति न संशयः ॥ ३५ ॥

यानिष्ट्वा तु पितॄन् श्राद्धैः क्रियाः काश्चित् करिष्यति ।
राक्षसा दानवा नागास्तासां प्राप्स्यन्ति ते फलम् ॥ ३६ ॥

श्राद्धैराप्यायिताश्चैव पितरः सोममव्ययम् ।
आप्याययाना युष्माभिर्वर्द्धयिष्यन्ति नित्यदा ॥ ३७ ॥

श्राद्धैराप्यायितः सोमो लोकानाप्याययिष्यति ।
समुद्रपर्वतवनं जङ्गमाजङ्गमैर्वृतम् ॥ ३८ ॥

श्राद्धानि पुष्टिकामाश्च ये करिष्यन्ति मानवाः ।
तेभ्यः पुष्टिं प्रजाश्चैव दास्यन्ति पितरः सदा ॥ ३९ ॥

श्राद्धे ये च प्रदास्यन्ति त्रीन् पिण्डान् नामगोत्रतः ।
सर्वत्र वर्तमानांस्तान् पितरः सपितामहान् ॥ ४० ॥

भावयिष्यन्ति सततं श्राद्धदानेन तर्पिताः ।
एवमाज्ञापितं पूर्वं ब्रह्मणा परमेष्ठिना ॥ ४१ ॥

इति तद्वचनं सत्यं भवत्वद्य दिवौकसः ।
पुत्राश्च पितरश्चैव वयं सर्वे परस्परम् ॥ ४२ ॥

Brahmājī said —

"O gods, do not worry! You are *brahmavādī*, namely, ones who know the secret of the *Veda*; they are the real fathers. But what they said to you is correct. You are the giver of their body so you are their *pitṛ* and on the other side they gave you knowledge so they are also your *pitṛ*s (*pati rakṣati*

= *pitā*). So you (gods) and your sons (*pitṛ*s) are father and son to each other." Then the gods returned to the *pitṛ* and told them: "You gave us knowledge so you are worthy to be called our father. Ask for some boon. You called us 'sons' so you are our fathers. Also *rākṣasa*, *daitya*, *nāga* and all the beings with a cruel nature who will adore you through *śrāddha* will obtain an auspicious outcome. Being satisfied by the *śrāddha* made by man you (*divya pitṛ*) will satisfy the *pitṛ*s on earth and they (*laukika pitṛ*s) being satisfied will satisfy our greatest *devatā*, Candramā. This is declared by *Chāndogya Upaniṣad*.[52] That is to say that, like in the 'Prāṇāgnihotra',[53] where satisfying the *adhyātma* the *adhidaiva* also is satisfied, in the same way by satisfying the *pitṛ*s Candramā also is satisfied. And when Candramā is satisfied, the seas, the forests, the mountains and all the movable and immovable beings are content. The *pitara*s will grant increase and progeny to the man who performs *śrāddha* desiring his own welfare. To the one who offers three *piṇḍa* in the rite of *śrāddha* after uttering his name and his family name (*gotra*), the *divya pitṛ*s, being pleased, will satisfy his *laukika pitṛ*s, wherever they may be. This is the order given by Brahmājī. In this way those words will be true: we are father and son to one another."[54] **[30-42]**

॥ इति श्री का० मा० पितृत्पत्तिवर्णनंनाम त्रिचत्वारिंशोध्यायः॥

Here ends the forty-third chapter of the Kāmpilyamāhātmya.

---

52. *sadyadbhaktaṁ prathamamāgacchet taddhomīyam.*

53. Name of a work and also of an Upaniṣad.

54. There are two *śreṇī* of *pitṛ*s: *devatāpitara*, who gave life to their sons; *putrapitara*, who gave the teaching to their fathers. According to *Manu-Smṛti* there are five kinds of fathers: *janitā*, the physical father; *upanitā*, the father who performs the *yajñopavīta saṁskāra*; *vidyādātā* or *ācārya*, who imparts knowledge; *annadātā*, who gives food; *bhayatrātā*, who protects from fears. — *janitā copanitā ca yāstu vidyāṁ prayacchati, annadātā bhayatrātā pañcayite pitarāḥ smṛtāḥ.*

44

The *Pitaṛs* can be *Amūrta* (Formless) or *Mūrtiman* (With Form)

FORMLESS pitṛs are praised by gods, and are divided into three classes:

(1) *Vairāja*, 'belonging or derived from Virāj', according to *Harivaṁśa Purāṇa*, or *Somasad* (name of the *pitṛ* of the *sādhyas*), according to *Manu-Smṛti*. They are sons of Virāj (*Hariv., Mn.*); they are worshippped by the *devatā* (according to the Purāṇas) or by the *sādhyaḥ* (*Mn.*). These *pitṛ*s stay in the *sanātanaḥ loka*, permanent, eternal, everlasting world. Their mind-born daughter is Menā, wife of Himālaya, whose three daughters were: (1) Aparṇā (Pārvatī), wife of Śiva; (2) Ekaparṇā, wife of Asitadevala and mother of Sannati (lit. 'humility personified'. She became the wife of Brahmadatta); (3) Ekapāṭalā, wife of Jaigīṣavya. Menā's son is Krauñca.

(2) *Agniṣvātta,* 'tasted by the funeral fire'; the Manes (*ṚV, X*, 15, 11) in *Mbh*. and in other Purāṇic texts they are a class of *pitṛ*, who on earth neglected the sacrificial fire, sons of Marīci (*Hariv., Mn.*), and worshipped by the *devatā* (*ibid.*). They stay in the *somapadaḥ loka*. Their mind-born daughters are Acchodā, wife of Paraśurāma, and Satyavatī, wife of Śāntanu. The latter's sons were Vyāsa, Vicitravīrya and Citrāṅgada.

(3) *Bahirṣad* ('outside the *sadas*', du. heaven and earth in *Hariv*., or the sacrificial assembly in *ṚV*). According to *Hariv.*

they are the sons of Pulastya, but according to *Mn.* they are Atri's sons. They are adored by the gods, and others. The *bahirṣad pitṛ* stay in the *vibhrāj loka.* Their mind-born daughter is Pīvarī, who was wife of Śukrācārya. Her sons were Kṛṣṇa, Gaura, Prabhu, Śambhu and her daughter, Kṛtvī, was the mother of Brahmadatta.

Mūrtimān, with form, *pitṛ* are worshipped by men. They are divided into four classes:

(1) *Sukālāḥ* (*Hariv.*) or *Sukālinaḥ* (*Mn.*), sons of Vasiṣṭha (both in *Hariv.* and *Mn.*). According to the *Purāṇas* they are adored by the *brāhmaṇas*, but according to *Mn.*, they should be worshipped by the *śūdras*. These *pitṛs* stay in *bhāsura loka.* Their mind-born daughter was Ekaśṛṅgā Garu, Śukrācārya's wife.

(2) *Havirbhujaḥ* (*Mn.*), sons of Aṅgirasaḥ (*Hariv., Mn.*). They are worshipped by the *kṣatriya* (*Hariv., Mn.*). Their abode is the *marīcigarbhā loka.* Their mind-born daughter is Yaśodā, wife of Viśvamahat, son of Vṛddhaśarmā. Her son was Dilīpa.

(3) *Susvadhāḥ* (*Hariv.*) or *Ājyapāḥ* (*Mn.*). The Purāṇic references (*MārkP.*, etc.) state that they are sons of Pulaha, whilst *Mn.* says that they are sons of Pulastya. They are considered the ancestors of the *vaiśya* order. Their world is *kāmagāḥ loka.* Their mind-born daughter was Virajā, wife of Nahuṣa and mother of Yayāti.

(4) *Sonapāḥ* (*Hariv.*) or *Somapā* (*Mn.*). Their father was Kavi (*Hariv., Mn.*). From the Purāṇic quotations they should be worshipped by the *śūdra,* but in *Mn.* their *pujārī* are the *brāhmaṇa.* They stay at *mānasāḥ loka.* Their mind-born daughter is Narmadā. Her husband was Purukṛtsa, son of Māndhātā. Her son was Trasadasyu.

	सं०	हरिवंशेनाम	मनुस्मृतौ	कस्यपुत्राः	मनुस्मृतौ	के पूजयन्ति	मनुस्मृतौ	लोकाः	मानसी क०	कस्य पत्नी	तत्सुताः
अमूर्त्तयस्त्रयः देवानां पूज्याः	१	वैराजाः	सोमसदः	विराजस्य	विराजः	देवाः	साध्याः	सनातनाः	मेना*	हिमवतः	मेनाकः तत्पुत्रः क्रौंचः
	२	अग्निष्वात्ता	अग्निष्वात्ता	मरीचेः	मरीचेः	देवाः	देवाः	सोमपदः	अच्छोदा सैवसत्यवती	पराशरस्य शान्तनोश्च	व्यास-विचित्र-वीर्य-चित्रांगद
	३	वर्हिषदः	वर्हिषदः	पुलस्त्यस्य	अत्रेः	देवादयः	देवादयः	विभ्राजाः	पीवरी	शुकस्य	कृष्णः-गौरः-प्रभुः शम्भुः
मूर्त्तिमन्तश्चत्वारः मानवानां पूज्याः	४	सुकालाः	सुकालिनः	वसिष्ठस्य	वसिष्ठस्य	ब्राह्मणाः	शूद्राः	भासुराः	एकशृङ्गगौ	शुकस्य	कन्या कृत्वी सत्सुतोब्रह्मद०
	५		हविर्भुजः	अङ्गिरसः	अङ्गिरसः	क्षत्रियाः	क्षत्रियाः	मरीचिगर्भा	यशोदा	वृद्धशर्मपुत्र-विश्वमहतः	दिलीपः
	६	सुस्वधाः	आज्यपाः	पुलहस्य	पुलस्त्यस्य	वैश्याः	वैश्याः	कामगाः	बिरजा	नहुषस्य	ययातिः
	७	सोमपाः	सोमपाः	कवेः	कवेः	शूद्राः	ब्राह्मणाः	मानसाः	नर्मदा	मांधातृपुत्र-पुरुकुत्सस्य	त्रसद्दस्युः

* मेनाकन्याः ३ (१) अपर्णा (पार्वती) शिवभार्या (२) एकपर्णा असितदेवलपत्नी तत्सुता संनतिः। (३) एकपाटला जैगीषव्यपत्नी।

सनत्कुमार उवाच -

सप्तैते यजतां श्रेष्ठ स्वर्गे पितृगणाः स्मृताः ।
चत्वारो मूर्त्तिमन्तश्च त्रयस्तेषाममूर्तयः ॥ १ ॥

सर्वेषां राजतैः पात्रैरथवा रजतान्वितैः ।
दत्तं स्वधां पुरोधाय श्राद्धं प्रीणाति वै पितॄन् ॥ २ ॥

पितॄन् प्रीणाति यो भक्त्या पितरः प्रीणयन्ति तम् ।
यच्छन्ति स्वर्गमारोग्यं यदन्यदपि चेप्सितम् ॥ ३ ॥

देवकार्यादपि मुने पितृकार्यं विशिष्यते ।
देवतानां हि पितरः पूर्वमाप्यायनं स्मृतम् ॥ ४ ॥

शीघ्रप्रसादा ह्यक्रोधा लोकस्याप्यायनं परम् ।
स्थिरप्रसादाश्च सदा तान् नमस्यस्व भार्गव ॥ ५ ॥

पितृभक्तोसि विप्रर्षे मद्भक्तश्च विशेषतः ।
श्रेयस्तेऽद्य विधास्यामि प्रत्यक्षं कुरू तत् स्वयम् ॥ ६ ॥

दिव्यं चक्षुः सविज्ञानं प्रदिशामि च तेऽनघ ।
गतिमेतामप्रमत्तो मार्कण्डेय निशामय ॥ ७ ॥

न हि योगगतिर्दिव्या पितॄणां च परा गतिः ।
त्वद्विधेनापि सिद्धेन दृश्यते मांसचक्ष षा ॥ ८ ॥

Sanatakumāra said —

In the heaven there are seven classes, *gaṇa* of *pitṛ*s, in whom four have a form (*mūrtimān*) and three are formless (*mūrti rahita*). They all get very happy when they are offered from a silver vessel some food in which some silver is mingled with the *mantra svadhā pitṛbhyaḥ*. Who satisfies them will be satisfied by them. They bestow heaven, protection from illness, and what more is wanted. O sage (Mārkaṇḍeya *ṛṣi*), the ritual function paid to the *pitṛ*s (*pitṛkārya*) is more important than the functions offered to the gods (*devakārya*), because the *pitṛ*s must be prayed before gods. The *pitṛ*s are easy to be pleased. They are rageless; they fulfil the whole world. They stay happy for a long time. You perform their *pujā*. Make the *pujā* to them and to me, and I will give you a *divya-dṛṣti* and complete experience, by which you will see the fruit of the *śrāddha*, because the *gati* of *yoga* and that of *pitṛ*s cannot be seen just with the eyes (of the gross body). **[1-8]**

Mārkaṇḍeya now tells the story of the 7 sons of Bharadvāja[55]

मार्कण्डेय उवाच -

स एवमुक्त्वा देवेशो मामुपस्थिमग्रतः ।
चक्षु दत्वा सविज्ञानं देवानामपि दुर्लभम् ॥ ९ ॥

जगाद पुनरेवाथ द्वितीयोग्निरिव ज्वलन् ।
आसन पूर्वयुगे तात भरद्वाजात्मजा द्विजाः ॥ १० ॥

योगधर्ममनुप्राप्ता भ्रष्टा दुश्चरितेन वै ।
महतः सरसः पारे मानसस्य विसंज्ञिताः ॥ ११ ॥

तमेवार्थमनुध्यान्तो नष्टमप्स्विव मोहिताः ।
अप्राप्य योगं ते सर्वे संयुक्ताः कालधर्मणा ॥ १२ ॥

ततस्ते योगविभ्रष्टा देवेषु सुचिरोषिताः ।
जाताः कौशिकदायादाः कुरुक्षेत्रे नरर्षभाः ॥ १३ ॥

हिंसया विहरिष्यन्तो धर्मं पितृकृतेन वै ।
ततस्ते पुनराजातिं भ्रष्टाः प्राप्स्यन्ति कुत्सिताम् ॥ १४ ॥

तेषां पितृप्रसादेन पूर्वजातिकृतेन वै ।
स्मृतिरुत्पद्यते प्राप्य तां तां जातिं जुगुप्सिताम् ॥ १५ ॥

ते धर्मचारिणो नित्यं भविष्यन्ति समाहिताः ।
ब्राह्मण्यं प्रतिलप्स्यन्ति ततो भूयः स्वकर्मणा ॥ १६ ॥

ततश्च योगं प्राप्स्यन्ति पूर्व जातिकृत पुनः ।
भूयः सिद्धिमनुप्राप्य स्थानं प्राप्स्यन्ति शाश्वतम् ॥ १७ ॥

योगो हि दुर्लभो नित्यमल्पप्रज्ञैः कदाचन ।
लब्ध्वापि नाशयन्त्येनं व्यसनैः कटुतामिताः ।
अधर्मेष्वेव वर्तन्ते प्रार्दयन्ते गुरूनपि ॥ १८ ॥

55. *Harivam.*, 19.

Mārkaṇḍeya said —

After saying that, Sanatkumāra gave me the *divya-dṛṣti*, the supernatural vision, and added: "In the previous *yuga* the *ṛṣi* Bharadvāja had seven sons. Due to some reason they failed in their *yoga* (*yogabhraṣṭa*). Then they started to search again for *yoga* in the depths of their heart but they could not find it. After death they went to the *devaloka* and stayed there for a long time.[56] Then they were born again in the family of Viśvāmitra in the country of Kurukṣetra. In the name of *śrāddha* they committed violence so that they got a lower birth. But even in an inferior birth, by virtue of the rites to the *pitṛ* previously made, they all could remember their past lives. So they could attain to the fruit of *yoga* and they achieved *mokṣa*. O *muni*, the dull-minded people cannot approach *yoga*, and if purely by chance they get to it they soon forget it as they are possessed by their cruel habits, like hunting and killing. Being engaged in the *adharma* they disrespect even their seniors. **[9-18]**

याचन्ते न त्वयाच्यानि रक्षन्ति शरणागतान् ।
नावजानन्ति कृपणान् माद्यन्ते न धनोष्मणा ॥ १९ ॥

युक्ताहारविहाराश्च युक्तचेष्टाः स्वकर्मसु ।
ध्यानाध्ययनयुक्ताश्च न नष्टानुगवेषिणः ॥ २० ॥

नोपभोगरता नित्यं न मांसमधुभक्षिणः ।
न च कामपरा नित्यं न विप्राऽसेविनस्तथा ॥ २१ ॥

नाऽनार्यसंकथासक्ता नालस्योपहतास्तथा ।
नात्यन्तमानसंसक्ता गोष्ठिष्वऽनिरतास्तथा ॥ २२ ॥

प्रशान्ताश्च जितक्रोधा मानाहङ्कारवर्जिताः ।
कल्याणभाजनं ये तु ये भवन्ति यतव्रताः ॥ २३ ॥

प्राप्नुवन्ति नरा योगं योगो वै दुर्लभो भुवि ।
एवंविधास्तु ते तात ब्राह्मणा ह्यभवस्तदा ॥ २४ ॥

---

56. *tathoktaṁ gītāsu* ।। *prāpya puṇyakṛtāṁ lokānuṣitvā śāśyatīḥ samā iti* ।

स्मरन्ति ह्यात्मनो दोषं प्रमादकृतमेव च ।
ध्यानाध्ययनयुक्ताश्च शान्ते वर्त्मनि संस्थिताः ॥ २५ ॥

योगधर्माद्धि धर्मज्ञ न धर्मोऽस्ति विशेषवान् ।
वरिष्ठः सर्वधर्मेषु तमेवाचर भार्गव ॥ २६ ॥

कालस्य परिणामेन लघ्वाहारो जितेन्द्रियः ।
तत्परः प्रयतः श्राद्ध योगधर्ममवाप्स्यसि ॥ २७ ॥

Whoever does not ask for anything from the base; whoever protects those who have come for shelter; whoever respects the miserable; whoever is not greedy of anyone's riches; the one who follows a right routine, who performs his duties with proper endeavour; who is concentrated and studious; who does not look for spoiled things; who is not always absorbed in enjoying; who does not eat meat nor drink wine, and is moderate in desires; the one who serves the *brāhmaṇa*s; who does not listen to the speech of the unworthy; who is not lazy and is free from egoism; who stays apart from the common society; who keeps in mind peaceful thoughts, without any anger; who does not make himself the best among the others and does not identify with his body; who is a container of welfare and is steady in his vows — That man can find *yoga*. On this earth *yoga* is difficult to find. O *muni*, the seven sons of Kauśika[57] were such *yogī*. They could remember the faults, *yogabhraṣṭa*, committed in their past lives and always absorbed in contemplation and study they became steady in calmness. O Mārkaṇḍeya there is not any *yoga* better than the *yogadharma*. You also become a *yogī*. Eat with moderation, control the senses, stay in purity, perform the *śrāddha* regularly, practice *yoga* daily. Then, at the proper time, you will attain the fruit of *yoga*." **[19-27]**

मार्कण्डेय उवाच -

इत्युक्त्वा भगवान् देवस्तत्रैवान्तरधीयत ।
अष्टादशैव वर्षाणि त्वेकाहमिव मेऽभवत् ॥ २८ ॥

57. Viśvāmitra, son or grandson of Kuśika.

उपासतस्तं देवेशं वर्षाण्यष्टादशैव मे ।
प्रसादात् कस्य देवस्य न ग्लानिरभवत् तदा ॥ २९ ॥
न क्षुत्पिपासे कालं वा जानामिस्म तदाऽनघ ।
पश्चाच्छिष्यसकाशाद् वै कालः संविदितो मया ॥ ३० ॥

Mārkaṇḍeya said —

After saying that, Sanatkumāra disappeared from my sight. Then I passed 18 years serving him, but to me that period seemed as one day. By his grace I passed 18 years without suffering any hunger or thirst, and I had no perception of the passing of time, until my disciples gave me proof of the elapsed time. **[28-30]**

॥ इति श्री का० मा० योगधर्ममहत्त्वकथनं नाम चतुश्चत्वारिंशोऽध्यायः॥

Here ends the forty-fourth chapter of the Kāmpilyamahātmya.

45

Mārkaṇḍeya Speaking on the Genealogy of King Brahmadatta[58]

मार्कण्डेय उवाच -

तस्मिन्नन्तर्हिते देवे वचनात् तस्य वै प्रभोः ।
चक्षुर्दिव्यं सविज्ञानं प्रादुरासीत् तदा मम् ॥ १ ॥

ततोहं तान पश्यं वै ब्राह्मणान् कौशिकात्मजान् ।
आपगेय कुरुक्षेत्रे यानुवाच विभुर्मम ॥ २ ॥

ब्रह्मदत्तो भवद्राजा यस्तेषां सप्तमो द्विजः ।
पितृवर्त्तीति विख्यातो नाम्ना शीलेन कर्मणा ॥ ३ ॥

शुकस्य कन्या कृत्वी तं जनयामास पार्थिवम् ।
अणुहात् पार्थिवश्रेष्ठात् काम्पिल्ये नगरोत्तमे ॥ ४ ॥

Mārkaṇḍeya said —

When Sanatakumāra went away I immediatly got the *divya-dṛṣṭi*. Then I saw the sons of Viśvāmitra in the field of Kurukṣetra. Among them the seventh was Pitṛvartī who daily performed the *śrāddha*. He became King Brahmadatta. His mother was Kṛtvī, daughter of Śukadeva and his father was Aṇuha (Nīpa), King of Kāmpilya. **[1-4]**

---

58. *Harivam.*, 20.

भीष्म उवाच -

यथोवाच महाभागो मार्कण्डेयो महातपाः ।
तस्य वंशमहं राजन् कीर्त्तयिष्यामि तच्छृणु ॥ ५ ॥

Bhīṣma said —

Yudhiṣṭhira, now listen to what I heard about the genealogy of Brahmadatta from Mārkaṇḍeya. **[5]**

युधिष्ठिर उवाच -

अणुहः कस्य वै पुत्रः कस्मिन् काले वभूव ह ।
धर्मभृतां श्रेष्ठो यस्य पुत्रा महायशाः ॥ ६ ॥

ब्रह्मदत्तो नरपतिः किंवीर्यः स वभूव ह ।
कथं च सप्तमस्तेषां स वभूव नराधिपः ॥ ७ ॥

नह्यल्पवीर्याय शुको भगवान् लोकपूजितः ।
कन्यां प्रादाद् यद्योगात्मा कृत्वीं कीर्त्तिमतीं प्रभुः ॥ ८ ॥

एतदिच्छांम्यहं श्रोतुं विस्तरेण महाद्युते ।
ब्रह्मदत्तस्थ चरितं तद् भवान् वक्तुमर्हसि ॥ ९ ॥

यथा च वर्त्तमानास्ते संसारे च द्विजातयः ।
मार्कण्डेयेन कथितास्तद् भवान् प्रब्रवीतु मे ॥ १० ॥

Yudhiṣṭhira said —

Whose son was King Aṇuha, and to which dynasty did he belong? What was his power and how was he born among the seven sons of Viśvāmitra? Śukadevajī, king of *yogī*, respected by all the world, surely could not give his daughter to a common man. I want to listen to this tale in detail. Please tell me. And also tell me the story of those seven sons that Mārkaṇḍeya told you. **[6-10]**

भीष्म उवाच -

प्रतीपस्य तु राजर्षेस्तुल्यकालो नराधिपः ।
पितामहस्य मे राजन् वभूवेति मया श्रुतम् ॥ ११ ॥

ब्रह्मदत्तो महाभागो योगी राजर्षिसत्तमः ।
रुतज्ञः सर्वभूतानां सर्वभूतहिते रतः ॥ १२ ॥

सखाऽऽस गालवो यस्य योगाचार्यो महायशाः ।
कण्डरीकश्च धर्मात्मा तस्यैव सचिवो महान् ॥ १३ ॥

जात्यन्तरेषु सर्वेषु सखायः सर्व एव ते ।
सप्तजातिषु सप्तैव वभूबुरमितौजसः ॥ १४ ॥

Bhīṣma said —

King Brahmadatta was the contemporary of my grandfather Pratīpa. He was a *yogī*, and he could understand the language of every living being. He was benevolent to everyone. He had two friends: Gālava (Pañcāla) and Kaṇḍarīka. The seven sons of Kauśika, these three and the other four, in every lives continued to mantain a mutual friendly disposition. **[11-14]**

वृहत्क्षत्रस्य दायादः सुहोत्रो नाम धार्मिकः ।
सुहोत्रस्यपि दायादो हस्ती यद्धस्तिनापुरम् ॥ १५ ॥

निर्मितं तस्य तनयास्त्रयः परमधार्मिकाः ।
अजमीढो द्विमीढश्च पुरुमीढस्तथैव च ॥ १६ ॥

अजमीढस्य धूमिन्यां जज्ञे बृहदिषुर्नृप ।
वृहद्धनुर्वृहदिषोः पुत्रस्तस्य महायशाः ॥ १७ ॥

वृद्धशर्मेति विख्यातो राजा परम धार्मिकः ।
सत्यजित् तनयस्तस्य विश्वजित् तस्य चात्मजः ॥ १८ ॥

तस्य त्वावन्तको राजा सेनजित् तत्सुता नृप ।
रुचिरः श्वेतकेतुश्च महिम्नारश्च वत्सकः ॥ १९ ॥

रुचिरस्य तु दायादः पृथुसेनो महायशाः ।
पृथुसेनसुतः पारः पारान्नीपः प्रजज्ञिवान ॥ २० ॥

नीपस्यैकशतं पुत्राः सर्वे नीपा इतिस्मृताः ।
तेषां वंशकरो राजा काम्पिल्ये समरोऽभवत् ॥ २१ ॥

समरस्य परः पारः सदश्व इति ते त्रयः ।
पुत्राः परमधर्मज्ञाः परपुत्रः पृथुर्वभौ ॥ २२ ॥

पृथोस्तु सुकृतो नाम सुकृतेनेह कर्मणा ।
जज्ञे सर्वगुणोपेतो विभ्राजस्तस्य चात्मजः ॥ २३ ॥

विभ्राजस्य तु पुत्रोभूदणु होनाम पार्थिवः ।
अणु धर्मरतो नित्यमणुं सोध्यगमत् पदम् ॥ २४ ॥

ददौ कन्यां शुकस्तस्मै कृत्वीं पूजितलक्षणाम् ।
सत्यशीलगुणोपेतां योगधर्मरतां सदा ॥ २५ ॥

पुत्रोऽणुहस्य राजर्षिब्रह्मदत्तोऽभवत् प्रभुः ।
ब्रह्मदत्तस्य पुत्रस्तु सर्वसेन इतिस्मृतः ॥ २६ ॥

चक्षुषी यस्य निर्भिन्ने पक्षिण्या पूजनीयया ।
सुचिरोषितया राजन ब्रह्मदत्तस्य वेश्मनि ॥ २७ ॥

अथास्यपुत्रस्त्वपरो ब्रह्मदत्तस्य जज्ञिवान् ।
विष्वक्सेन इति ख्यातो महाबलपराक्रमः ॥ २८ ॥

योगात्मा तपसा युक्तो ब्रह्मदत्तपितामहः ।
विभ्राजः पुनरायातः स्वकृतेनेह कर्मणा ॥ २९ ॥

विष्वक्सेनस्य पुत्रोऽभूद् दण्डसेन इति स्मृतः ।
भल्लाटोऽस्य कुमारोऽभूद् राधेयेन हतः पुरा ॥ ३० ॥

भल्लाटपुत्रो दुर्बुद्धिर्नीपानामन्तकृन्नृप ।
उग्रायुधेन यस्यार्थे सर्वे नीपा विनाशिताः ॥ ३१ ॥

उग्रायुधो मदोत्सिक्तो मया विनिहतो युधि ।
दर्पान्वितों दर्परुचिः सततं चानये रतः ॥ ३२ ॥

Bṛhatkṣatra had a son named Suhotra. His son was Hastī, who resided at Hastināpura. Hastī had three sons: Ajamīḍha, Dvimīḍha and Purumīḍha. Ajamīḍha had a son called Bṛhadiśu from his wife Dhūminī. His son was Bṛhadśarmā, whose son was Satyajīt, from whom Viśvajīt was born. His son was Senajīt, the king of Ujjain. He had four sons: Rucira, Śvetaketu, Mahimnāra, Vatsaka. From Rucira Pṛthusena was born, who had Pāra, who was the father of Nīpa. He had 100 sons. Among them one was Samara who reigned at Kāmpilya. Samara's three sons were Para, Pāra and Sadāśva. Para had Pṛthu. From Pṛthu Sukṛta, who was followed by Vibhrāja, who had Aṇuha. He was a *yogī* and knower of the subtle matter. Śukadevajī gave him his daughter Kṛtvī, endowed with *yogadharma*, in marriage. Aṇuha's son was Brahmadatta, whose first son Sarvasena had his eyes pierced by the bird Pūjanīyā. The second son of Brahmadatta was Viśvaksena, a *yogī* who was the reincarnation of Vibhrāja. From Viśvaksena Daṇḍasena was born, then Bhallāṭa, who was killed by Karṇa. The son of Bhallāṭa was Janamejaya, *Durbuddhi*, who caused the ruin of the Nīpas, destroyed by Ugrāyuddha. And I (Bhīṣma) killed the persecutor Ugrāyuddha. **[15-32]**

॥ इति का० मा० ब्रह्मदत्तवंशवर्णनं नाम पञ्चचत्वारिंशोऽध्यायः॥

Here ends the forty-fifth chapter of the Kāmpilyamahātmya.

46

On the Dynasty of Ugrāyuddha, the Destroyer of the Nīpas[59]

युधिष्ठिर उवाच -

उग्रायुधः कस्य सुतः कस्मिन् वंशे स जज्ञिवान्।
किमर्थं चापि भवता निहतस्तद् ब्रवीहि मे ॥ १ ॥

Yudhiṣṭhira said —

Whose son was Ugrāyuddha? To which genealogy did he belong and why did you kill him? **[1]**

भीष्म उवाच -

द्विमीढस्य तु दायादो विद्वान् राजा यवीनरः।
धृतिमांस्तस्य पुत्रस्तु तस्य सत्यधृतिः स्मृतः ॥ २ ॥

जज्ञे सत्यधृतेः पुत्रो दृढनेमिः प्रतापवान्।
दृढनेमिसुतश्चापि सुधर्मानाम पार्थिवः ॥ ३ ॥

आसीत् सुधर्मणः पुत्रः सार्वभौमः प्रजेश्वरः।
सार्वभौम इति ख्यातः पृथिव्यामेकराड विभुः ॥ ४ ॥

तस्यान्ववाये महति महान् पौरवनन्दनः।
महतश्चापि पुत्रस्तु राजा रुक्मरथः स्मृतः ॥ ५ ॥

पुत्रो रुक्मरथस्यापि सुपार्श्वो नाम पार्थिवः।
सुपार्श्वतनयश्चापि सुमतिर्नाम धार्मिकः ॥ ६ ॥

---

59. *Harivam.*, 20.

सुमतेरपि धर्मात्मा संनतिर्नाम वीर्यवान् ।
तस्य वै संनतेः पुत्रः कृतो नाम महाबलः ॥ ७ ॥

शिष्यो हिरण्यनाभस्य कौशल्यस्य महात्मनः ।
चतुर्विंशतिधा येन संप्रोक्ताः सामसंहिताः ॥ ८ ॥

स्मृतास्ते प्राच्यसामानः कार्तयोनाम सामगाः ।
कार्तिरुग्रायुधः सोथ वीरः पौरवनन्दनः ॥ ९ ॥

वभूव येन विक्रम्य पृषतस्य पितामहः ।
सहदेवो महातेजाः पञ्चालाधिपतिर्हतः ॥ १० ॥

उग्रायुधस्य दायादः क्षेम्यो नाम महायशाः ।
क्षेम्यात् सुवीरो नृपतिः सुवीरात् तु नृपंजयः ।
नृपंजयाद् बहुरथ इत्येते पौरवाः स्मृताः ॥ ११ ॥

Bhīṣma said —

Dvimīḍha had a son called Yavīnara.[60] His son was Dhṛtamān. Then came Satyadhṛti, Dhṛḍhanemi, Sudharma. His son was the king Cakravartī Sarvabhauma. His son was Mahān, who had Rukmaratha. After him Supārśva, Sumati, Sannati, Kṛta. King Kṛta was the disciple of Hiraṇyanābha Kauśalya.[61] He defined the 24 *saṁhitā* of the *Sāmaveda*, which are well known as Kārti Prācyasāman. The son of Kṛta was Ugrāyuddha, who had Kṣemya, who had Suvīra, who had Nṛpañjaya whose son was Bahuratha. **[2-11]**

स चाप्युग्रायुधस्तात दुर्बुद्धिरभवत् तदा ।
प्रवृद्धचक्रो बलवान् नीपान्तकरणो महान् ॥ १२ ॥

---

60. Even though in the *Harivaṁśa* Yavīnāra is said to be Ajamīḍha's son, in the *Bhāgavata Purāṇa* he is the son of Dvimīḍha. We have respected both the versions, because we know it to be the proper method.

61. Hiraṇyanābha Kauśalya was the 16th generation from Śrī Rāmacandrajī. He was the disciple of the *ṛṣi* Jaimini and teacher of the *yogī* Yājñavalkya. *Bh.P.*, 9, 12.

स दर्पपूर्णो हत्वाजौ नीपानन्यांश्च पार्थिवान्।
पितर्युपरते मह्यं श्रावयामास किल्विषम्॥ १३॥

माममात्यैः परिवृतं शयानं धरणीतले।
उग्रायुधस्य राजेन्द्र दूतोऽभ्येत्य बचोऽब्रवीत्॥ १४॥

अद्य त्वं भीष्म जननीं गन्धकालीं यशस्विनीम्।
स्त्रीरत्नं मम भार्थार्थे प्रयच्छ कुरुपुङ्गव॥ १५॥

एवं राज्यं च ते स्फीतं धनानि च न संशयः।
प्रदास्यामि यथाकाममहं वै रत्नभाग भुवि॥ १६॥

मम प्रज्वलितं चक्रं निशाम्येदं सुदुर्जयम्।
शत्रवो विद्रवन्त्याजौ दर्शनादेव भारत॥ १७॥

राष्ट्रस्येच्छसि चेत् स्वस्ति प्राणानां वा कुलस्य वा।
शासने मम तिष्ठस्व नहि ते शान्तिरन्यथा॥ १८॥

अधः प्रस्तारशयने शयानस्ते न चोदितः।
दूतान्तर्हितमेतद् वै वाक्यमग्निशिखोपमम्॥ १९॥

ततोऽहं तस्य दुर्बुद्धेर्विज्ञाय मतमच्युत।
आज्ञापयं वै युद्धार्थं सेनाध्यक्षाश्च सर्वशः॥ २०॥

विचित्रवीर्यं बालं च मदुपाश्रयमेव च।
दृष्ट्वा क्रोधपरीतात्मा युद्धायैव मनो दधे॥ २१॥

निगृहीतस्तदाहं तैः सचिवैर्मन्त्रकोविदैः।
ऋत्विग्भिर्वेदकल्पैश्च सुहृद्भिश्चार्थदर्शिभिः॥ २२॥

स्निग्धैश्च शास्त्रविद्भिश्च संयुगस्य निवर्त्तने।
कारणं श्रावितश्चास्मि युक्तरूपं तदाऽनघ॥ २३॥

King Ugrāyuddha was very malicious. He destroyed all the Nīpas. After killing the Nīpas and other kings he sent a messenger to me. At that time my father Śāntanu had just passed away and I was impure due to his death. I was lying on the ground and my counsellor (*mantrī*) was sitting near me. Then the messenger arrived and said: "O Bhīṣma, now give me in marriage your mother Satyavatī. She is a jewel among women and I like jewels. If you accept this I will give you many lands and riches. My rule is very severe and my enemies run away when they see me. Respect my desire if you value your country, your life and the welfare of your family. Otherwise there will be no happiness." Lying on the bed of *kuśa* grass I listened to the entire message of the envoy. And considering him wicked I ordered my soldiers to put him in jail. At that time 'my little brother' Vicitravīrya, still a boy, was guarding me, and I decided to give the command to be ready for the battle. But my counsellors, friends and priests stopped me. Other well-wishers spoke against my intervention with the army. **[12-23]**

मन्त्रिण ऊचुः -

प्रवृत्तचक्रः पापोसौ त्वं चाशौचगतः प्रभो ।
न चैष प्रथमः कल्पो युद्धं नाम कदाचन ॥ २४ ॥

ते वयं सामपूर्वं वै दानं भेदं तथैव च ।
प्रयोक्ष्यामस्ततः शुद्धा दैवतान्यभिवाद्य च ॥ २५ ॥

कृतस्वस्त्ययनो विप्रैर्हुत्वाऽग्नीनर्च्य च द्विजान् ।
ब्राह्मणैरभ्यनुज्ञातः प्रयास्यसि जयाय वै ॥ २६ ॥

सामदानादिभिः पूर्वमपि भेदेन वा ततः ।
तं हनिष्यसि विक्रम्य शम्बरं मघवानिव ॥ २७ ॥

अस्त्राणि न प्रयोज्यानि प्रवेश्यश्च सङ्गरः ।
आशौचे वर्त्तमाने तु वृद्धानामिति शासनम् ॥ २८ ॥

The Counsellors said —

Ugrāyuddha does not respect any *dharma*. And it is not suitable for you to go to battle whilst in mourning clothes. With conciliation, gifts and reasoning we will try to stop him; after becoming pure and saluting the gods, having the *svastivācana* uttered by the *brāhmaṇa*s and performing a *havana*, then with the permisson of the *brāhmaṇa*s you will be able to set out on a victorious journey. If he does not accept our conciliation, gifts and reasoning then you will have to fight with heroism, as Indra killed Śaṁvara. Wise men avoid using weapons or fighting in battle whilst under the impurity of mourning. **[24-28]**

भीष्म उवाच -

प्राज्ञानां वचनं काले वृद्धानां च विशेषतः।
श्रोतव्यमिति तच्छ्रुत्वा निवृत्तोस्मि तदाऽनघ ॥ २९ ॥

ततस्तैः संक्रमः सर्वः प्रयुक्तः शास्त्रकोविदैः।
तस्मिन् काले कुरुश्रेष्ठ कर्म चारब्धमुत्तमम ॥ ३० ॥

स सामादिभिरेवादावुपायैः प्राज्ञचिन्तितैः।
अनुनीयमानो दुर्बुद्धिरनुनेतुं न शक्यते ॥ ३१ ॥

प्रवृत्तं तस्य तच्चक्रमधर्मनिरतस्य वै।
परदाराभिलाषेण सद्यस्तात निवर्तितम् ॥ ३२ ॥

न त्वहं तस्य तज्जाने निवृत्तं चक्रमुत्तमम्।
हतं स्वकर्मणा जाने पूर्वं सद्भिर्विगर्हितम् ॥ ३३ ॥

कृतशौचः शरी चापी रथी निष्क्रम्य वै पुरात्।
कृतस्वस्त्ययनो विप्रैः प्रायोधयमहं रिपुम् ॥ ३४ ॥

ततः संसर्गमागम्य बलेनास्त्रबलेन च।
त्र्यहमुन्मत्तवद् युद्धं देवासुरमिवाभवत् ॥ ३५ ॥

स मयाऽस्त्रप्रतापेन निर्दग्धो रणमूर्द्धनि।
पपाताभिमुखं शूरस्त्यक्त्वा प्राणानरिंदम ॥ ३६ ॥

Bhīṣma said —

One should respect the advice of his intelligence and of the sages, so I decided not to go into battle. Then my counsellors tried in every way to appease Ugrāyuddha but he did not desist. The wicked army of Ugrāyuddha, lusting for other women, did not turn back. But I heard that the army of this evil-doer had been spiltted and destroyed. After becoming pure, with my bow and arrows, sitting on my chariot, I went out of town. After having the *svastivācana* uttered by the *brāhmaṇa*s I went to fight against Ugrāyuddha. For three days we clashed and engaged in hand-to-hand fighting and throwing missiles. In the end I killed him and he fell in front of me.[62] **[29-36]**

62. Even at the time of death the heroes do not show their back to the dying enemy.

एतस्मिन्नन्तरे तत्र काम्पिल्ये पृषतोऽभ्ययात् ।
हते नीपेश्वरे चैव हते चोग्रायुधे नृपे ॥ ३७ ॥

आहिच्छत्रं स्वकं राज्यं पित्र्यं प्राप महाद्युतिः ।
द्रुपदस्य पिता राजन् ममैवानुमते तदा ॥ ३८ ॥

ततोऽर्जुनेन तरसा निर्जित्य द्रुपदं रणे ।
आहिच्छत्रं सकाम्पिल्लं द्रोणायाथापवर्जितम् ॥ ३९ ॥

प्रतिगृह्य ततो द्रोण उभयं जयतां वरः ।
काम्पिल्यं द्रुपदायैव प्रायच्छद् विदितं तव ॥ ४० ॥

एष ते कथितो राजन् ब्रह्मदत्तस्य चैव ह ।
वंशःकात्स्न्र्येन कौन्तेय नीपस्योग्रायुधस्य च ॥ ४१ ॥

O King, Ugrāyuddha destroyed the king of Nīpa Durbuddhi and I destroyed Ugrāyuddha. Then with my consent King Pṛṣata, father of Drupada, became King of Kāmpilya and Ahicchatra. Then Arjuna defeated Drupada and gave to Droṇācārya both Kāmpilya and Ahicchatra. Then Droṇācārya gave back to King Drupada Kāmpilya, and this you know already. O Kaunteya, so I have told you the genealogy of Brahmadatta, Durbuddhi and Ugrāyuddha. **[37-41]**

॥ इति श्री का० मा० उग्रायधवधो नाम षट्चत्वारिंशोऽध्यायः॥

Here ends the forty-sixth chapter of the Kāmpilyamahātmya.

47

The Story of Brahmadatta and Pūjanīyā[63]

युधिष्ठिर उवाच -

किमर्थं ब्रह्मदत्तस्य पूजनीया शकुन्तिका ।
अन्धं चकार गाङ्गेय ज्येष्ठं पुत्रं पुरा विभो ॥ १ ॥

चिरोषिता गृहे चापि किमर्थं चैव यस्य सा ।
चकार विप्रियमिदं तस्य राज्ञो महात्मनः ॥ २ ॥

पूजनीया चकारासौ किं सख्यं तेन चैव ह ।
एतं मे संशय छिन्धि सर्वमुक्त्वा यथातथम् ॥ ३ ॥

Yudhiṣṭhira said —

Why did the bird Pūjanīyā blind Sarvasena, the son of Brahmadatta? Why did Pūjanīyā do that to him, the person whose house she had stayed for so many years? How did the friendship between Pūjanīyā and the king grow? Please dispel my doubts. **[1-3]**

भीष्म उवाच -

शृणु सर्वं महाराज यथा वृत्तमभूत् पुरा ।
ब्रह्मदत्तस्य भवने राजर्षेस्तु युधिष्ठिर ॥ ४ ॥

काचिच्छकुन्तिका राजन् ब्रह्मदत्तस्य वै सखा ।
शितिपक्षा शोणशिराः शितिपृष्ठा कृशोदरी ॥ ५ ॥

---

63. This story is referred to in *MBh.*, XII, 139, 5137-5246.

सखी सा ब्रह्मदत्तस्य सुद्रढं वद्धसौहृदा ।
तस्याः कुलायमभवत् गेहे नरोत्तम ॥ ६ ॥

सा सदाऽहनि निर्गत्य तस्य राज्ञो गृहोत्तमात् ।
चचाराम्भोधितीरेषु पल्वलेषु सरस्सु च ॥ ७ ॥

नदीपर्वतकुञ्जेषु वनेषूपवनेषु च ।
प्रफुल्लेषु तडागेषु कल्हारेषु सुगन्धिषु ॥ ८ ॥

कुमुदोत्पलकिञ्जल्कसुरभीकृतवायुषु ।
हंससारसघुष्टेषु कारण्डवरुतेषु च ॥ ९ ॥

चरित्वा तेषु सा राजन् निशि काम्लिल्लमागमत् ।
नृपतेर्भवनं प्राप्य ब्रह्मदत्तस्य धीमतः ॥ १० ॥

राज्ञा तेन सदा राजन् कथायोगं चकारह ।
आश्चर्याणि च द्रष्टानि यानि वृत्तानि कानिचित् ॥ ११ ॥

Bhīṣma said —

O King, now listen to the story of Brahmadatta and Pujanīyā. Brahmadatta was a king. He had a bird called Pujanīyā. Her wings were white, her head was red and the back was black; her abdomen was shaded. Between the two there was a deep affection, and the bird had its nest inside the king's castle. Daily, Pūjanīyā used to go out for a tour to some small ponds[64] near the sea and from there flying all around she could see rivers, mountains, groves forests, tigers, *kalhāra*[65] and many other perfumed flowers, swans and herons with big beaks. She remembered all the things she had seen during the day and at night she used to tell the king everything. **[4-11]**

चरित्वा विविधान् देशान् कथयामास सा निशि ।
कदाचित् तस्य नृपतेर्ब्रह्मदत्तस्य कौरव ॥ १२ ॥

पुत्रो भूद्राजशार्दूल सर्वसेनेतिविश्रुतः ।
पूजनीयाऽथ सा तस्मिन् प्रासूताण्डं तथैव च ॥ १३ ॥

---

64. *Palval*, a lake; *jhīla*, is bigger than a territory occupied by 16000 elephants.

65. A white lotus flowering at sunset.

तस्मिन् नीडे पुरा ह्येकं तत् किल प्रास्फुटत् तदा ।
स्फुटितो मांसपिण्डस्तु बाहुपादास्यसंयुतः ॥ १४ ॥

बभ्रु वक्त्रोऽक्षिहीनश्च वभूव पृथिवीपते ।
चक्षुष्मानप्यभूत् पश्चादीषत्पक्षोत्थितश्च ह ॥ १५ ॥

अथ सा पूजनीया वै राजपुत्रस्वपुत्रयोः ।
तुल्यस्नेहात् प्रीतिमती दिवसे दिवसेऽभवत् ॥ १६ ॥

आजहार सदा सायं चंच्वाऽमृतफलद्वयम् ।
अमृतास्वादसदृशं सर्वसेनस्वपुत्रयोः ॥ १७ ॥

स बालो ब्रह्मदत्तस्य पूजनीया सुतश्च ह ।
ते फले भक्षयित्वा पृथुकौ प्रीतमानसौ ॥ १८ ॥

One day King Brahmadatta had a son, Sarvasena, and on the same day Pūjanīyā also laid an egg. At the proper time, from it a little bird hatched. Out of love Pūjanīyā brought in her beak two *amṛtaphala*, the fruit of immortality, and she gave one to the king's son and one to hers. The two infants took the fruits and became very happy at once. **[12-18]**

अभूतां नित्यमेवेह खादेतां तौ च ते फले ।
तस्यां गतायामथ च पूजन्यां वै सदाऽहनि ॥ १९ ॥

शिशुना चटकेनाथ धात्री तं तु शिशु नृप ।
तेन प्रक्रीडयामास ब्रह्मदत्तात्मजं सदा ॥ २० ॥

नीडात् तमाकृष्य तदा पूजनीयाकृतात् ततः ।
क्रीडता राजपुत्रेण कदाचिच्चटकः स तु ॥ २१ ॥

निगृहीतः कन्धरायां शिशुना दृढमुष्ठिना ।
दुर्भङ्गमुष्ठिना राजन्नसून् सद्यस्त्वजीजहत् ॥ २२ ॥

तं तु पंचत्वमापन्नं व्यात्तास्यं बालघातितम् ।
कथंचिन्मोचितं दृष्ट्वा नृपतिर्दुःखितोऽभवत् ॥ २३ ॥

वात्रीं तस्य जगर्हे तां तदाऽश्रुपरमो नृपः ।
तस्थौ शोकान्वितो राजन् शोचंस्तं चटकं तदा ॥ २४ ॥

पूजनीयापि तत्काले गृहीत्वा तु फलद्वयम् ।
ब्रह्मदत्तस्य भवनमाजगाम बनेचरी ॥ २५ ॥

अथाऽपश्यत् तमागम्य गृहे तस्मिन् नराधिप ।
पञ्चभूतपरित्यक्त शोच्यं तं स्वतनूद्भवम् ॥ २६ ॥

मुमोह दृष्ट्वा तं पुत्रं पुनः संज्ञामथालभत् ।
लब्धसंज्ञा च सा राजन् विललाप तपस्विनी ॥ २७ ॥

On the days when Pūjanīyā went out, the wet-nurse used to take the little bird from the nest and let him play with the king's son. One day while playing together the son of the king grasped the little bird by the neck and killed him. The king felt distressed when he saw the dead bird and the nurse became angry. Because of her grief, tears started to flow from her eyes. At that moment Pūjanīyā arrived from the jungle with two fruits and seeing her son dead she lost consciousness. When she awoke she started wailing. **[19-27]**

न तु त्वमागतां पुत्र वाशन्तीं परिसर्पसि ।
कुर्वंश्चाटु सहस्राणि अव्यक्तकलया गिरा ॥ २८ ॥

व्यादितास्यः क्षुधार्त्तश्च पीतेनास्येन पुत्रक ।
शोणेन तालुना पुत्र कथमद्य न सर्पसि ॥ २९ ॥

पक्षाभ्यां त्वां परिष्वज्य ननु वाशामि चाप्यहम ।
चीची कूचीतिवाशन्तं त्वामद्य न शृणोम किम् ॥ ३० ॥

मनोरथो यस्तु मम पश्येयं पुत्रकं कदा ।
व्यात्तास्यं वारि याचन्तं स्फुरत्पक्षं ममाग्रतः ॥ ३१ ॥

स मे मनोरथो भग्नस्त्वयि पञ्चत्वमागते ।
विलप्यैवं बहुविधं राजानमथ साब्रवीत् ॥ ३२ ॥

ननु मूर्द्धाभिषिक्तस्त्वं धर्मं वेत्सि सनातनम् ।
अथ कस्मान्मम सुतं धात्रया घातितवानसि ॥ ३३ ॥

तव पुत्रेण चाकृष्य क्षत्रियाधम शंस मे ।
न च नूनं श्रुता तेऽभूदियमाङ्गिरसो श्रुतिः ॥ ३४ ॥

उपद्रतः शत्रुभिश्च क्षुधार्त्तः शरणागतः ।
चिरोपितश्च स्वगृहे पातव्यः सर्वदा भवेत् ॥ ३५ ॥

अपालयन् नरो याति कुम्भीपाकमसंशयम् ।
कथमस्य हविर्देवा गृह्णन्ति पितरः स्वधाम् ॥ ३६ ॥

Pūjanīyā said —

O son, I have returned from outside and even when I called you, you did not come to me and you did not answer with your parrot-like voice. Your head has fallen down and is already yellow. You must be hungry. I want to speak with you and I want to hear something from your beak; so why do you not answer? I wanted to see my son fluttering to me, but by your death my enthusiasm has also died. Weeping she spoke to the king: "Even if you were born a warrior you still do not know the *sanātana dharma*. Why has your wet-nurse taken my son out of the nest and killed him? Explain this to me. O wretch, you have not listened to the words of the sage Aṅgirā. Now listen: one should always protect those who have been defeated by the enemy, the hungry, those who approach for shelter, those who are house-bound. Whoever does not protect these will go to hell and his food offerings will be refused by gods and ancestors." **[28-36]**

सैवमुक्त्वा महाराज दशधर्मगत+सती ।
शोकार्त्ता तस्य बालस्य निर्विभेदाथ चक्षुषी ॥ ३७ ॥

कराभ्यां राजपुत्रस्य ततस्तच्चक्षुरस्फुटत् ।
कृत्वा चान्धं नृपसुतमुत्पपात ततोम्बरम ॥ ३८ ॥

अथ राजा सुतं द्रष्ट्वा पूजनीयामुवाच ह ।
विशोका भव कल्याणि कृतं ते भीरु शोभनम् ॥ ३९ ॥

गतशोका निवर्तस्य अयर्यं सख्यमस्तु ते ।
पुरेव बस भद्रं ते निवर्तस्व रमस्व च ॥ ४० ॥

पुत्रपोडोद्भवश्चापि न कोपः परमस्त्वयि ।
ममास्ति सखि भद्रं त कर्त्तव्यं च कृतं त्वया ॥ ४१ ॥

O Mahārāja (Yudhiṣṭhira), after saying this Pūjanīyā, without any discrimination[66] and falling prey to despair, pierced with

66. There are ten attributes, *dharma*, by which one loses his discrimination: (1) drunkness, (2) insanity, (3) possession by evil spirits, (4) tiredness, (5) anger, (6) hunger, (7) impatience, (8) fear, (9) greed, and (10) lust.

her beak both the eyes of the king's son and flew away. Then the king, seeing his son blind, said to Pūjanīyā: "Do not grieve, you did right. Come back to me, we will be friends as we were before. It is not your fault if my son is blind, you have done the right thing." **[37-41]**

पूजनीयोवाच -

कुपुत्रं च कुराजानं कुमित्रं च कुमित्रताम्।
कुदेशं च कुभार्यां च दूरतः परि वर्जयेत्॥ ४२॥

कुपुत्रे च कुतः पिण्डः सर्वतोऽसुखमेवहि।
कुराजनि भयं नित्यं नापि सत्यं कदाचन॥ ४३॥

कुमित्रे सौहृदं नास्ति क्व विश्वासः कुसौहृदे।
कुदेशे जीवनं नैव कुभार्यायां कुतो रतिः॥ ४४॥

अपकारिणि विस्रम्भं यः करोति नराधमः।
अनाथो दुर्बलो यद्वन्नचिरं स तु जीवति॥ ४५॥

न विश्वसेदविश्वस्ते ऽविश्वस्ते नातिविश्वसेत्।
विश्वासाद् भयमुत्पन्नं मूलान्यपि निकृन्तति॥ ४६॥

राजसेविषु विश्वासं गर्भसङ्करितेषु च।
यः करोति नरो मूढो न चिरं स तु जीवति॥ ४७॥

अप्युन्नतिं प्राप्य नृपात् प्रावारः कीटको यथा।
स विनश्यत्यसन्देहमाहैवमुशना नृप॥ ४८॥

अपि मार्दवभावेन गात्रं संलीय बुद्धिमान्।
अरिं नाशयते नित्यं यथा वल्लिर्महाद्रुमम्॥ ४९॥

मृदुरार्द्रः कृशो भूत्वा शनैः संलीयते रिपुः।
वल्मीक इव वृक्षस्य पश्चान्मूलानि कृन्तति॥ ५०॥

न चासन्ने निवस्तव्यं सवैरे वर्द्धिते रिपौ।
पातयेत् तं समूलं हि नदीवेगो यथा द्रुमम्॥ ५१॥

अद्रोहसमयं कृत्वा मुनीना मग्रतो हरिः।
जघान नमुचिं पश्चादपां फेनेन पार्थिव॥ ५२॥

कृत्वा सम्बन्धकं चापि विश्वसेच्छत्रुणा न हि।
पुलोमानं जघानाजौ जामाता सन् शतक्रतुः॥ ५३॥

निधाय मनसा वैरं प्रियं वक्तोह यो नरः ।
उपसर्पेन्न तं प्राज्ञः कुरङ्ग इव लुब्धकम् ॥ ५४ ॥

हसते जल्पते वैरी एक पात्रे भुनक्ति च ।
आरोहत्यासनं चैकं स्मरते तच्च किल्विषम् ॥ ५५ ॥

सुप्तं मत्तं प्रमत्तं वा घातयन्ति रिपुं नराः ।
विषेण वह्निना वापि शस्त्रेणाऽप्यथ मायया ॥ ५६ ॥

शत्रुशेषमृणाच्छेषं शेषमग्नेश्च भूमिप ।
पुनर्वर्द्धेत सम्भूय तस्माच्छेषं न शेषयेत् ॥ ५७ ॥

इत्येता ह्युशनोगीता गाथा धार्या विपश्चिता ।
कुर्वता चात्मरक्षां हि नरेण पृथिवीपते ॥ ५८ ॥

मया सकिल्विषं तुभ्यं प्रयुक्तमतिदारूणम् ।
पुंत्रमन्धं प्रकुर्वत्या तस्मान्नो विश्वसे त्वयि ॥ ५९ ॥

Pūjanīyā said —

A bad king, a bad friend, a bad friendship, a bad son, a bad country, a bad woman. These six are to be abandoned, if they are near they are source of horrible fears. Fearful is the bad king, under whom truth is not spread. Unworthy of faith is the bad friend and the bad friendship. A bad son afflicts his parents' life, and later even if he offers *piṇḍa*, the ancestors do not receive any pleasure. If the king has a bad conduct all the kingdom will act badly. There will be only fear. Neither truth nor justice can ever be there. There is no friendship with bad friends. If the country is bad how can one live there? The wicked person who keeps faith in the one who has done bad to him, becomes helpless, weak and doesn't live long. None should believe those who are unworthy to be believed, and even if they are believable, not excess belief should be done. From faith fear sprouts. And that fear can cut the hardest roots. The foolish fellow who trusts the servants of the king and the bastards cannot live long. Any person who gets progressive status from the king, is sure to be destroyed by the king. This is said by Uśanā (Śukrācārya). As insects like ants, receive wings when they are to die. Or just as a creeper clings to a big tree and destroys it so the wise man being humble to his enemies and mixing with them gets destroyed. Such a person should daily kill his enemies. By being humble, melted in nature and showing himself weak, a person is gradually attacked by the enemy. The enemy cuts off the very roots of a person, in course of time like the ants first make their residence around a tree and ultimately destroy it. If the enmity with some person has increased one should not live near him. As the currents of a river uproots the tree in the proximity of its banks so the enemy may uproot the person near him. O king, Viṣṇu even making a contract in front of the sages, killed Namuci with the water-foam of the sea. One should not believe any relation with the enemy. Indra, being son-in-law, killed Pulomā in the battle. The wise should avoid the one who keeps enmity in mind and speaks sweet words to his rival, as the deer doesn't go to the hunter. Even if the enemy talks, shows love, eats in the same vessel and sleeps on the same *āsana*, his mind always keeps the enmity. The enemy kills the person while he is sleeping under the effect of intoxication or in any such condition, by poison, fire, weapon or by intrigues. The remains of enemy, the remains of debt, the remains of fire, O king, they last and can increase again, therefore none should leave any residue. These statements are said by Uśanā (Śukrācārya). The wise man should always keep them in mind, thus he can protect himself from the king. You are sinful, that is why I have used this harsh punishment to blind your son: I have committed an awful act, I have ruined your son forever, for this reason I have neither faith in you nor in any relation with you. There will not be any affection between us. **[42-59]**

भीष्म उवाच -

एवमुक्त्वा प्रदुद्राव तदाऽऽकाशे पतङ्गिनी ।
शोकार्ता राजसदनं परित्यक्त्वा महीपते ॥ ६० ॥

इत्येतत् ते मया ख्यातं पुराभूतमिदं नृप ।
ब्रह्मदत्तस्य राजर्षेर्यद् वृत्तं पूजनीयया ॥ ६१ ॥

श्राद्धं च पृच्छसे यन्मां युधिष्ठिर महामते ।
अतस्ते वर्त्तयिष्येहमितिहासं पुरातनम् ॥ ६२ ॥

गीतं सनत्कुमारेण मार्कण्डेयाय पृच्छते ।
यथा च मम कौन्तेय मार्कण्डेयेन वर्णितम् ॥ ६३ ॥

Bhīṣma said —

After her speech Pūjanīyā flew away from the palace. O king, I have told you the story of Brahmadatta and Pūjanīyā. Now I will tell you about the fruit of the *śrāddha*, as you have asked before. Now listen to what Sanatkumāra has said to Mārkaṇḍeya and Mārkaṇḍeya has said to me. **[60-63]**

॥ *इति श्री का० मा० पूजनीयोपाख्यानं नाम सप्तचत्वारिंशोऽध्यायः* ॥
Here ends the forty-seventh chapter of the Kāmpilyamahātmya.

48

The Story of the Seven Sons of Viśvāmitra[67]

मार्कण्डेय उवाच -

ततोहं तात धर्मिष्ठान् कुरुक्षेत्रे पितृव्रतान्।
सनत्कुमारनिर्दिष्टानपश्यं सप्त वै द्विजान ॥ १ ॥

कौशिकस्य सुतास्ते तु शिष्या गार्ग्यस्य भारत।
पितर्युपरते सर्वे व्रतवन्तस्तदाऽभवन् ॥ २ ॥

विनियोगाद् गुरोस्तस्य गां दोग्ध्रीं समकालयन्।
समानवत्सां कपिलां सर्वे न्यायागतां तदा ॥ ३ ॥

तेषां पथि क्षुधार्त्तानां बाल्यान्मोहाच्च भारत।
क्रूरा बुद्धिः समभवत् तां गां वै हिंसितुं तदा ॥ ४ ॥

तान् कविः खसृमश्चैव याचेतां नेति वै तदा।
न चाशक्यन्त ते ताभ्यां तदा वारयितुं द्विजाः ॥ ५ ॥

पितृवर्ती तु यस्तेषां नित्यं श्राद्धान्हिको द्विजः।
स सर्वानब्रवीद् भ्रातॄन् कोपाद् धर्मे समाहितः ॥ ६ ॥

यद्यवश्यं प्रहन्तव्या पितॄनुद्दिश्य साध्विमाम्।
प्रकुर्वीमहि गां सम्यक् सर्वं एव समाहिताः ॥ ७ ॥

एवमेषापि गौर्धर्मं प्राप्स्यते नात्र संशयः।
पितॄनभ्यर्च्य धर्मेण नाधर्मोऽस्मान् भविष्यति ॥ ८ ॥

तथेत्युक्त्वा तु ते सर्वे प्रोक्षयित्वाथ गां ततः।
पितृभ्यः कल्पयित्वैनामुपायुञ्जन्त भारत ॥ ९ ॥

---

67. This story is referred in *Padma P.*, I, 10., though the narrator there is Pulastya speaking with Bhīṣma.

द्वौ दैवे भ्रातरौ कृत्वा त्रीन् पितृनथ चापरान् ।
तथैकमतिथिं कृत्वा श्राद्धकृत् पितृवर्त्यभूत् ॥ १० ॥

एवं सा प्रोक्षिता धेनुः कपिला कौशिकात्मजैः ।
भक्षयित्वाथ तां सर्वे गुरोस्तस्य न्यवेदयन् ॥ ११ ॥

शार्दूलेन हता धेनुर्वत्सोऽयं गृह्यतामिति ।
आर्जवात् स तु तं वत्सं प्रतिजग्राह वै द्विजः ॥ १२ ॥

मिथ्योपचर्य ते तं तु गुरुमन्यायतो द्विजाः ।
कालेन समयुज्यन्त सर्व एवायुषः क्षये ॥ १३ ॥

Mārkaṇḍeya said —

O Bhīṣma, then I saw the seven sons of Viśvāmitra that Sanatkumāra had described. While their father was performing asceticism they were disciples of the *ṛṣi* Gārgya. Following the instructions of their *guru* they went to the forest to graze the cow Kapilā and her calf, both of brownish colour. On the road they felt very hungry. Out of ignorance and youth, in four of them, Vāgaduṣṭa (harsh-speaking), Krodhana (inclined to wrath), Hisra (cruel), Piśuna (back-biter) grew the will to slaughter the cow. Two of them, Kavi and Khasṛma, tried to stop them but they were ignored. Then the seventh brother, Pitṛvartī, who daily used to perform *śrāddha*, said: "If the murder of this cow is necessary then you should offer it to the *pitṛ*s, by whose grace we could get this cow. In this way we will not incur *adharma*." Everyone accepted his words and after sprinkling the cow with water as required before an animal sacrifice, they slaughtered her. Then they offered the meat to the *pitṛ*s and shared it among themselves. Respecting the order of Pitṛvartī, two of the brothers were to sit at the place of Viśvedeva,[68] three as *pitṛ*s, one as guest and he himself

---

68. The thirteen sons of Viśvā, daughter of Dakṣa, and their names are as follows: Vasu, Satya, Kratu, Dakṣa, Kāla, Kāma, Dhṛti, Kuru, Purūravas, Mādravas, Rocaka or Locana and Dhvani; they are particularly worshipped at *śrāddha*s and at *vaiśvadeva* ceremony.

participated in the sacrifice as the *yajamāna*. In such a way the sons of Viśvāmitra ate the cow and went to their *guru*'s place, giving him back only the calf. They told him that the cow had been eaten by a tiger and they were able only to save the calf. The *guru* believed their false-sincerity and accepted the calf back. That time they all lied to their teacher in words and deeds. After much time they all fell under the sway of death. **[1-13]**

ते वै क्रूरतया हिंस्रा अनार्यत्वाद् गुरौ तथा ।
उग्रा हिंसा विहाराश्च सप्ताजायन्त सोदराः ॥ १४ ॥

जाता व्याधा दशार्णेषु सप्त धर्मविचक्षणाः ।
स्वकर्मनिरताः सव लोभामृतविवर्जिताः ॥ १५ ॥

तावन्मात्रं प्रकुर्वन्ति यावता प्राणधारणम् ।
शेषं ध्यानपराः कालमनुध्यायन्ति कर्म तत् ॥ १६ ॥

तैरेवमुषितैस्तात हिंसाधर्मरतैः सदा ।
माता च पूजिता वृद्धा च परितोषितः ॥ १७ ॥

यदा माता पिता चैव संयुक्तौ कालधर्मणा ।
तदा धनूंषि ते त्यक्त्वा वने प्राणानवासृजन् ॥ १८ ॥

They were reborn in the country of Daśārṇa as sons of a *bhīla*. Even though they had been born in a low womb they could remember their past fault. So they abandoned falsity and lust, and reduced so much their violence against the world as to take from it just the amount of food to substain their lives. They spent the rest of their existence thinking about the slaughter of the cow and the lie to their *guru*. They satisfied their parents by serving them, and when their father and mother died they all went to the forest, and after throwing down the bow they performed *yoga* until death came. **[14-18]**

शुभेन कर्मणातेन जाता जातिस्मरा मृगाः ।
त्रासानुत्पाद्य संविग्ना रम्ये कालञ्जरे गिरौ ॥ १९ ॥

तमेवार्थमनुध्यान्तो जातिस्मरणसंभवम् ।
आसन् वनचराः क्षान्ता निर्द्वन्द्वा निष्परिग्रहाः ॥ २० ॥

ते सर्वे शुभकर्माणः सधर्माणो वनेचराः ।
जहुः प्राणान् मरुं साध्य लध्वाहारा जितेन्द्रियाः ॥ २१ ॥

तेषां मरुं साधयतां पदस्थानानि भारत ।
तथैवाद्यापि दृश्यन्ते रम्ये कालंजरे नृप ॥ २२ ॥

Then they were born as deer in the country of Kālañjara. There they could remember the *pujā* they used to perform for their *bhīla* parents and disgust for the violence committed in their past lives started to grow in them. Always remembering their past faults they went on cultivating forgiveness, non-violence, chastity, lonliness, frugality in food and control over the senses. Keeping the vow of abstinence from water they roamed here and there. O king, even today it is possible to see the footprints of these ascetic deer. **[19-22]**

कर्मणा तेन ते तात शुभेनाशुभवर्जिताः ।
शुभाच्छुभतरां योनिं चक्रवाकत्वमागताः ॥ २३ ॥

शुभे देशे शरद्वीपे सप्तैवासन् जलौकसः ।
त्यक्त्वा सहचरीधर्मं मुनयो ब्रह्मचारिणः ॥ २४ ॥

ते तत्र पक्षिणः सर्वे शकुना धर्मचारिणः ।
निराहारा जहुः प्राणांस्तपोयुक्ताः सरित्तटे ॥ २५ ॥

The good behaviour performed as deer made them be reborn in Pañcāla, at the Śardvīpa *tīrtha*, in the form of *cakravāka* (partridge), the best birth among the acquatic birds. They stayed chaste all their lives and through *yoga* they renounced solid food. They left their bodies on the banks of the Gaṅgā. **[23-25]**

अथ ते सोदरा जाता हंसा मानसचारिणः ।
जातिस्मराः सुसंयुक्ताः सप्तैव ब्रह्मचारिणः ॥ २६ ॥

विप्रयोनौ यतो मोहान्मिथ्योपचरितो गुरुः ।
तिर्यग्योनौ ततो जाताः संसारे परिबभ्रमुः ॥ २७ ॥

यतश्च पितृवाक्यार्थः कृतः स्वार्थे व्यवस्थितैः ।
ततो ज्ञानं च जातिं च ते हि प्रापुर्गुणोत्तराम् ॥ २८ ॥

तेषां तु तपसा तेन पूर्वजातिकृतेन वै ।
योगस्य चापि निर्वृत्या प्रतिभानाच्च शोभनात् ॥ २९ ॥

विप्रजन्मनि यद् ब्रह्म श्रुतं गुरुकुलेतु तैः ।
तथैवावस्थिता बुद्धिः संसारेष्वपि वर्त्तताम् ॥ ३० ॥

ते ब्रह्मचारिणः सर्वे विहङ्गा ब्रह्मवादिनः ।
योगधर्म मनुध्यान्तो बिहरन्तिस्म तत्र ह ॥ ३१ ॥

After this they were all born as *haṁsa*, goose, at Mānasarovar, a lake also called Ciḍiyātāla about half a *kosa* from Kampil in the western direction. The name Ciḍiyā is a reminder of those birds. Also there they could remember their previous lives and passed their time as chaste *yogīs*. They had to be born many times for the faults committed to their *guru* in their lives as *brāhmaṇa*. But they could also remember the *śrāddha* performed that time by Pitṛvartī's advice, so that they progressively obtained a better birth. In virtue of their asceticism, *yoga*, and the possibility of remembering their past lives, the knowledge that they had learnt as *brāhmaṇa*s remained constant in them throughout all their births. Also in this birth, as *haṁsa*, they were acquainted with *brahma-jñāna*, and being *yogī*s they wandered around. **[26-31]**

॥ *इति श्री का० मा० कौशिकात्मजोपाख्यानं नामाष्टचत्वारिंशोऽध्यायः* ॥

Here ends the forty-eighth chapter of the Kāmpilyamahātmya.

49

Haṁsa Yogi Life of the Seven Sons of Viśvāmitra

मार्कण्डेय उवाच -

ते योगधर्मनिरत्ताः सप्त मानसचारिणः ।
वाय्वम्बुभक्षाः सततं शरीराण्युपशोषयन् ॥ १ ॥

तेषां तत्र विहङ्गानां चरतां सहचारिणाम् ।
नीपानामीश्वरो राजा विभ्राजः पौरवान्वयः ॥ २ ॥

विभ्राजमानो वपुषा प्रभावेण समन्वितः ।
श्रमानन्तःपुरवृतो वनं तत् प्रविवेश ह ॥ ३ ॥

स्वतन्त्रश्च विहङ्गोऽसौ स्पृहयामास तं नृपम् ।
दृष्ट्वा यान्तं श्रियोपेतं भवेयमहमीदृशः ॥ ४ ॥

यद्यस्ति सुकृतं किञ्चित् तपो वा नियमोऽपिवा ।
खिन्नोस्मि ह्युपवासेन तपसा निःफलेन च ॥ ५ ॥

ततस्तं चक्रकायौ द्वाबूचतुः सहचारिणौ ।
आवां ते सचिवौ स्यावस्तव प्रियहितैषिणौ ॥ ६ ॥

तथेत्युक्त्वा च तस्यासीत् तदा योगात्मिका गतिः ।
एवं ते समयं चक्रुः शुचिवाक् तमुवाच ह ॥ ७ ॥

यस्मात् कामप्रधानस्त्वं योगधर्ममपास्य वै ।
एवं वरं प्रार्थयसे तस्माद् वाक्यं निवोध मे ॥ ८ ॥

राजा त्वं भविता तात काम्पिल्ले नात्र संशयः ।
भविष्यतः सहायौ च द्वाविमौ सचिवौ तव ॥ ९ ॥

शप्त्वा चानभिभाष्यांस्तांश्चत्वारश्चक्रुरण्डजाः ।
तांस्त्रीनभीप्सतो राज्यं व्यभिचारप्रधर्षितान् ॥ १० ॥

Mārkaṇḍeya said —

All seven used to consume only water and air and after sometime their bodies started to dry up. They were living together near Ciḍiyātāla. One day the king of Nīpas, Vibhrāja, arrived there. He was very powerful and with him there were his queens. The seventh *haṁsa*, Svatantra hoped to get such a royal birth some day as the fruit of his asceticism because he was tired of the penance and the vows done so far. Then the fifth and the sixth said to him: "We want to be your counsellors." He consented to this. Then he kept silent. Suddenly the second *haṁsa*, Śucivāka, said: "You want to leave the *yoga* to enjoy the sensesory experiences. You will become the king of Kampil and these two will be your counsellors." After saying this the four *haṁsa* stopped speaking to those three *haṁsa*, ruiners of their own asceticism. **[1-10]**

शप्ताः खगास्ततस्ते तु योगभ्रष्टा विचेतसः ।
तानयाचन्त चतुरस्त्रयस्ते सहचारिणः ॥ ११ ॥

तेषां प्रसादं ते चक्रुरथैतान् सुमनाऽब्रवीत् ।
सर्वेषामेव वचनात् प्रसादानुगतं वचः ॥ १२ ॥

अन्तवान् भविता शापो युष्माकं नात्र संशयः ।
इतश्च्युताश्च मानुष्यं प्राप्य योगमवाप्स्यथ ॥ १३ ॥

सर्वसत्त्वरुतज्ञश्च स्वतन्त्रोयं भविष्यति ।
पितृप्रसादो ह्यस्माभिरस्य प्राप्तः कृतेन वै ॥ १४ ॥

गां प्रोक्षयित्वा धर्मेण पितृभ्य उपकल्प्य ताम् ।
अस्माकं ज्ञानसंयोगः सर्वेषां योगसाधनः ॥ १५ ॥

इमं च वाक्यसंदर्भं श्लोकद्वयमुदाहृतम् ।
पुरुषान्तरितं श्रुत्वा ततो योगमवाप्स्यथ ॥ १६ ॥

The three corrupted *haṁsa*, worried by this curse, begged pardon from the four *yogi-haṁsa*. Then among them the first *haṁsa*, Sumanā, said: "The end of this curse will be only when after taking human birth, in the next life, you will secure the welfare of your kingdom. And among you,

Svatantra will be able to understand all the modes of speaking of the animals, because by the grace of our ancestors we have all received the *jñāna-yoga*. The means that this *yoga* has been granted owing to the offering to the *pitṛ*s we performed on the occasion when we slaughtered Gārgya's cow. In that human existence when you three will listen to the two *śloka*s uttered now by me, *sapta vyādha ityādi*, pronounced by another man, and you will become *yogī* again, and the curse will end." **[11-16]**

॥ *इति श्री का० मा० हंसशापोनामैकोनपञ्चाशत्तमोऽध्यायः* ॥

Here ends the forty-ninth chapter of the Kāmpilyamahātmya.

50

The Story of Seven *Haṁsa*[69]

मार्कण्डेय उवाच -

राजा विभ्राजमानस्तु वपुषा तद्वनं तदा ।
चचारान्तःपुरवृतो नन्दनं मघवानिव ॥ १ ॥

स तानपश्यत् खचरान् योगधर्मात्मकान् नृप ।
निर्वेदाच्च तमेवार्थमनुध्यायन् पुरंययौ ॥ २ ॥

अणुहोनाम तस्यासीत् पुत्रः परमधार्मिकः ।
स्थापयित्वाथ तं राज्ये विभ्राजः पृथिवीपतिः ॥ ३ ॥

आमन्त्र्य पौरान् प्रीतात्मा ब्राह्मणान् स्वस्ति वाच्य च ।
प्रायात् सरस्तपश्चर्तुं यत्र ते सहचारिणः ॥ ४ ॥

स वै तत्र निराहारो वायुभक्षो महातपाः ।
त्यक्त्वा कामांस्तपस्तेपे सरसस्तस्य पार्श्वतः ॥ ५ ॥

तस्य सङ्कल्प आसीच्च तेषामेकतरस्य वै ।
पुत्रत्वं प्राप्य योगेन युज्येयमिति भातर ॥ ६ ॥

कृत्वाऽभिसन्धिं तपसा महता स समन्वितः ।
महातपाः स विभ्राजो विरराजांशुमानिव ॥ ७ ॥

ततो विभ्राजितं तेन वैभ्राजं नाम तद् वनम् ।
सरस्तच्च कुरुश्रेष्ठ वैभ्राजमिति संज्ञितम् ॥ ८ ॥

यत्र ते शकुना राजंश्चत्वारो योगधर्मिणः ।
यकेगभ्रष्टस्त्रयश्चैव देहन्यासकृतोऽभवन् ॥ ९ ॥

---

69. *Harivam.*, 23.

काम्पिल्ये नगरे ते तु ब्रह्मदत्तपुरोगमाः ।
जाताः सप्त महात्मानः सर्वे विगतकिल्विषाः ॥ १० ॥

ज्ञानध्यानतपः पूता वेदवेदाङ्गपारगाः ।
स्मृतिमन्तोऽत्र चत्वारस्त्रयस्तु परिमोहिताः ॥ ११ ॥

Mārkaṇḍeya said —

O Bhīṣma, King Vibhrāja was roaming like an Indra in the Vandana forest. When he saw the seven *haṁsa* performing *tapasyā*, the attitude of renunciation started to grow in his heart. On his way back home he was thinking: "If even birds can do asceticism how much can a man do?" King Vibhrāja had a son, Aṇuha, who was seated in the place of his father. And Vibhrāja, with the approval of the citizens, after the reciting of the *svasti mantra* by the *brāhmaṇa*s, went near the pond where the *haṁsa* were practising self-mortification. There he gave up eating and fixed his mind on *tapasyā*. While performing asceticism in his mind came the will: "I would like to have as a son one of those *haṁsa*, so that he could really practise *yoga*." With this thought in mind he increased his ascetic effort, so that he became resplendent like the sun. His brightness was so strong that the forest and the lake were always illuminated; for this reason the pond is also called Vaibhrāja. There were also the four *yogi-haṁsa* and their three brothers who had spoiled their *yoga*. Those seven *haṁsa* became Brahmadatta and other characters in the town of Kāmpilya. Because of the memory of their past lives, four of them were endowed with knowledge, practising concentration and self-renouncement and were well-versed in *Veda* and *Vedāṅga*. The other three were ignorant. **[1-11]**

स्वतन्त्रस्त्वणुहाज्जज्ञे ब्रह्मदत्तो महायशाः ।
यथासीत् पक्षिभावेस्य संङ्कल्पः पूर्वचिन्तितः ॥ १२ ॥

छिद्रदर्शी सुनेत्रश्च रथा वाभ्रव्यवत्सयो×ः ।
जातौ श्रोत्रियदायादौ वेदवेदाङ्गपारगौ ॥ १३ ॥

सहायौ ब्रह्मदत्तस्य पूर्वजातिसहोषितौ ।
पांचालः पांचिकश्चैव कण्डरीकस्तु षष्ठकः ॥ १४ ॥

पांचालो वव्हृचस्त्वासीदाचार्यत्वं चकार ह ।
द्विवेदः कण्डरीकस्तु छन्दोगोऽध्वयुरेव च ॥ १५ ॥

सर्वसत्त्वरुतज्ञस्तु राजासीदणुहात्मजः ।
पांचालकण्डरीकाभ्यां तस्य सख्यमभूत् तदा ॥ १६ ॥

ते ग्राम्यधर्मनिरताः कामस्य वशवर्तिनः ।
पूर्वजातिकृतेनासन् धर्मकामार्थकोविदाः ॥ १७ ॥

अणुहस्तु नृपश्रेष्ठ ब्रह्मदत्तमकल्मसम् ।
राज्येऽभिषिच्य योगात्मा परां गतिमवाप्तवान् ॥ १८ ॥

ब्रह्मदत्तस्य भार्या तु देवलस्यात्मजाऽभवत् ।
असितस्य हि दुर्द्धर्षा संनतिर्नाम नामतः ॥ १९ ॥

कौशिकस्यात्मजैः पूर्वं निहता कपिला गुरोः ।
पितृकार्ये नियुक्तातः साभवद् योगधर्मिणी ॥ २० ॥

ब्रह्मदत्तात्मजस्तस्यां स वैभ्राजस्त्वजायत ।
योगात्मा तपसा युक्तो विष्वक्सेन इति स्मृतः ॥ २१ ॥

शेषा विहङ्गमाये वै काम्पिल्ये सहचारिणः ।
ते जाताः श्रोत्रियकुले सुदरिद्रे सहोदराः ॥ २२ ॥

The seventh *haṁsa*, Svatantra, was the son of Aṇūha, as it had been envisaged by the ascetic King Vibhrāja. The fifth *haṁsa* was born as the counsellor Vābhravya's son, Pāñcāla. He was expert in the *Ṛgveda* and a good teacher. The sixth *haṁsa*, Sunetra was the son of the counsellor Vatsa, and his name was Kaṇḍarīka. Because he was skilled in *Yajurveda* and *Sāmaveda* he was called Dvivedī. King Brahmadatta could understand the mode of speaking of all the creatures. His ministers were Pāñcāla and Kaṇḍarīka. In spite of their familiarity with *dharma*, *artha* and *karma* from the *haṁsa* existence, they were addicted to the pleasures. King Aṇūha put his son Brahmadatta on the throne and left the body as a *yogī*, attaining the highest path. The wife of Brahmadatta was that same cow Kapilā that the seven sons of Kauśika had slaughtered and then offered to the *pitṛ*s. She was born as the daughter of Asita Devala *ṛṣi*, and was a follower of *yogadharma*. Her name was Sannatī. They had a son Viśvaksena, who was a (second) manifestation (*avatāra*) of the king Vibhrāja, and was also a *yogī*. **[12-22]**

धृतिमान् सुमना विद्वान् तत्वदर्शी च नामतः ।
वेदाध्ययनसम्पन्नाश्चत्वारश्छिद्रदर्शिनः ॥ २३ ॥

तेषां संवित् तथोत्पन्ना पूर्वजातिकृता तदा ।
ते योगनिरताः सिद्धाः प्रस्थिताः सर्व एव हि ॥ २४ ॥

आमन्त्र्य पितरं तात पिता तानब्रवीत् तदा ।
अधर्म एष युष्माकं यन्मां त्यक्त्वा गमिष्यथ ॥ २५ ॥

दारिद्र्यमनपाकृत्य पुत्रार्थांश्चैव पुष्कलान् ।
शुश्रूषामप्रयुज्यैव कथं वै गन्तुमर्हथ ॥ २६ ॥

ते तमूचुर्द्विजाः सर्वे पितरं पुनरे व च ।
करिष्यामो विधानं ते येन त्वं वर्त्तयिष्यसि ॥ २७ ॥

इमौ श्लोकौ महार्थौ द्वौ राजानं सहमन्त्रिणम् ।
श्रावयेथाः समागम्य ब्रह्मदत्तमकल्मषम् ॥ २८ ॥

प्रीतात्मा दास्यति स ते ग्रामान् भोगांश्च पुष्कलान् ।
यथेप्सितांश्च सर्वार्थान् गच्छतात यथेप्सितम् ॥ २९ ॥

एतावदुक्त्वा ते सर्वे पूजयित्वा च तं गुरुम् ।
योगधर्ममनुप्राप्य परां निर्वृतिमाययुः ॥ ३० ॥

The other four *haṁsa* were born as the sons of a poor *brāhmaṇa* of Kāmpilya. They were Dhṛtimān, Sumanā, Vidvān, Tattvadarśī. These four were readers of the Veda and they could see the fault in sensory pleasures. They all remembered the knowledge of their previous lives. When they went to ask permisson from their father to become *yogī*, their father answered: "You are going to commit *adharma*, by leaving me here alone. You have not removed poverty, and you have not even undertaken the family life. Moreover you are not making any service to me: how can you go?" So they answered: "We have the remedy that will give you what is necessary for your life. When you will utter the *mantra*: *sapta vyādha ityādi*" (see chap. 49, 16; 51, 29-30) to King Brahmadatta together with his two ministers, he will get very happy and give you many villages and riches.[70] O father, now go. After saying that they bowed their heads down to their fathers feet and went to practise *yoga* in the jungle. **[23-30]**

॥ इति श्री का० मा० ब्रह्मदत्ताद्युत्पत्तिवर्णनं नाम पंचाशत्तमोऽध्यायः ॥

Here ends the fiftieth chapter of the Kāmpilyamahātmya.

---

70. The oral tradition hands down that King Brahmadatta on that occasion gave to the *brāhmaṇa* twelve villages for everyone of his brother: 12 multiplied by 7 = 84. The *brāhmaṇas* residing in those villages are still called Caurāsiyā, eighty-four.

51

How the Queen Sannati Felt Offended by King Brahmadatta, and How he with Two of his Brothers Hearing the *Śloka* Utterd by a *Brāhmana* Obtained Jatismarana and Mukti[71]

मार्कण्डेय उवाच -

कदाचिद् ब्रह्मदत्तस्तु भार्यया सहितो वने ।
विजहार प्रहृष्टात्मा यथा शच्या शचीपतिः ॥ १ ॥

पिपीलिकरुतं तत्र स शुश्राव नराधिपः ।
कामिनीं कामिनस्तस्य याचतः क्रोशतो भृशम् ॥ २ ॥

पिपीलिकामधोवक्त्रां पुरतः स पिपीलिकः ।
पंचबाणाभितप्ताङ्गः सगद्गदमुवाच ह ॥ ३ ॥

न त्वया सदृशी लोके कामिनी विद्यते क्वचित् ।
मध्ये क्षीणाऽतिजघना बृहद्वक्त्राऽतिगामिनी ॥ ४ ॥

सुवर्णवर्णसदृशी सद्वक्त्रा चारुहासिनी ।
आलक्ष्यते ते वदनं गुडशर्करवत्सलम् ॥ ५ ॥

भोक्ष्यसे मयि भुक्ते त्वं स्नासि सनाते तथा मयि ।
प्रोषिते मयि दीना त्वं क्रुद्धे तु भयचञ्चला ॥ ६ ॥

किमर्थं वद कल्याणि त्वमधोवदना स्थिता ।
सा तमाह ज्वलत्कोपा किमालपसि रे शठ ॥ ७ ॥

त्वया मोदकपचूर्णं हि मां विहायापि भक्षितम् ।
प्रादास्त्वं मामतिक्रम्य तदन्यस्यै समन्मथः ॥ ८ ॥

---

71. *Harivam.*, 24.

Mārkaṇḍeya said —

One day King Brahmadatta and his wife Sannatī were walking around in the garden like Indra and Indrāṇī. There they saw a couple of ants quarrelling. The lustful ant-husband was addressing his angry ant-wife. She was keeping her head down and he, standing in front of her, with choked voice was saying: "O dear, in this world there is not a beautiful ant-lady like you. Your waist is slender, your legs are long, your face is noble; you move with agility, you have a pleasant mouth and a nice smile, your mouth wants to eat sugar and jaggery. You will bath after my bathing. When I go abroad you will remain poor, I am acting angrily just to make you afraid. Why do you stay with your face down?" At once she became angry and said: "O rascal, you are leaving me after feeding my co-wife and yourself." **[1-8]**

पिपीलिक उवाच -

त्वत्साद्धश्यान्मया दत्तमन्यस्यै वरवर्णिनि ।
तदेकमपराऽधः मे क्षन्तुमर्हसि भामिनि ॥ ९ ॥

नैवं पुनः करिष्यामि त्यज कोपं शुभस्तनि ।
स्पृशामि पादौ सत्येन प्रणतस्य प्रसीद मे ॥ १० ॥

भत्वयां त्वयि सुश्रोणि मृत्युर्मे पुरतो भवेत् ।
तुष्टायां त्वयि वामोरु पूर्णाः सर्वे मनोरथाः ॥ ११ ॥

पूर्णचन्द्रोपमं वक्त्रं स्वादेऽमृतरसोपमम् ।
निर्भरं तव कल्याणि पातुमिच्छामि कामुकः ॥ १२ ॥

Pipīlika (the ant-husband) said —

I have used that subterfuge with you, because I had an offence to be forgiven by her. From now on I will follow the path of truth; and I am touching your feet. Please leave your anger. Your frown is my death, and your happiness is what I wish for. Let me kiss your face round like the full-moon and sweet like ambrosia. **[9-12]**

मार्कण्डेय उवाच -

श्रुत्वा तु याच्यमाना तां क्रुद्धां सूक्ष्मां पिपीलिकाम्।
ब्रह्मदत्तो महाहासमकस्मादेव चाकरोत्॥ १३॥

ततः सा संनतिर्दीना ब्रीडितेवाभवत् तदा।
निराहारा बहुतिथं वभूव वरवर्णिनी॥ १४॥

प्रसाद्यमाना भर्त्रा सा समुवाच शुचिस्मिता।
त्वया च हसिता राजन् नाहं जीवितुमुत्सहे॥ १५॥

स तत्कारणमाचख्यौ न च सा श्रद्दधाति तत्।
उवाच चैनं कुपिता नैष भावोऽस्ति मानुषे॥ १६॥

को वै पिपीलिकरुतं मानुषो वेत्तुमर्हति।
ऋते देवप्रसादाद् वा पूर्वजातिकृतेन वा॥ १७॥

तपोबलेन वा राजन् विद्यया वा नराधिप।
यद्येष वै प्रभावस्ते सर्वसत्त्वरुतज्ञता॥ १८॥

यथाहमेतज्जानीयां तथा प्रत्याययस्व माम्।
प्राणान् वापि परित्यक्ष्ये राजन् सत्येन ते शपे॥ १९॥

तत् तस्या वचनं श्रुत्वा महिष्याः परुषाक्षरम्।
स राजा परमापन्नो देवश्रेष्ठमगात् ततः॥ २०॥

शरणं सर्वभूतेशं भक्त्या नारायणं हरिम्॥।
समाहितो निराहारः षड्रात्रेण महायशाः॥ २१॥

ददर्श दर्शने राजा देवं नारायणं प्रभुम्।
उवाच चैनं भगवान् सर्वभूतानुकम्पकः॥ २२॥

ब्रह्मदत्त प्रभाते त्वं कल्याणं समवाप्स्यसि।
इत्युक्त्वा भगवान् देवस्तत्रैवान्तरधीयत॥ २३॥

Mārkaṇḍeya said —

At once Brahmadatta, understanding the anger of the she-ant and the insistence of the he-ant, burst out laughing. Then Queen Sannatī got sad and ashamed and for many days she did not take any food. "The king wanted to ask her why she was upset. The queen answered: That time you laughed at me and now I just want to die." King Brahmadatta explained that he was laughing because of the ants' talk, but the queen did not believe him. She got angry and replied: "No human being can do such a performance. Man could understand the speech of ants only by the grace of gods or by the effect of past lives, or by virtue of asceticism, or of the knowledge of *yoga*. If you really have the capacity to understand the mode of speaking of the animals, then show it to me. If not I will commit suicide." Listening to the harsh speech of the queen King Brahmadatta felt distressed and took refuge in Lord Viṣṇu. For six days he fasted. Then the Lord appeared to him and spoke thus: "O King, tomorrow your problem will be resolved." Saying so, the Lord disappeared. **[13-23]**

चतुर्णां तु पिता योऽसौ ब्राह्मणानां महात्मनाम्।
श्लोकौ सोधीत्य पुत्रेभ्यः कृतकृत्य इवाभवत्॥ २४॥

स राजानमथान्विच्छन् सहमन्त्रिणमच्युतम्।
न ददर्शान्तरं किंचित् श्लोकौ श्रावयितुं तदा॥ २५॥

अथ राजा सरःस्नातो लब्ध्वानारायणाद् वरम्।
प्रविवेश पुरीं प्रीतो रथमारुह्य कांचनम्॥ २६॥

तस्य रश्मीन् प्रत्यगृह्णात् कण्डरीको द्विजर्षभः।
चामरं व्यजनं चापि पांचाल्यः समवाक्षिपत॥ २७॥

इदमन्तरमित्येव ततः स ब्राह्मणस्तदा।
श्लोकौ तौ श्रावयामास राजानं सचिवौ च तौ॥ २८॥

सप्त व्याधा दशार्णेषु मृगाः कालंजरे गिरौ।
चक्रवाकाः शरद्वीपे हंसाः सरसि मानसे॥ २९॥

तेऽभिजाताः कुरुक्षेत्रे ब्राह्मणा वेदपारगाः।
प्रस्थिता दीर्घमध्वानं यूयं किमवसीदथ॥ ३०॥

तच्छ्रुत्वा मोहमगमद्ब्रह्मदत्तो महीपतिः।
सचिवश्चास्य पांचालः कण्डरीकश्च भारत॥ ३१॥

स्रस्तरश्मिप्रतोदौ तौ पतितव्यजनावुभौ।
दृष्ट्वा वभूवुरस्वस्थाः पौराश्च सुहृदस्तथा॥ ३२॥

Meanwhile the poor *brāhmaṇa*, father of the four *yogī*s, after learning from his sons the two *śloka*s went to the town but he could not find the king and his two ministers together in order to utter those two *śloka*s. But when the king returned to the city with his chariot after getting the boon from Lord Viṣṇu and bathing in the pond, the two ministers Kaṇḍarīka and Pāñcāla were with him, driving his chariot. So he realised this was the right occasion, as the three were together, to utter the two *śloka*s: "Those who were seven *bhīla* in the country of Daśārṇa (at the south of Vindhyācala), deer on the mountain of Kālīñjara, partridges at the lake of Śardvīpa, then became seven *haṁsa* at the Mānasa lake. Among them we four were born as *brāhmaṇa*s in Kāmpilya; we have studied the *Veda*s in Kurukṣetra and now we are going to practise *yoga*. Why are you, who have spoiled your *yoga*, still here?" The three heard those verses[72] and fell unconscious, and everyone worried when the chariot entered the town uncontrolled. **[24-32]**

मुहूर्तमेव राजा स सह ताभ्यां रथे स्थितः ।
प्रतिलभ्य ततः संज्ञां प्रत्यागच्छदरिंदमः ॥ ३३ ॥

ततस्ते तत् सरः स्मृत्वा योगं तमुपलभ्य च ।
ब्राह्मणं विपुलैरर्थैर्भोगैश्च समयोजयन् ॥ ३४ ॥

अभिषिच्य स्वराज्ये तु विष्वक्सेनमरिंदमम् ।
जगाम ब्रह्मदत्तोथ सदारो बनमेव ह ॥ ३५ ॥

अथैनं संनतिर्धीरा देवलस्य सुता तदा ।
उवाच परमप्रांता योगाद् वनगतं नृपम् ॥ ३६ ॥

जानन्त्या ते महाराज पिपीलकरुतज्ञताम् ।
चोदितः क्रोधमुद्दिश्य सक्तः कामेषु वै मया ॥ ३७ ॥

---

72. *sapta vyādha daśarṇeṣu mṛgāḥ kālañjare girau । cakravākāḥ śardvīpe haṁsa sarasi mānase ॥ te'bhi jātāḥ kurukṣetre brāhmaṇā vedapāragāḥ । prasthitā dīrghamadhvānaṁ yūyaṁ kimavasīdatha ॥*

इतो वयं गमिष्यामो गतिमिष्टामनुत्तमाम् ।
तव चान्तर्हितो योगस्ततः संस्मारितो मया ॥ ३८ ॥

स राजा परमप्रीतः पत्न्याः श्रुत्वा वचस्तदा ।
प्राप्य योगं बलादेव गतिं प्राप सुदुर्लभाम् ॥ ३९ ॥

ज्ञानध्यानतपः पूतो वेदवेदाङ्गपारगः ।
जैगीषव्योपदेशेन योगतन्त्रं चकार ह ॥ ४० ॥

कण्डरीकोपि धर्मात्मा सांख्यये गमनुत्तमम् ।
प्राप्य योगमतिः सिद्धौ विशुद्धस्तेन कर्मणा ॥ ४१ ॥

क्रमं प्रणीय पांचाल्यः शिक्षां चोत्पाद्य केवलाम् ।
योगाचार्यगतिं प्राप यशश्चाग्र्यं महातपाः ॥ ४२ ॥

For sometime the king and his two ministers were unable to move, and they stayed on the chariot. When they regained consciousness they went home. Then they remembered the lake and the *yoga* performed (when they had born in the family of Bhardvāja). Later the three, the king and the two ministers, gave many riches and villages to the *brāhmaṇa* and sent him off. King Brahmadatta left his kingdom to his son Viśvaksena and, with his wife, went into the jungle. The queen was happy and when they reached the forest, she said: "O Mahārāja, I knew that you could understand the languages of the animals, but you were still attached to pleasures. So I have used the subterfuge of getting angry with you just to enlighten your *yoga*. Now we will get to the highest path." The king was very happy on hearing the queen's speech and with the strength of *yoga* reached a high spiritual rank, difficult to attain. Purified by knowledge and concentration and skilled in Veda and Vedāṅga, the king got the *yogatantra* initiation from the *ṛṣi* Jaigīśavya. Kaṇḍarīka through the teaching of Sāṅkhyayoga attained perfection and *mokṣa*. Also Pāñcāla with the repetition of the Vedic *mantra* achieved the status of *yogācārya* and in the end was realesed from *saṁsāra*. **[33-42]**

एवमेतत् पुरा वृत्तं मम प्रत्यक्षमच्युत ।
तद् धारयस्व गाङ्गेय श्रेयसा योक्ष्यसे ततः ॥ ४३ ॥

ये चान्ये धारयिष्यन्ति तेषां चरितमुत्तमम् ।
तिर्यग्योनिषु ते जातु न गमिष्यन्ति कर्हिचित् ॥ ४४ ॥

श्रुत्वा चेदमुपाख्यानं महार्थं महतां गतिम् ।
योगधर्मो हृदि सदा परिवर्त्तति भारत ॥ ४५ ॥

स तेनैवानुबन्धेन कदाचिल्लभते शमम् ।
ततो योगगतिं याति शुद्धां तां भुवि दुर्लभाम् ॥ ४६ ॥

O Bhīṣma, I have seen with my eyes the power and the greatness of the rite of *śrāddha*. Remember all this and you will prosper. And whoever understands this will never be born from a lower womb. By listening to this great tale the elevated souls will be able to keep their minds steady. Then at any time, with a serene mind, through the *yogadharma*, they can be freed from rebirth. **[43-46]**

वैशम्पायन उवाच -

एवमेतत् पुरा गीतं मार्कण्डेयेन धीमता ।
श्राद्धस्य फलमुद्दिश्य सोमस्याप्यायनाय वे ॥ ४७ ॥

Vaiśampāyana said —

O King (Janamejaya), Mārkaṇḍeya told this story of the greatness of the fruit of *śrāddha*: with this rite Soma, the moon, is magnificated and through the moon the *pitṛ*s residing in the *svarga* and those residing on earth become satisfied. **[47]**

॥ इति श्री का०मा० ब्रह्मदत्तादिमोक्षो नामैकपंचाशत्तमोऽध्यायः॥

Here ends the fifty-first chapter of the Kāmpilyamahātmya.

अथ श्रवणविधिः

Method of Listening

एतत् काम्पिल्यमाहात्म्यं शृणुयाद् भक्तियुङ् नरः ।
ब्रह्मचारी जितक्रोधो लध्वाहारा जितेन्द्रियः ॥ १ ॥

विघ्नेश पूजयित्वादौ गन्धपुष्पाक्षतादिभिः ।
पुस्तकं वाचकं चापि शृणयात सत्कथामिमाम् ॥ २ ॥

ततोग्निं तर्पयेच्छक्त्या सर्पिषा पायसेन च ।
ब्राह्मणान् भोजयेत् सप्त कौशिकात्मजतुष्ट ये ॥ ३ ॥

सवत्सां कपिलां दोग्ध्रीं ततो दद्याद् द्विजातये ।
कपिलायाः प्रदानेन संतुष्टा संनतिर्भवेत् ॥ ४ ॥

पितृश्राद्धं प्रकुर्वीत तंतः प्रयतमानसः ।
एवं कृते व्रजेन्मर्त्यः पदं योगिसुदुर्लभम् ॥ ५ ॥

Listen to this *Kāmpilyamahātmya* with devotion. Chaste, without anger, after having taken light food and with the senses under control. A *pujā* to Gaṇeśa should be done first with sandalwood paste, rice, etc. Then, after the *pujā* of the book and of the reader, one should listen to this story. After the recitation of this tale a *havana* with *ghī* or *khīr* should be performed. For the happiness of the sons of Kauśika food should be offered to seven *brāhmaṇa*s. And the milk of a Kapilā cow (brown colour) should also be offered to delight the Queen Sannatī. Finally the *śrāddha* to the *pitra*s should be done: in this way the man can attain such a state that is hard to reach even by *yogī*s. [1-5]

उपसंहार
Epilogue

योऽवस्थिवंशसरसीरुहलोकबन्धुः
सिन्धुर्गिरा हरदयालुरितिप्रसिद्धः।
तस्यात्मजस्य तनयेन सुचिन्त्य सम्यक्
कास्पिल्यकस्य निरमायि महत्त्वमेतत्॥ १॥

निधिवसुनवेकवर्ष तपसि मिते भार्गवे पूर्णिमायाम्।
कास्पिल्यस्य महत्त्वं सम्पूर्णत्व गतं शुभं भवतु॥ २॥

The nephews of Paṇḍit Haradayāl, like a sun in his lineage and ocean of knowledge, have composed this *Kāmpilyamāhātmya* after deep consideration. In the Vikramāditya year 1989 (AD 1933), Pūrṇimā, Friday, this work has been completed.

Śubhamastu

अथ कविवंशावर्णनम्

Description of the Genealogy of the Poet

कश्यपफल अवरंस प्रथम द्विज धनीराम वर ॥ तासु कनिष्ठ तनूज वसे औनहा जु खेचर ॥ तिनकिय अवसथ यज्ञ लह्यो अवलथिय आलपद ॥ दसविसबा मर्जाद दइय कनबजपति जयचँद ॥ तिहि वंश दाससविता तनय चिंतामनि पंडित चतुर ॥ औनहा त्याजि किहुकाजवस वसे आनि बिलहौरपुर ॥ १ ॥

In the beginning there was a brilliant *paṇḍita* called Dhanirām of the Kaśyapa progeny, whose little son stayed in Aunahā Jū Khecar. In this village he performed an important sacrifice, by which he obtained ten measures of land from the King Jayacand of Kannauj. Belonging to the same *brāhmaṇa* family there was a *paṇḍita* Cintāmaṇi, son of mother Savitā, who for some reasons left Aunahā to stay in Bilhaurpur. [1]

चिन्तामनि कुल विपुलमव्य द्विज विश्वनाथ भनि ॥ नारायन तिहि तनय श्यामसुन्दर तिहि तनुमनि ॥ जगन्नाथपरसाद मऊ जैराज द्विवेदिय ॥ कंपिल नगर निवास तास तनपा सपान सिय ॥ सो जगन्नाथ दीनी सुतासुन्दर श्यानम अवस्थि घर ॥ तिहि जठर जनमि घनश्याम सो बसे आनि कपिल नगर ॥ २ ॥

His son was Viśvanāthamaṇi, who had Nārāyaṇa, who got a son called Śyāmasundara. His son was Jagannāthapraśāda, by whom Jayarāja Dvivedī. When he was staying in Kampil he had a daughter, Sapanā. Jagannātha arranged her marriage by which she got Ghanśyāma, who came to stay in the town of Kampil. [2]

तिहिसुत खेतलदाल तासुसुत लाल जवाहर ॥ रामलाल तिहितनय तासु तनुजात सातवर ॥ लेखराज तिन मध्य भये विद्यागुन भारिय ॥ टोंक नगर नव्बाव मीरखानह दर बारिय ॥ तिन तनुज मनुजअवतार गुरु हरदयाल पंडित कहिय ॥ सजि लोभ मोह जिन निस दिवसि अध्यापन अध्यायन किय ॥ ३ ॥

His son was Khetaladāl whose son was Lāl Javāhar, by whom Rāmalāl was born. He had seven sons. The third of them, who used to stay at the court of the *navāb* of Ṭoknagar, Mīrkhān, was Lekharāja endowed with much knowledge. His third son was Haradayāl *paṇḍita*. Free from greed and infatuation he used to pass night and day learning and teaching at his home. [3]

भूनिवास तिन तनय भये पंडित अरु कविवर ॥ सकल कला परवीन ज्ञान विज्ञान ध्यान हर ॥ गृहबसि उनतिस बरस भयउ निविन्न सुचित्तह ॥ वारानसी पयान कियहु शिबथान तुरित्तह ॥ तहँ निवसि उभय सप्ताह पुनि सुरधुनितट निजदेह तजि ॥ कैलासवास पायो अटल शंकरचरण सरोज भजि ॥ ४ ॥

Bhunivas appeared as his third son, a great *paṇḍita* and best among poets. He was expert in all the arts, sciences and knowledge. When he was twenty-nine he went to Banāras where he stayed near Viśvanātha. After sometimes he left his body on the banks of Gaṅgā and in grace of his firm devotion to Śiva he attained the abode on Kailāsa. [4]

भू निवास तनुजनम नाम मम दुर्गादत्तह ॥ सेय पितामह चरण कमल पायो कछु तत्तह ॥ तिनही को धरि ध्यान चित्त निज करि अति साहस ॥ कंपिल नगर महत्व कियो सुरनर भाषा रस ॥ जिहि पढत बढत चित हरष अति कलिकलुषित विनसति कुमति ॥ हरि चरणकमल विगसतु हृदय तिहि सुभिगति सुभिगति भवति ॥ ५ ॥

Bhunivas had me as his son, called Durgadatta. Following the example of his forefathers and with much attention and great effort he wrote a poetical work to expound the fame of the town of Kampil. By reading his work the mind becomes content and the lower tendencies, typical of *kaliyuga*, are abandoned; attraction to the feet of Hari and welfare are obtained. [5]

जय विरंचि बरदान देनि जय विष्णु जगावनि ॥ जय मधुकैटभ हनन हेतु जय सुर दुख द्रावनि ॥ जय महिषासुर हननि चड अरु मुंड विनासिनि ॥ जय खल बल दल दहनि जयति हिमभधर वासिनि ॥ जय शरण समागत दत्त कवि दुख हारिन कारिनि अभय ॥ जय मातु निशुम्भ विनाशिनी शुंभ नाशिनी जयति जय ॥ ६ ॥

Victory to the one who granted a boon to Brahmājī and awakened Śrī Viṣṇu; to the one who killed Madhu and Kaiṭabha, victory to the destroyer of demons, of Mahīṣāsura and of Caṇḍa and Muṇḍa. To the destroyer of the wicked, victory, to the one who stays in the mountains, victory to the mother who cleansed the devoted poet Durgadatta from every pain and made him fearless. Victory to the destroyer of Śumbha and Niśumbha. May it always be your victory. [6]

दोहा

वक्ता श्रोता चिर जियौ सुखी रहौ सच सत्व।
इत्येव पूरन भयो कम्पिल नगर महत्व॥

Those who read or listen to this *Kāmpilyamahātmya* will live a long and happy life, this is true!

Thus, the *Kāmpilyamahātmya* is complete.

Glossary

adharma: the disorder, an irreligious situation.

adhidaiva: the Supreme Deity or the divine agent operating in material objects; the Macrocosm.

adhyātma: the Supreme Spirit manifested as the individual self; the Microcosm.

āgneyāstra: a fire-missile, a rocket.

apsarā: water nymphs.

aratni: the distance between the elbow and the fist.

artha: attainment of riches or wordly prosperity, regarded as one of the four aims of human existence, the other three being *dharma*, *kāma* and *mokṣa*.

aśoka: (lit. without sorrow) name of a tree having red flowers, (*Jonesia Asoka Roxb.*).

āśrama: 'refuge'; the house of the teacher, where the disciples stay to live a spiritual discipline.

aśvamedha: a horse sacrifice.

ātman: the self, the individual soul, the principle of life and sensation.

belpatra, bilvapatra: the leaf of the *Aegle Marmelos* or wood-apple.

bharaṇī: name of the second constellation containing three stars.

bhikṣā: begging alms; mendicancy.

bhīl: name of a tribal people of central India.

brahmacarya: 'moving with the *Brahman*', synonym of being unmarried and pure; the first stage of the life of the *dvija*.

Brahman: the unconditioned and non dual Supreme principle.

brāhmaṇa: priest, member of the higher caste; the knower of the *Brahman*.

cāṇḍāla: a sub-caste amongst the *śūdra* taken to be the lowest in the traditional Hindu caste hierarchy.

candravaṁśa: the lunar race, one of the two major *kṣatriya* dynasties that flourished in ancient India.

cāraṇa: a celestial singer, heavenly chorister.

caturdaśī: the fourteenth day of a lunar fortnight.

daitya: a son of Diti, a *rākṣasa*, a demon.

dakṣiṇā: a present or gift to *brāhmaṇa*s or to the teacher (at the completion of a religious rite or a sacrifice).

dānava: a class of demons.

darśana: sight; visiting a shrine or worshipping an idol.

devaloka: the 'locus' of the gods, the sphere of a particular deity.

devapratiṣṭhā: the rite of immission of life into any statue.

devatā: the 'bright ones', the gods.

dhanurvidyā: the art of archery.

dhana: property, wealth; trasure.

dhanuṣa: a bow.

dharma: the Universal law; the religious duties; the Hinduism.

dhūpa: incense; light or heat of the sun.

dīkṣā: consecration for a religious ceremony, instruction from a teacher, initiation.

dīpaka: a light, a lamp (often offered to a deity).

divya-dṛṣṭi: the divine faculty of vision.

divyavastra: divine cloths.

dvija: twice-born; every member of the three highest castes having got the sacred thread.

gaṇa: multitude; in laterage, dwarf *yakṣa*.

gandharva: class of demi-gods; subtle being.

gāyatrī-mantra: a Vedic metre; the name of a particularly sacred verse of the *Ṛgveda*.

ghī: clarified butter.

gotra: an exogamous sub-division of the a caste group.

gṛhastha-dharma: the duty and the obligations of the stage of householder.

guhyaka: name of a class of demi-gods, who, like the *yakṣa*s, are attendants of Kubera and guardians of his treasures.

guru: master, teacher, especially in the initiation context.

haṁsa: a swan, goose, duck, flamingo; the Supreme Soul, *Brahman*.

hasta: the hand; the forearm (as a measure).

havana: a fire offering, sacrifice; an oblation of *ghī*.

indriya: the ten faculties of sense and action plus the mind.

iṣṭa-devatā: the favoured deity of a family, or of an individual.

jāti-smaraṇa: the memory of previous birth.

jayamālā: garland of victory; garland placed round a bridegroom's neck by his wife.

kāma: the desire, the passional love.

kamaṇḍalu: a water-pot used by ascetics, and by other devout person.

karman: deed, action; rite.

khīra: a dish of rice boiled in milk, with sugar.

kinnara: half man and half horse spirits, reckoned among the *gandharva* as divine musicians or singers.

kosa (*krośa*): a measure of distance (approx. two miles).

kṣatriya: the members of the second caste, the warriors.

kumbhakāra, kumhāra: potter.

kuṇḍa: a wide-mouthed deep basin; pit as for sacrificial fire; a pool as consecrated to a person or to a deity.

kuśa (or *darbha*): herb consecrated to Viṣṇu (*Desmostachya bipinnata*?).

lava: an istant, a moment; a fragment, a particle.

liṅgam: a phallic image in which the form Śiva is worshipped.

māhātmya: eulogy.

maṇḍapa: an open hall, pavillion; a building consecrated to a deity.

mantram: Vedic verses; syllable or word with a vibrating effect, right for offering a support for the spiritual realisation.

manuṣyaloka: the world of mortals, the earth.

maruta: wind, air, breeze; vital-air or breath.

mitra mantrī: the King's nearest counsellor.

mokṣa: the Liberation from every bondage, supreme aim of the man.

muhūrta: a moment; a period of time; a period of 48 minutes.

muni: a sage, a holy man, saint, an ascetic enjoying the spiritual loneliness.

nakṣatra: a star in general; an asterism in the moon's path, lunar mansion.

nirguṇa: devoid of all properties; the Supreme Spirit.

nirjalā ekādaśī: name of the eleventh day in the bright half of the month of Jyeṣṭha.

pañcākṣara mantram: the five-syllabled *mantra*.

parikramā: circumambulation; walking around in reverence.

pātāla: one of the seven infernal regions; the underworld; hell.

piṇḍa: sweet ball offered to the *pitara* or gods in several rites.

piṇḍadāna: the *piṇḍa* offered with the purpose of reuniting the recent dead person with the *pitṛ*.

pitṛ (pl. *pitara*): ancestor. Favourable or unfavourable state of the deceased people waiting for the rebirth.

pradakṣiṇā: ritual deambulation to right hand, following the apparent moving of the Sun.

prakṛti: Universal Substance, material Cause of the Cosmos.

pūjā: not sacrificial rite focussed on the Images worship.

purāṇa-puruṣa: an epithet of Viṣṇu; an old man.

puraścaraṇa: a preparatory or initiatory rite; repetition of the name of a deity accompained with burnt offerings.

purṇāhuti: complete oblation: the burnt offering which concludes a ceremony.

purohita: the *brāhmaṇa* playing the role of Court chaplain.

purī: a town, city; abode, palace; fig. the body.

rājasika: concerning or arising from passion, *rajas*.

rākṣasa: an evil spirit, demon; night devils.

rāmanaumī: the ninth day in the bright half of the month of Caitra, the anniversary of the birth of Śrī Rāmacandra.

ṛṣi: Vedic seer.

ṛtvija: the priest performer of the sacrifice.

sādhu: religious mendicant about to become a *saṁnyāsin*.

saguṇa: having attributes or qualities; the Supreme Being seen as positively qualified or personal.

samādhi: direct contemplation; a way to express the death of the *saṁnyāsin*; funeral monument for a *saṁnyāsin*.

saṁhitā: the Vedic hymn.

sanātana dharma: eternal *dharma*: Hinduism as involving acceptance of *śruti* and *smṛti*, orthodox belief and practice.

sāttvika: endowed with the quality of purity, *sattva*, genuineness, honesty.

siddha: category of *yogin* pursuing the control of the eight supernatural powers (*siddhī*).

siddhāsana: a typical sitting posture.

śivarātri: Śiva's night; a Hindu festival observed on the fourteenth day of the dark lunar fortnight of the month of Phālgun.

somavatī amāvasyā: a Monday coinciding with the last day of the dark fortnight (celebrated as a festival and bathing day).

śrāddha: offering of *piṇḍa*s leading the *preta* to *pitṛloka*.

śṛṅgī devatā: gods who are engaged in the 'heroic' practice synonym of *vīra sādhaka*.

śrotrya: those *brāhmaṇa*s in whose family the *Veda* is recited from ten generations.

śūdra: a member of the fourth and lowest division in the traditional hierarchical set-up of the Hindu society.

sūryavaṁśa: the solar race, one of the two major *kṣatriya* dynasties that flourished in ancient India.

svarga: Heaven, abode of the gods.

svastivācana: benedictory words.

svayaṁvara: public choice of a bridegroom by the bride from among her assembled suitors.

tāmasika: pertaining to, related with or inspired by the quality of inertia, ignorance, *tamas*.

tāmbūla: betel, especially betel leaf.

tapas: the heat produced by the asceticism.

tattva: every production of *prakṛti*.

tejas: the element of fire; the vital warmth; energy, strength.

tīrtha: ford; places of pilgrimage close to a sacred river, lake or sea.

upaveda: class of writings dealing with four branches of knowledge, attached to and subordinate to the four *Veda*s.

vaikuṇṭha: the heaven of Viṣṇu, paradise.

vaiśya: a member of the third division of Hindu society with trade as its main profession.

vajra: a thunderbolt; the thunderbolt of Indra.

varṇasaṅkara: a person of mixed caste or blood.

vidyā: science, analytic knowledge, wisdom.

vimāna: a self-moving aerial chariot.

vipra: a *brāhmaṇa*; a family priest.

vrata: the ascetic vow.

yajamāna: the institutor of a sacrifice.

yajña: a sacrifice.

yakṣa: a subtle being, like an elf.

yantra: an instrument; a mystical diagram.

yoga: union (=*mokṣa*); a way to reach the *mokṣa*; the doctrine theorised by Patañjali.

yogabhraṣṭa: the failure in the practice of *yoga*.

yogin: the human being having realised the union with the *Brahman*.

yuga: one of the four ages of the History of a Humanity.

Bibliography

Primary Sources

Bhāgavata Purāṇa, in 5 vols., translated into English by G.V. Tagare, Motilal Banarsidas, Delhi, 1994.

Harivaṁśapurāṇa, translated into Hindi by Pandi Rāmanārāyaṇadatta Śāstrī Pāṇḍey, Gita Press, Gorakhpur, undated.

Mahābhārata of Vedavyāsa, in 6 vols., translated into Hindi by Pandit Rāmanārāyaṇadatta Śāstrī Pāṇḍey, Gita Press, Gorakhpur, undated.

Padmapurāṇa of Vedavyāsa, in 10 vols., translated into English by N.A. Deshpande, Motilal Banarsidas, Delhi, 1988.

Skandamahāpurāṇa, Nag Publishers, New Delhi, 1991.

Śivapurāṇa, in 5 vols., translated into English by G.V. Tagare, Motilal Banarsidas, Delhi, 1994.

Viṣṇupurāṇa, Nag Publishers, New Delhi, 1995.

Secondary Sources

Dallaporta, Annamaria, Filippi, Gian Giuseppe and Marcolongo, Bruno, 'Cercando Kāmpilya', *Asiatica Venetiana*, no. 1, Venice,1996, pp. 232-33.

Dallaporta, Annamaria, Filippi, Gian Giuseppe and Marcolongo, Bruno, 'Kāmpilya Rediscovered', *I for Italy*, no. 5, III, New Delhi, September-October 1996, pp. 24-29.

Filippi, G.G., 'The Archaeological Indo-Italian Kāmpilya Project',

Heartland Eurasian Review of Geopolitics, Hong Kong-Rome, n. 3, 2001, pp. 93-95.

Filippi G.G., *Mṛtyu, Concept of Death in Indian Traditions*, D.K. Printworld (P) Ltd., Delhi, 1996.

Filippi, G.G., & Marcolongo, B., (ed.), *Kāmpilya: Quest for a Mahābhārata City*, New Delhi, D.K. Printworld, V.A.I.S. Series no. 2, 1999, pp. 1-82.

Marcolongo, B., (ed.) *First International Symposium on Kāmpilya Project*, Padua, CNR, 2001, pp. 35-38.

Puchetti C., *History and Archaeology of the Kāmpilya Region*, unpublished Ph.D. thesis at B.H.U., Varanasi, 2002.

Sri Karpattriji, *Bhakti Sudhā*, Sri Radhakrisna Dhanuka Prakashan Sansthan, Delhi, 2000, pp. 228-233.